THE CLASSICS OF WESTERN SPIRITUALITY
A Library of the Great Spiritual Masters

President and Publisher
Kevin A. Lynch, C.S.P.

EDITORIAL BOARD

Editor-in-Chief
John Farina

Editorial Consultant
Ewert H. Cousins—Professor, Fordham University, Bronx, N.Y.

John E. Booty—Professor of Church History, Episcopal Divinity School, Cambridge, Mass.

Joseph Dan—Professor of Kaballah in the Department of Jewish Thought, Hebrew University, Jerusalem, Israel.

Albert Deblaere—Professor of the History of Spirituality, Gregorian University, Rome, Italy.

Louis Dupré—T.L. Riggs Professor in Philosophy of Religion, Yale University, New Haven, Conn.

Rozanne Elder—Executive Vice President, Cistercian Publications, Kalamazoo, Mich.

Anne Fremantle—Teacher, Editor and Writer, New York, N.Y.

Karlfried Froehlich—Professor of the History of the Early and Medieval Church, Princeton Theological Seminary, Princeton, N.J.

Arthur Green—Associate Professor in the Department of Religious Studies, University of Pennsylvania, Philadelphia, Pa.

Stanley S. Harakas—Professor of Orthodox Christian Ethics, Holy Cross Greek Orthodox Seminary, Brookline, Mass.

Jean Leclercq—Professor, Institute of Spirituality and Institute of Religious Psychology, Gregorian University, Rome, Italy.

Miguel León-Portilla—Professor of Mesoamerican Cultures and Languages, National University of Mexico, University City, Mexico.

George A. Maloney, S.J.—Director, John XXIII
Ecumenical Center, Fordham University, Bronx, N.Y.

Bernard McGinn—Professor of Historical
Theology and History of Christianity, University of Chicago
Divinity School, Chicago, Ill.

John Meyendorff—Professor of Church History, Fordham
University, Bronx, N.Y., and Professor of Patristics and Church History,
St. Vladimir's Seminary, Tuckahoe, N.Y.

Seyyed Hossein Nasr—Professor of Islamics, Department of Religion,
Temple University, Philadelphia, Pa., and Visiting Professor, Harvard
University, Cambridge, Mass.

Heiko A. Oberman—Director, Institute fuer Spaetmittelalter und
Reformation, Universitaet Tuebingen, West Germany.

Alfonso Ortiz—Professor of Anthropology, University of New
Mexico, Albuquerque, N. Mex.; Fellow, The Center for Advanced Study,
Stanford, Calif.

Raimundo Panikkar—Professor, Department of Religious Studies,
University of California at Santa Barbara, Calif.

Jaroslav Pelikan—Sterling Professor of History and Religious Studies,
Yale University, New Haven, Conn.

Fazlar Rahman—Professor of Islamic Thought, Department of Near
Eastern Languages and Civilization, University of Chicago, Chicago, Ill.

Annemarie B. Schimmel—Professor of Hindu Muslim Culture,
Harvard University, Cambridge, Mass.

Sandra M. Schneiders—Assistant Professor of New Testament
Studies and Spirituality, Jesuit School of Theology, Berkeley, Calif.

Huston Smith—Thomas J. Watson Professor of Religion,
Adjunct Professor of Philosophy, Syracuse University, Syracuse, N.Y.

John R. Sommerfeldt—Professor of History, University of Dallas,
Irving, Texas.

David Steindl-Rast—Monk of Mount Savior Monastery,
Pine City, N.Y.

William C. Sturtevant—General Editor, Handbook of North
American Indians, Smithsonian Institution, Washington, D.C.

David Tracy—Professor of Theology, University of Chicago Divinity
School, Chicago, Ill.

Victor Turner—William B. Kenan Professor in Anthropology, The
Center for Advanced Study, University of Virginia, Charlottesville, Va.

Kallistos Ware—Fellow of Pembroke College, Oxford;
Spalding Lecturer in Eastern Orthodox Studies, Oxford University,
England.

JOHN of the CROSS
SELECTED WRITINGS

EDITED WITH AN INTRODUCTION BY
KIERAN KAVANAUGH, O.C.D.

PREFACE BY
ERNEST E. LARKIN, O. CARM.

PAULIST PRESS
NEW YORK • MAHWAH

Cover art: JOHN LYNCH, a Capuchin Franciscan friar, is a seminarian at Garrison N.Y. He obtained his degree in commercial art from Dutchess Community College in Poughkeepsie N.Y., and his degree in psychology from Iona College in New Rochelle, N.Y.

Copyright © 1987 by
the Washington Province of Discalced Carmelite Friars, Inc.

All rights reserved. No part of this book may be reproduced or transmitted in any form or by any means, electronic or mechanical, including photocopying, recording, or by any information storage and retrieval system without permission in writing from the publisher.

Library of Congress Cataloging-in-Publication Data

John of the Cross, Saint, 1542–1591.
   St. John of the Cross.

   (The Classics of Western spirituality)
   Translated from the Spanish by the editor.
   Bibliography: p.
   Includes indexes.
   Contents: The ascent of Mount Carmel—The dark night—The spiritual canticle—[etc.]
     1. Mysticism—Catholic Church. 2. Spiritual life—Catholic authors. 3. Catholic Church—Doctrines. I. Kavanaugh, Kieran, 1928–
II. Title. III. Title: Saint John of the Cross.
IV. Title: Selected writings. V. Series.
BV5080.J642   1987   248.2'2   86-30421

ISBN 0-8091-0384-2
ISBN 0-8091-2839-X (pbk.)

Published by Paulist Press
997 Macarthur Boulevard
Mahwah, New Jersey 07430

Printed and bound in the United States of America

Contents

Foreword	1
Preface	3
General Introduction	7
The Ascent of Mount Carmel	41
The Dark Night	155
The Spiritual Canticle	211
The Living Flame of Love	285
Selected Bibliography	317
Index	323

Editor of this Volume

KIERAN KAVANAUGH was born in Milwaukee, Wisconsin, in 1928 and entered the Discalced Carmelites in 1946. After ordination and completion of theology at the Teresianum in Rome, he spent a year in the Carmelite "desert" in France. Since his return to the United States in 1957, he has taught spiritual theology within his order and at Catholic University.

His major academic effort has been an English translation of the works of both St. Teresa of Avila and St. John of the Cross. In 1982, he lived with the Carmelites in Avila, Spain, and also traced the journeys of Teresa and John through the various towns and cities where they lived and made foundations. He was a founder and past president of the Institute of Carmelite Studies and continues to be actively engaged in its work of publishing and scholarly research.

Author of the Preface

ERNEST E. LARKIN, O. CARM. has spent practically all of his forty years as a Carmelite priest in educational work. He taught in his own major seminary and at Catholic University for twenty years before going to Phoenix, where he helped found the Kino Institute. Since 1981 he has been active in retreats, workshops, and writing, especially in promoting contemplative prayer and popularizing the teachings of the two Carmelite saints, Teresa of Avila and John of the Cross. He is the author of *Silent Presence* (1981) and *Christ within Us* (1984).

Foreword

A public lecture on St. John of the Cross makes you almost sense in the air an impending question. How must one go about reading this awesome mystic? The answers might be as varied as the question sure to come. In sorting out these selections from John's complete works, I have had foremost in mind the need that such a question discloses. The themes and essential points of any spiritual synthesis may be illustrated, but John shows a tendency to illustrate with a kind of detail that he himself sometimes hesitates over. This tendency presses him on, especially in *The Ascent of Mount Carmel*, into a labyrinth of divisions and subdivisions, in which the reader may well bog down, although John's admirers would never want that he had written a word less. Each of the works contains the nucleus of his synthesis; each contains as well a particular perspective, its own thrust and style, and as a result John propounds in each certain aspects of spiritual development more carefully than in the other works. This fact makes it possible to present the major works in a certain sequential order so that the first prepares the reader for the lure of the next, and so on with the others. In choosing these selections, then, I have sought those texts that concentrate on the core message and main spiritual situation found in the individual work. In a word, I am presenting this volume as one possible and, I hope, fruitful way for beginners to read St. John of the Cross. But seasoned readers might also profit from this opportunity to limit their attention to these substantial passages. No choice of selections should mean that what is not included is unimportant, and readers may have favorite passages that they regret are absent from these pages; let them know I share this regret.

Another question sure to come forth in the public lecture on John's writings concerns commentaries. Are there any good commentaries we might read? The truth of the matter is that little has been published in

FOREWORD

English. The research of recent years has come forth mostly in foreign languages and is published in periodicals not always easy to come by. With this situation in mind, I have tried in the general and particular introductions, as well as in the notes to the text, to lay before the reader some of the fruits of the excellent scholarship of the past years. Also, the general introduction includes a brief biographical sketch of John, in which I expand a little on several important related topics for the sake of background information: the social, political, and religious conflicts of the age; St. Teresa's relationship with John; and the complex struggles that arose within the Carmelite order over the Teresian reform.

Finally, in choosing these selections, I have gone over the translation I did in the early 1960s with my colleague Otilio Rodriguez and have made a number of stylistic changes as well as some other modifications where I thought the translation could be improved on for the sake of clarity.

Since editors have numbered the paragraphs in John's writings for easy reference, I have preserved this traditional numbering even though some numbers may include more than one paragraph. The ellipsis points will signal readers where omissions are being made in the text, and from the numbering of the books, chapters, stanzas, and paragraphs, the reader can judge where the omissions are lengthy and where brief. Everything that appears in brackets is the work of editors and absent from the early manuscript copies of John's works.

Special thanks go to I.C.S. Publications for allowing me to use freely my earlier book *The Collected Works of St. John of the Cross* in the translations and selections for this volume. I am deeply indebted to the Carmelites Eulogio Pacho and Federico Ruiz Salvador for the vast amount of material they have contributed to *sanjuanist* studies. The introductions and notes in their Spanish editions of the works of St. John of the Cross have benefited me greatly in my research and in the preparation of this volume. I must express gratitude to Steven Payne, O.C.D., for his contributions to the bibliography, for reading a first draft of these introductions, and for his valuable suggestions. And finally, my thanks to John Farina, the editor of *The Classics of Western Spirituality*, who gave me some helpful ideas and the encouragement needed for this undertaking.

Preface

Both seasoned and new readers of St. John of the Cross are in the debt of Kieran Kavanaugh and the Paulist Press for the present volume. Highly esteemed for his translations of St. Teresa of Avila and St. John of the Cross, Kieran Kavanaugh is probably the best informed English-speaking scholar on the lives and teaching of the two Carmelite doctors. His choice of texts, therefore, is an expert opinion on what is key in John's synthesis. For newcomers the selections provide easier access to the sometimes prolix author. John's writings lend themselves to this kind of presentation: Certain chapters stand out for their power, lucidity, and summary quality. In short, the volume is a wonderful breviary of the essential John of the Cross.

But is he not an author for specialists only, for the scholar or the saint? The editors of the Classics of Western Spirituality apparently think otherwise. I agree and applaud their decision to produce this collection. While John needs to be read judiciously, he has something for everyone, as he himself suggests in the prologue to *The Ascent of Mount Carmel*. His goal is that "everyone who reads this book will in some way discover the road he is walking, and the one he ought to follow if he wants to reach the summit" (n. 7).

John of the Cross offers a profound and solid spirituality, suitable for all manner of vocations in the Church today. He is not just a curiosity from the late Middle Ages. He is recognized by the Catholic community as *the* mystical doctor. A taste for his teaching is a mark of spiritual maturity.

The entire corpus of his works describes the process of assimilation into the Paschal Mystery. There are three phases: It begins with the halcyon days of first conversion, when the gifts of creation, especially other human beings, lead the person into deeper appreciation and love of God; then there is the eclipse of that optimism

PREFACE

in the purifying dark nights; finally the journey culminates in divine union, when transcendence and incarnation are complete and the divine and the human interpenetrate. John does not dwell on the first phase, though it is there. His emphasis falls on purification, which is largely the work of contemplation, and divine union. Sometimes people are not aware of his beginnings. I recall in my ardent Charismatic Renewal days friends would sometimes chide me for belonging to the Renewal and at the same time claiming discipleship under John of the Cross. Was this not a contradiction? I would reply that John would have been delighted with the Renewal, but that he would also say: "Now that you have discovered the Lord, read my books."

The conditions for entering the narrow way are utter simplicity: eyes on Jesus and total honesty. John discloses the secret sins of a self-centered piety. He speaks of renunciation and detachment, not because of any excessively negative view of the human condition, but because of the goal proposed: the divine presence incarnate in the whole of human reality. Transcendence, not moral depravity, is the key to this teaching. In our idiom the language of integration better conveys the meaning. All of life is to be rooted in Jesus Christ. In the process human values may appear to be left in the shadows, but that is a temporary side-effect. After purification they reappear in their true glory, grounded in the pure soil of divine union.

No one has any quarrel with the sublimity of this teaching, but in our anthropocentric times there are sometimes doubts about John's commitment to the human and the world. Let it be said unequivocally that he does not undercut creation. He exalts it, not in its truncated, fragmented form apart from God, but in its truth with God in the center.

Without doubt John's eyes are fixed on God, but the living God, not a counterfeit domesticated and betrayed by human projections. To encounter the real God is not easy; it demands a radical and total redemption of heart and mind. But if our author is the enemy of easy, self-serving ways, he is also the protagonist of the fullest human development. His overriding point is that Christian humanism demands Christ at the center of things.

Herein lies the relevance of St. John of the Cross. He offers the deepest foundation for the promotion of human values. He gives no strategy for changing things from the outside, such as liberation theology or Christian involvement in any form. But he offers something

PREFACE

even more important: a soul for the renewal of persons, Church, and world. However foreign his culture or strange his language, however dated his world view or different his life-style, he supplies a spiritual anthropology that has not been superseded by any other author. May this new collection of his thought flourish.

General Introduction

St. John of the Cross is a major figure in the history of Spanish literature and Christian mysticism. From the time Pius XI declared him a Doctor of the Church, in 1926, a large amount of historical, doctrinal, and critical research has taken place, providing us with a much better grasp of the depth of his personality and work.

The most widely known biographies of St. John of the Cross are those of the French scholar Bruno de Jésus-Marie and the Spanish historian and theologian, Crisógono de Jesús. Padre Crisógono's biography is especially valuable for its thorough treatment and abundance of documentation. The complaint made is that although these authors had worked with the manuscripts and had attempted to be faithful to the witnesses of John's time, they continued a tradition of hagiography. In this tradition, the complaint goes, John's human qualities are either forgotten or lost among all the trappings that sixteenth-century Spain considered requisite in the life of a true saint. Some basic knowledge about John's life, despite the hagiographical problems, can prove immensely helpful for the interpretation of his personality and works.[1]

---

1. See Bruno de Jésus-Marie, *Saint John of the Cross* (New York: Sheed & Ward, 1932); and Crisógono de Jesús Sacramentado, *The Life of St. John of the Cross* (London: Longman, Green & Co., 1958). For a more contemporary but much less thorough approach, see Richard P. Hardy, *Search for Nothing: The Life of John of the Cross* (New York: Crossroad, 1982); see also Hardy's methodological articles on this question: "Early Biographical Documentation on Juan de la Cruz," *Science et Esprit* 30 (Oct.–Dec. 1978): 313–23; and "A Personality Sketch," *Ephemerides Carmeliticae* 29 (1978): 507–18.

GENERAL INTRODUCTION

Early Years
(1542–1563)

Juan de Yepes was born in 1542 in Fontiveros, a little town about twenty-four miles northwest of Avila, a rocky and barren part of Spain. His father, Gonzalo de Yepes, had come from an upper-class family of silk merchants, probably of Jewish origin, but was disowned by the family when he insisted on marrying a poor weaver, Catalina Alvarez. The parents of the future saint entered a marriage based on love, one demanding the sacrifice of wealth and worldly status to the nobler aspirations of a married union in intimacy and friendship. Juan was the last of the three boys born to the marriage. A lingering illness gradually destroyed the life of Gonzalo, who died when Juan was about three. The story of Catalina with her three children then became a sad one of unemployment, rejection, and hunger. Soon Luis, the middle son, also died, leaving the mother with only her oldest, Francisco, and her youngest. When Juan was nine, the family moved to Medina del Campo, one of the great market centers of Spain. Here Catalina succeeded in placing Juan in a school for poor children where he could receive food and shelter, a rudimentary education, and a trade that would fit him for life. But the young lad did not feel any enthusiasm for the trades he tried out at the school. Rather, his gentleness and patience led to the discovery of his gift of caring for the sick, and he was given a job as nurse and alms seeker for one of the fourteen hospitals in Medina.

While he was working at the hospital, an opportunity for attending classes in Latin and rhetoric at the nearby Jesuit school came along and another of Juan's gifts was revealed—a sharp intellect. His love for studies stirred him to find time for them at night when he was free of his duties connected with the hospital. Thus Juan de Yepes with his gifts and curiosity of mind received a basic education and came into contact with the classics and the imagery found in them. He learned about literary technique, was encouraged to write his own compositions and poems, and opened himself sensitively to the world around him. These years of hospital work and study, tasks that called for responsibility and diligence, complemented his early experiences of poverty.

GENERAL INTRODUCTION

Spanish Reform and a Carmelite Vocation (1563–1578)

When Juan was twenty-one, the hospital administrator, Don Alonso Alvarez de Toledo, offered him ordination to the priesthood and the post of chaplain at the hospital. Economically, this would have provided Juan with a secure future, but he refused, deciding instead to enter the Carmelite order, which had a monastery in Medina. His desire for solitude and the contemplative life, as well as his devotion to our Lady, may have prompted him most to make this fateful decision.

Receiving the name Fray Juan de Santo Matía, he passed his novitiate year, one would suppose, studying the rule and learning about the order's ancient, eremitical origins. In *The Book of the First Monks*, considered by Carmelites at the time to be their manual of spirituality, the following teaching brings to mind John's own doctrine:

> The goal of this life is twofold. One part we acquire, with the help of divine grace, through our efforts and virtuous works. This is to offer God a pure heart, free from all stain of actual sin. We do this when we are perfect and in Cherith, that is, hidden in that charity of which the Wise Man says: "Charity covers all sins" (Prv 10:12). God desired Elijah to advance thus far when he said to him: "Hide yourself by the brook Cherith" (1 Kgs 17:3–4). The other part of the goal of this life is granted us as the free gift of God: namely, to taste somewhat in the heart and to experience in the soul, not only after death but even in this mortal life, the intensity of the divine presence and the sweetness of the glory of heaven. This is to drink of the torrent of the love of God. God promised it to Elijah in the words: "You shall drink from the brook." It is in view of this double end that the monk ought to give himself to the eremitic and prophetic life.[2]

Entering the monastery did not demand of Fray Juan the denial of studies. After making profession at the completion of his one-year no-

---

2. *The Book of the First Monks*, trans. Michael Edwards (Boars Hill, Oxford: Teresian Press, 1985). For a historical account of the use of this text in the Spanish Carmels of John's time, see Otger Steggink, *Experiencia y Realismo en Santa Teresa y San Juan de la Cruz* (Madrid: Editorial de Espiritualidad, 1974), pp. 99–122.

GENERAL INTRODUCTION

vitiate, he departed for the bustling university city of Salamanca, where for four years (1564–1568) he studied philosophy and theology. He attended courses at the University of Salamanca as well as at the Carmelite College of San Andrés. Stimulating and excellent in quality, the intellectual surroundings in which Fray Juan found himself gave him the opportunity of coming into contact with some of the outstanding teachers of the times. It was a period in which all systems were discussed and any opinion could be held as long as faith was not called into question. Exactly which lectures Fray Juan attended remains unknown. That he was recognized for his intellectual talents is evident in the fact that he was appointed prefect of studies at the College of San Andrés. This office required him to conduct some classes, defend theses, and answer objections—assignments that meant he had to be in command of the material. Later on, in the university cities of Alcalá and Baeza, Fray Juan was noted for his knowledge of Scripture, the Fathers, and theology, and also for his keen mind. But at Salamanca witnesses remembered him as well for the austere and contemplative way of life he had set up for himself during these student years.

Despite the rich intellectual experience in Salamanca and his bent for intellectual work, Fray Juan at the time of his ordination was feeling an attraction to a full contemplative life and thinking of transferring to the Carthusian order. When he went back to Medina in 1567 to sing his first Mass, he met St. Teresa of Avila, who was then fifty-two and looking for friars to help her adapt for them the new contemplative form of life she was establishing among the Carmelite nuns. Teresa was delighted with what she found in the small friar (four feet eleven inches in height), and Fray Juan decided to devote himself to this work and way of life she so enthusiastically and fervently explained to him.

Teresa's interest in founding small communities of contemplatives must be seen as part of a larger movement of reform spreading through sixteenth-century Spain. Certain common characteristics marked the spirit of this Spanish reform: the return to one's origins, to primitive rules and the founders; a strict life lived in community with practices of poverty, fasting, silence, and enclosure; and, as the most important element, the life of prayer. The communities that were formed as a result were referred to descriptively as "reform," "observant," "discalced," or "hermit" communities.

The efforts at reform had their beginnings in the fifteenth century, taking the shape of a response to the upheavals in religious life that were caused by the Black Death. The early attempts, with an anti-intellectual tone, especially among the Franciscans, stressed affectivity, external ceremonies, devotions, and community vocal prayer. These communities of religious spent no less than seven hours a day on the Divine Office and more on Sundays and feast days. One of the promoters of this kind of reform, Pedro de Villacreces (1350–1429), urged that this vocal prayer of the Divine Office not be disturbed or shortchanged by manual labor. But so much vocal prayer day after day, for so many hours, could only become tedious and mechanical; it bore little noticeable fruit, unless in breeding a desire for forms of spiritual life and prayer more interior in their dimensions. As a matter of fact, a way called "recollection," whose followers were called *recogidos*, began to develop in many Franciscan houses. This way, or spirituality, made union with God through love its most important concern, while it sought its nourishment in Sacred Scripture and other classic spiritual works by authors such as Augustine, Gregory the Great, Bernard, and Bonaventure.

A Franciscan friar, Francisco de Osuna (c.1492–c.1540), took up the task of elaborating this spirituality and achieved his goal in *The Third Spiritual Alphabet*.[3] Teresa in her *Life* speaks of the happiness brought her by this book, a gift from her uncle, and how, though a Carmelite nun, she first learned about prayer from its pages. She then began to follow earnestly the path of recollection recommended by Osuna.

Osuna taught that to advance on the path of union, one must practice recollection, imitating Jesus Christ who went alone into the desert to pray secretly and spiritually. By this recollection, Osuna explained, you withdraw from people and noisy places and enter within yourself. By it you recollect the exterior person, the senses and bodily members, withdraw into the heart, unite the powers of the soul with the soul's highest part where the image of God is imprinted. Finally, this prayer joins God and the soul, that is, "the soul participates in the Lord himself and is perfectly recollected in him." This way of recollection, also called mental prayer, had to involve one's whole life. You lived a life of recollection, a life of mental prayer. Finally, though the practitioners of recollection gave greater importance to recollection, they did not abandon vocal prayer.

In another simultaneous development, a movement whose mem-

---

3. Francisco de Osuna, *The Third Spiritual Alphabet*, trans. and intro. Mary E. Giles (New York: Paulist Press, 1981).

GENERAL INTRODUCTION

bers were later called *alumbrados* rejected vocal prayer entirely and counseled a type of abandonment in which the soul would remain suspended in God. In this suspended state of abandonment in God you could not sin, nor did you need to bother with meditation on the Passion of Christ, or with fasts and abstinences, and rites and ceremonies; the use of images was useless, the religious life a hindrance. This abandonment placed you at the summit of perfection; you could find no quicker and safer way to union with God. But the practice did not prevent the members of this movement, called *dejados*, from showing at times an aggressive contempt for tradition. Coming as no surprise, the belief in one's incapacity to sin ended with immoral sexual practices in a number of instances.

A further aberration to appear at the time was the attraction to ecstasy and other extraordinary phenomena. These experiences were presented as something to be sought, but such esteem led to fraud and then suspicion as news about bogus ecstatics, visionaries, and stigmatics made its way through Spain.

To begin to understand the suspicion that became a part of the fabric of the Spain of this time, one must go back to the reign of the Catholic monarchs Ferdinand and Isabella. Toward the beginning of the sixteenth century, Granada was finally conquered and a country formerly divided was united and pacified. The authority of the Crown became absolute, and the country assumed its full role in the arena of European politics and diplomacy; at the same time a whole New World was discovered. In addition, Isabella's enthusiasm for the new learning of the Renaissance infused the kingdom with renewed cultural activity. But in her attempts to pacify and unite her people, Isabella gave in to pressures and imposed religious orthodoxy as a means of preserving political unity and social stability. The Inquisition was set up as a coercive tool for Christian orthodoxy. Moslems and Jews had either to convert or leave Spain. A land in which Christians, Moslems, and Jews were able to live side by side relatively peacefully now bred intolerance and a climate of mistrust.

With regard to the *alumbrado* movement, the Inquisition suspected that, though fundamentally different, it was closely connected with Lutheranism, since both stressed internal religion at the expense of outward ceremony. And the *recogidos* themselves were often confused with those in the *alumbrado* movement.

Teresa, in forming small, simplified communities of Carmelite nuns devoted to a life of recollection, was influenced partly by her fa-

GENERAL INTRODUCTION

milarity with the movement of the *recogidos* but even more by the extraordinary mystical favors God was granting her. In either case, considering the temper of the times, she too was vulnerable to the suspicions and accusations of others and, in fact, suffered no small amount from the mistaken opinions formed about her.

Philip II, who began to reign in 1556, had received the notion from his father, the emperor Charles V (grandson of the Catholic monarchs), that one of the reasons for the spread of Protestantism in Europe was the laxity of religious orders. It is not difficult to understand, then, that Philip took much interest and engaged actively in the reform of religious communities. The prior general of the Carmelite order, John Baptist Rossi, to whom Teresa referred, in a Spanish rendering, as Rubeo, was also interested in reform. In 1566, traveling sometimes by mule sometimes on horseback, he set about a journey throughout the Iberian peninsula on a mission of pastoral visitation and reform of his Carmelite communities. He came to Avila in 1567 and there Teresa first met him. She had been living for nearly five years in a little monastery of discalced, or contemplative, Carmelite nuns that she had founded. Since she had arranged that the community be placed under the jurisdiction of the local bishop, she was anxious about what Rubeo would decree. To her delight, he was impressed by the life she had established and urged her to make more foundations similar to the one she had made in Avila. But only reluctantly did he grant her request to found two houses for friars who, while living in a manner resembling that of her nuns, would also engage in pastoral ministry as the occasion arose. Since Rubeo had met with resistance in his efforts to bring about reform among the rival factions of Carmelites in Andalusia, he specified that the friars who would join Teresa should be subject to the province of Castile. To forestall any trouble, as though peering into the future, he gave further orders: There must be no attempt to seek separation from the province through the favor of princes or with briefs and other concessions from Rome.

At sundown on August 9, 1568, Teresa, with a small group, set off on a journey from Medina del Campo to Valladolid, where she intended to make another foundation. Traveling with the group was her new recruit, Fray Juan de Santo Matía, whom the Mother Foundress was bringing along to teach about the contemplative way of life she had been establishing. Fray Juan enjoyed the beauties of the sky spreading over the small caravan in that journey by night and spoke knowingly and brilliantly to Teresa and the others about the wonders of God and

GENERAL INTRODUCTION

the mysteries of the divine goodness, so knowingly in fact that the group began to refer to him as "God's archives." When they arrived in Valladolid the small friar began to learn firsthand how Teresa's nuns had adopted a mode of life in which, unlike that of the foundress's former monastery, the numbers were few and all class distinctions were eliminated. As a result of her personal mystical experience, Teresa envisioned her communities as small groups of friends of Christ and the contemplative life, the way of recollection, as a life of intimacy with Jesus, who continued forever to be human as well as divine. The manner of reciting the Divine Office was now simpler, an hour in the morning and an hour in the evening was set aside for mental prayer, and the nuns lived their day mostly in silence and solitude, engaging, alone in their cells, in the manual labor of spinning to help support themselves. The friar also learned, as Teresa takes pains to point out, "about the recreation we have together . . . to provide a little relief so that the rule may be kept in its strictness." In her account of this event in her *Foundations*, Teresa confesses that she felt that Fray Juan was so good that she could have learned more from him than he from her.[4] She nonetheless persevered in her role as teacher so that he would have a better notion of how to initiate the Teresian life among the friars. On finishing this brief novitiate under Teresa's guidance, Fray Juan left Valladolid to start working to convert into a monastery the little farm house acquired by Teresa for her first friars. It was situated in a lonely spot of Castile, called Duruelo, midway between Avila and Salamanca.

On November 28, 1568, with two of his confreres, Fray Juan inaugurated the new contemplative life that Teresa had taught him. The three friars in the presence of their provincial promised to follow the primitive Carmelite rule without mitigation. At this time Juan de Santo Matía changed his name to Juan de la Cruz; or in English, John of the Cross. History has respected this choice, and he has been known by this name ever since. The cross, indeed, lay at the core of his life and teaching, and it became for him a title of glory in the mystery of Jesus Christ. Although Rubeo had wanted the new group of friars to be known as the contemplative Carmelites, the popular name "discalced" won out. They were called discalced because initially they went bare-

---

4. See Chapter 13 of *The Foundations* in *The Collected Works of St. Teresa of Avila*, vol. 3, trans. Kieran Kavanaugh and Otilio Rodriguez (Washington, D.C.: I.C.S. Publications, 1985).

GENERAL INTRODUCTION

foot, a practice in vogue among the more eremitical groups of those times.

The former prior of Medina, Antonio de Heredia, became the first superior of the new foundation, and John of the Cross, the first novice master. John thus began what was to become one of his major ministries, an apostolate of spiritual direction, undertaken with exceptional responsibility and seriousness. In the years that followed, he moved with the community to larger quarters in nearby Mancera; he also traveled to Pastrana to help with the organization of a new novitiate there, and later became rector of the first college for discalced friars, in Alcalá de Henares. (Rubeo had given permission for four more communities of Teresa's friars in addition to the first two, which were Duruelo and Pastrana.)

At the very time Rubeo had been in Spain on his mission of reform, Philip II obtained a brief *Maxime cuperemus* from Pius V entrusting the reform of religious orders to the bishops and instructing them to carry out visitations. These visitations were to be done through delegates who in turn were to be accompanied by serious religious appointed by the provincial of the respective religious order. But in the case of the Carmelites, Trinitarians, and Mercedarians an exception was made. These orders were thought to be lacking in "observants," that is, those who observed the practices of the rule, as opposed to the "conventuals," who had acquired various privileges after the Black Death. The observants, it was thought, would be the most appropriate assistants to the bishops in the visitations. Another brief, *Superioribus mensibus*, was obtained a year later, in 1567. This brief instructed that, in the case of the above three orders, two Dominicans were to accompany the bishop's delegate. The Carmelites themselves claimed to have already renounced all forms of conventuality—in a word, that their houses were houses of observance and that the brief made little sense in their regard. But the king had his doubts about this because of the way things were going among the Carmelites of Andalusia. In the end, all the king's above efforts at reform failed, and Pius V decided to remove the visitation from the hands of the bishops. On January 13, 1570, the pope turned to another solution and put the work of reform into the hands of the generals, each being responsible for his own order. He again, though, at the intervention of the king, made an exception with respect to the Carmelites, Trinitarians, and Mercedarians, entrusting their reform to Dominican friars who would remain in their offices as apostolic commissaries for four years.

GENERAL INTRODUCTION

Two Dominicans were named visitators of the Carmelites; Pedro Fernández for those in Castile and Francisco Vargas for those in Andalusia, where the real trouble lay. They received ample powers: They could move religious from house to house and province to province, assist superiors in their offices, and depute other superiors from among either the Dominicans or the Carmelites. They were entitled to perform all acts necessary for the visitation, correction, and reform of both head and members of all houses of friars and nuns.

Since these powers seemed to ignore the privilege of religious exemption held by the orders involved and also the decree of the Council of Trent that entrusted reform to religious superiors, Rubeo responded anxiously, dispatching twenty commissaries to defend the rights of the Carmelite order in Spain. On account of the various interpretations that the authorities in question gave to the powers granted them by the Holy See, much controversy ensued between Teresa's friars, fast growing in numbers, and the other Carmelites.

The Dominican Fernández tactfully and diplomatically carried out his responsibilities within the normal legislative channels of the Carmelite order. A deep mutual respect and an easy working relationship developed between him and Teresa. In 1571 he appointed the Mother Foundress prioress of her former monastery, the Incarnation in Avila, hoping she would be able to find solutions for that large community of nuns crippled by its many economic and social problems. But soon Teresa realized that there was need for an understanding confessor and skilled spiritual director to assist the nuns to follow seriously their religious call. She arranged with Fernández to have John of the Cross come as a spiritual guide, and for five years he carried out this ministry among the nuns with exceptional results. In these years he learned much about God's way of communing with souls, and also had the opportunity to work closely with Teresa as her spiritual director; he was present when she reached the highest stage of her inward journey to the center of the soul where the Holy Trinity dwells, a stage she, and John himself, was later to refer to as the spiritual marriage. In one of her letters Teresa expressed her opinion of John of the Cross, referring to him as a "divine and heavenly man," and she affirmed that she had found no spiritual director like him in all Castile.[5] She found

---

5. See letter to Ana de Jesús, December 1578, in *The Letters of St. Teresa*, vol. 2, trans. E. Allison Peers (London: Burns Oates & Washbourne, 1951).

GENERAL INTRODUCTION

deep satisfaction in his learning and intelligence and significantly, if not also humorously, when she later in her letters had to choose code names for her associates lest any harm come to them if the letters were intercepted, referred to John as Seneca. But John was not only helpful to saints and nuns during these years. His ministry of spiritual direction extended to a wide variety of people, including public sinners. He found time for everyone and even room in his schedule to teach the poor children in the vicinity how to read and write.

Whereas Fernández exercised his authority prudently and in harmony with the Carmelite provincial of Castile, Francisco Vargas proceeded independently and requested the discalced friars to make foundations in Seville, Granada, and La Peñuela, all in Andalusia. These foundations went against the prior general's explicit orders, and Rubeo was alarmed that monasteries were being founded against his prohibition.

At a chapter convened at Piacenza on May 22, 1575, the Carmelite order, addressing the question of its discalced friars in Andalusia, but before all the facts were in about the happenings in Spain, came to some stern decisions. Those who had been made superiors against the obedience due superiors within the order itself, or who had accepted offices or lived in monasteries or places prohibited by the same superiors, should be removed. The following determinations exemplify those of the Chapter Acts:

> And because there are some, disobedient, rebellious and contumacious, commonly called discalced friars, who against the patent letters and statutes of the prior general have lived and do live outside the province of Old Castile, in Granada, Seville, and near the small place known as La Peñuela, and who, excusing themselves with fallacies, cavilling, and misrepresentations, have been unwilling humbly to accept the mandates and letters of the prior general, it shall be intimated to the said discalced Carmelites, under apostolic penalties and censures, including, if necessary, the aid of the secular arm, that they shall submit within the space of three days, and if they resist they shall be severely punished.

To enforce the statutes of the chapter of Piacenza, Jerónimo Tostado received the appointment of visitator to Spain with all the powers the order could bestow on him for this task.

GENERAL INTRODUCTION

The previous year, on August 13, 1574, Gregory XIII, the new pope, had declared an end to the Dominican visitation and ordained that from then on the Carmelites should be visited by the prior general and his delegates. However, what had been established by the Dominican visitators was to remain in effect. Offended because the visitation had been called officially to a close without a word to him, the king imperiously declared Gregory's papal brief to be invalid because it lacked his royal placet. Afterward, the papal nuncio, Nicolás Ormaneto, received assurance that the recall of the Dominican visitators in no way affected his own powers as nuncio to visit and reform religious orders. He appointed Jerónimo Gracián, who had entered the discalced and become a close collaborater with Teresa, as visitator in Andalusia and then even provincial of all Teresa's friars and nuns.

It should be pointed out that the prestige of the papacy was not then what it was later to become. The pontiff was considered a political prince as much as head of the Catholic Church. He had his states just as did any other earthly ruler. Castilians, from the time of the Catholic monarchs, had grown accustomed to seeing in the king a kind of pope by reason of the many powers he had in Church affairs; he was looked upon as the protector of Catholicism, the protector as well of a reform that went beyond that of the Council of Trent, one that in the Castilian mind proved more effective.

This maze of claims and counterclaims, this wrangling over who had what authority, ultimately led to the little house next to the Incarnation where John was living. As chaplain and confessor to the nuns he became the cause of tension and jealousy. The office belonged by rights to the Carmelites of the observance and not to the new group of Teresa's friars. John himself, after the expiration of Teresa's term of office in 1574, had wished also to leave, and again at other times had requested to leave and so lessen the conflicts that had arisen over his presence in Avila. But the nuncio Ormaneto ordered him to stay on.

When Ormaneto died, in June 1577, the friars of the observance snatched their opportunity and hurried to enforce the ordinations of the chapter of Piacenza, an undertaking the nuncio, through his actions, had been forestalling. During the night of December 2, 1577, John was blindfolded and carried off as prisoner by order of Tostado. Perhaps the argument for his arrest followed the reasoning that though he was not living in one of the houses of Andalusia whose members were classified as rebels, he incurred the same penalties for living outside an approved monastery. But John lived where he did at the request of

GENERAL INTRODUCTION

Fernández, the visitator, remained there by the authority of the nuncio, Ormaneto, and had been subject as well to Gracián. The small discalced friar hung on when Tostado tried to make him renounce the Teresian way of life, and for that he was declared contumacious and a rebel. Imprisonment, flogging, fasting on bread and water, were standard penalties in religious orders of the time. And in John's case they were severely applied in the monastery of Toledo. On the day following his capture, Teresa wrote to the king protesting and pleading with him for the love of God to order that the innocent friar be set free. John was locked up in a small room, six feet wide by ten feet long, that for a window had only a tiny opening, two inches wide, high up in the wall. There, for about nine months, he suffered in darkness and alone, with little to eat and hardly a change of clothing. In the midst of this severe deprivation, he attempted to find some relief by composing poems in his mind, among which were the first thirty-one verses of *The Spiritual Canticle*, one of the greatest lyric poems in Spanish literature. These verses reveal that in that cramped and barren prison, deprived of all earthly comfort, in the dark night of the soul, John received some rays of light and was divinely touched by glory in the substance of his being. Here, too, in his stark experience of emptiness, a spiritual synthesis began to take shape in his mind, in which the way to union moved directly up a path he later designated by the word *nada*, meaning "nothing." "Nothing, nothing, nothing, and even on the Mountain nothing."

One hot night in the month of August, the emaciated friar undertook a dangerous escape from his prison and fortunately succeeded. He found refuge first with Teresa's nuns in Toledo, and then, through their intervention, at the nearby hospital of Santa Cruz, where he was secretly cared for.

In the meantime the new nuncio, Felipe Sega, was showing displeasure with Teresa and her friars. He removed Gracián from his office as visitator, and was looking to Tostado for help in bringing about some kind of order. On October 9, 1578, with near desperation, the discalced friars, despite doubts about its legality, convened a chapter in Almodóvar del Campo. The excuse put forth was that they merely wanted to execute what they had agreed on in a previous chapter called by Gracián in 1576 while Ormaneto was still alive. By this time the number of discalced friars had increased to over three hundred. John of the Cross, at this chapter, was appointed vicar of El Calvario, a house situated in a mountainous solitude near Beas in Andalusia. In this isolated place he would be more secure against attempts to recapture him.

When Sega learned of the chapter at Almodovar, he fumed, declared it null and void, angrily sent Gracián and others to prison, and placed the discalced friars and nuns under the authority of the provincials of the observance. But the king, with some appropriate maneuvering, seeking to temper Sega's zeal, had previously appointed a commission to study the accusations made against the discalced. What the commission finally did, in April of 1579, was place Angel de Salazar, a former provincial of the observant Carmelites, in charge of Teresa's friars and nuns. The latter were jubilant, and Gracián spoke of Salazar as a gentle and discreet man whose main concern was to console the afflicted and promote peace. Ultimately, Gregory XIII, in a brief dated June 22, 1580, allowed Teresa's friars and nuns to form a separate province and govern themselves. Teresa best summed up the final results: "Now we are all at peace, calced and discalced; no one can hinder us from serving our Lord."[6]

Superior and Writer (1578–1588)

When John arrived at El Calvario, a place of spectacular beauty, to take up his office, he was far enough away from jurisdictional conflicts and threats to be able to enjoy a tranquillity in his surroundings that by contrast must have been extraordinary.

But after less than a year as superior in the remote solitude of El Calvario (1578–1579), he moved to the city of Baeza to serve as rector (1579–1582) of the new college founded there for the young discalced students in the south. Afterward, he resided in Granada, first as prior (1582–1585), then as vicar provincial of Andalusia (1585–1587), and then again as prior (1587–1588). An important aspect of a superior's role in those times was the spiritual direction of the community. Besides this work and his other duties as prior, John also, at the request of Teresa, began to assist the discalced nuns as spiritual director. This ministry among friars, nuns, and many others who approached the doors of the monastery for help led to his vocation as a writer, in which he composed treatises on spirituality that have become classics.

---

6. See *The Foundations*, ch. 29, no. 32.

GENERAL INTRODUCTION

His duties and offices, especially later as vicar provincial, also obliged him to travel frequently and led him to important cities: Baeza, Granada, Córdoba, Seville, Málaga, Caravaca, Jaén, and even Lisbon.

At Baeza, as at Salamanca and Alcalá, he once more came into contact with university people and soon found himself known and esteemed as an expert in Scripture, theology, and spirituality. As vicar provincial he had to attend to all the houses of both friars and nuns in Andalusia, visiting each formally at least once a year. During these years, he also founded seven monasteries.

In the historic and picturesque city of Granada, in a monastery with an outstanding view of the Sierra Nevada and adjacent to the property of the Alhambra, that magnificent palace of the Moslem kings, John wrote the bulk of his works. His writing, then, was squeezed into a life that presented many other obligations and burdens.

In the summer of 1588 John was elected a councillor to the vicar general, Nicolás Doria, and had to return north to Castile, where in his capacity as councillor he also became prior of Segovia.

His Personality

Early deprivations, the later misunderstandings and prison sufferings within the order, his own contemplative dark nights—all of these affected John positively in the sense that through them he discovered an opportunity to grow in love and compassion for others who suffer. He felt drawn especially to assist those laboring under heavy loads, and has received the title "patron of the afflicted."

Remembering his own experiences of poverty, he did not restrict himself to seeking the good of his penitents in spiritual matters but sought as well to assist them in their material needs. Sometimes he gave alms from the small funds of the monastery; sometimes he begged alms from devout people to help them. The poor, begging at the monastery entrance, he tried to assist concretely with food or money. His compassion for them merged with an intense sympathy for the needs and sufferings of the sick. They too, having lost their physical well-being, stood among the deprived.

His method of governing included a gentleness that was rare for the times. He taught that no one could be persuaded to the love of God through harshness, that severity only produced pusillanimity in the

GENERAL INTRODUCTION

works of great virtue. Seeking to promote a positive spirit of cheerfulness and good humor, he was able to assist those inclined toward sadness and depression.

According to John, individuals who grow in the love of God desire, in the measure they do, that other people also love Him; and the greater their love the more they will labor for these people both in prayer and in all other kinds of work. In his ministry John spared neither time nor energy seeking to liberate individuals from their spiritual illnesses; nor did he shrink, when necessary, from pointing out to them these illnesses. With a special awareness of the dignity and high destination of each individual, he found time for everyone, from university professors to uneducated shepherds' wives. Sinners as well as saints searched him out and found him a blessing to talk with.

In directing others, he focused on the life of faith, hope, and love, and thus became known as a moderator of penances (which frequently were practiced rigorously by contemporary spiritual seekers) and warned against excessive reliance on external practices and customs. Holiness came from God as His gift; you could not acquire it by some kind of prowess but only dispose yourself for it, particularly through detachment and the simplicity of contemplative prayer.

Skilled in practical matters, not at all expected in the stereotype of a poet or mystic, he designed the monasteries of Granada and Segovia, and also an aqueduct for the former to bring water down from the Alhambra. Opposed to the teachings of the *alumbrados* that manual labor should not be undertaken by those living in abandonment to God, he helped the workmen in the construction of the monasteries both at Granada and Segovia. On days when he resided at the nuns' communities to give them spiritual conferences and direction, he would spend his free time laying bricks, setting up partition walls, working in the garden, and so on.

A lover of nature and of the beauty of creation, he preferred the country to the city. While rector in Baeza he purchased a piece of property in the country so that the friars would have an opportunity to escape from the noise and commotion of the city. He would often take his friars to the mountains, sometimes so that they could relax, at other times so that they could spend the day in solitude and prayer.

Beneath the simplicity of his manner lay a soul on fire with love, as evidenced particularly in his poetry. Admitting his intimacy with God, he once remarked in Granada: "God communicates the mystery of the Trinity to this sinner in such a way that if His Majesty did not strengthen my weakness by a special help, it would be impossible for me to live." A good part of the night he would spend in contemplation before the tabernacle, or in the garden, or at the window of his cell.

The sublimity of his contemplation did not diminish his esteem for liturgical prayer. The liturgical seasons were the occasions for an interior transformation in the spirit of the mystery being celebrated. In his prison cell in Toledo, after months of physical deprivation and suffering, he was asked on the vigil of the feast of the Assumption what he was thinking of, and he replied: "I was thinking that tomorrow is the feast of our Lady and that it would give me great joy to say Mass." His love for the Bible, the word of God, contributed further to his devotion to the liturgy.

Accused at times of being too calm in the midst of need, he made determined efforts to free people from anxiety and worry through trust in God's providence. He wanted them to learn through experience that as he explained in his writings the endurance of a trial with equanimity not only brings about spiritual blessings but enables the afflicted one to come more easily to a right judgment about the difficulty at hand.

The Last Years (1588–1591)

In Segovia John continued his ministry of spiritual direction in addition to his other responsibilities. At the ill-fated chapter of June 1591, however, the fabric of his life was changed. He was not elected to any office. He had dared to differ with the astute, strong-willed vicar general, Nicolás Doria, especially in regard to the government of the nuns and the way the vicar general wanted to deal with Jerónimo Gracián. In the end, Doria managed to have Gracián expelled from the discalced. As a kind of rebuff, John was sent away to La Peñuela, an isolated monastery in Andalusia; but, as years before in Duruelo and Calvario, he once again enjoyed the solitude and appreciated the time he had for more prayer. Indeed, seemingly undisturbed by this turn of affairs, he wrote to Madre Ana de Jesús (Jimena), who had been hoping that he would be the one chosen superior for the nuns: "If things did not turn out as you desired, you ought rather to be consoled and thank God profusely. Since His Majesty has so arranged matters, it is what suits everyone."

Some ugly news spoiled the silence of his desert. Word reached

GENERAL INTRODUCTION

John about an investigation conducted against him by two friars who, apparently out of resentment, were engaged in a process against him, not without intrigue and defamation of his character. They were trying to expel him from the order. Because of fears stirred up by this investigation, the nuns destroyed many of the letters and counsels John had written for them, and posterity lost a precious heritage. A serious illness afflicting John prevented his accusers from carrying their plan to its final conclusion.

Because of a persistent fever and an inflammation of the leg, he had to journey to the town of Ubeda, where he could receive medical help. There he met no cheerful welcome from the prior, Padre Crisóstomo, who considered the little sick friar from Castile both a nuisance and an added expense. Shortly after John arrived, the disease, erysipelas, broke out more severely. The medical and surgical treatments caused excruciating pain, but the inflammation and ulceration continued to spread. By mid-December, John knew that his time was at hand. Begging forgiveness from the prior for the bother and expense, John one day had the happiness of witnessing a sudden change in Padre Crisóstomo, who began to undergo a complete conversion of heart, appealing for forgiveness, and leaving the sick friar's cell in tears. At midnight on December 14, 1591, shortly after the bell for Matins sounded, Fray John of the Cross died, repeating the words of the psalmist, "Into your hands, O Lord, I commend my spirit."

He was beatified by Clement X in 1675, canonized by Benedict XIII in 1726, and declared a Doctor of the Church by Pius XI in 1926.

Poet, Mystic, and Theologian

The letters of St. Teresa of Avila contain references to couplets and carols and other kinds of poems that went back and forth between her monasteries and were shared with other friends. These compositions were destined to give some extra solemnity to a liturgical feast or other special day, such as the day of one's patron saint. Like today's greeting card, a poem represented Teresa's simple means of providing joy and recreation for a special occasion.

In 1959 a newly discovered fragment in Teresa's hand was first published among her letters. Writing to her brother Lorenzo, Teresa says in it: "Here are some little lyric verses composed by Fray John of

GENERAL INTRODUCTION

the Cross who sent them to me from the Incarnation." At this time Fray John of the Cross was serving as chaplain at the monastery of the Incarnation in Avila. The fragment indicates that before his imprisonment in Toledo John had joined in that Teresian form of diversion which consisted in the writing and sharing of verses. It comes as little surprise, then, that John sought to divert himself in his cramped, barren prison cell by composing verses. In fact, the largest block of the saint's twenty poems was composed in the prison of Toledo.

John had been better instructed in the art of poetry than Teresa and her nuns and was familiar with contemporary poets such as Boscán and Garcilaso. Yet literary works were not his sole guide. He drew his materials from popular works also, though the main sources of his poetic inspiration were the Bible and his own experience.

Mystics may undergo an irrepressible urge toward some kind of outward expression of their experiences of God, at least of the more intense ones. The root of this need lies in the indissoluble bond between the body and the living experience of the spirit. The outward expression prolongs in the body that which spiritually resonates within. At the same time, this outward expression can so stir the emotions that these latter in turn may add to the spiritual experience. The concrete form of expression depends on the capacity and inclinations of the subject.

Having the soul of an artist, John expressed himself outwardly in a number of forms. There is his sketch of Christ on the cross, still extant. He enjoyed carving and sculpting. His architectural design of the monastery in Granada was so successful that it was then used as a model for other monasteries. Today we can still see and admire the cloister he designed in Segovia and the aqueduct in Granada. He composed little dramas that the nuns and friars performed for various liturgical feasts. At times he was known to dance under the power of strong religious emotion. On his journeys, he used to pass the time singing hymns and songs, some of which he himself composed. But poetry became John's best vehicle of self-expression. In it we find the traces of his other gifts: color, form, sonority, dramatic movement. Not only do the words have their function, but also the rhythm, the music, the accents, and the coloring.

To be sure, poetry involves the use of symbols. Symbol is a preponderant element in John of the Cross's work. Through symbolic images, he speaks directly of experiences on another plane. His symbols have both a strong base in sense experience and a strict link with spiritual and divine realities. Allowing his forceful impressions of natural things to suggest and allude to divine things, he showed a remarkable sensitivity to natural beauty. This does not mean so much that he raised himself from the world around him to higher things but that in an enlightened way he succeeded in breaking through nature to the transcendent mystery. In commenting on one of his verses from *The Spiritual Canticle*, "the silent music,"[7] he explains that the soul, in a knowledge coming from the divine light, becomes aware of Wisdom's wonderful harmony in the variety of creatures and that each of them, endowed with a certain likeness of God, gives voice to what God is in it. Each in its own way and according to its capacity bears God within itself and magnifies Him. Thus we find in John, besides the experience of natural reality and divine Reality, the experience of their compenetration. This friar poet teaches that as individuals become more detached from possessiveness in natural things, they become more sensitive and begin to see with greater efficacy until all of sensible reality becomes a pure sacrament.

Having escaped from prison, John, in true Teresian fashion, began to share his prison poems with the friars and nuns, and they started asking questions about different stanzas, especially those of the mysterious *Canticle*. The result was that he began writing his commentaries with the goal of offering spiritual assistance and inspiration.

The commentaries provide John with the occasion to communicate with his readers as a mystic, poet, teacher, and ardent lover of God. In order to instruct he uses his knowledge as theologian, psychologist, and spiritual director. From symbol he takes us to a conceptual system with its own language and applications. If John makes use of his poems as occasions for presenting his teaching, however, he never means to restrict our use of the poems. His commentaries ought to lead us back to the poem and to a more fruitful reading. In his own words he reminds his readers of the freedom they ought to feel in reading the poem: "Though we give some explanation of these stanzas, there is no reason to be bound to this explanation."[8]

---

7. In stanzas 14–15.
8. C. prol., 2. References to John's works will be made as follows: A = *The Ascent of Mount Carmel*, which will be followed by the book number, chapter, and paragraph number; N = *The Dark Night*, followed by the book number, chapter, and paragraph number; C = *The Spiritual Canticle*, followed by the stanza number and paragraph number; F = *The Living Flame of Love*, followed by the stanza and paragraph number.

GENERAL INTRODUCTION

For some three hundred years after John's death his poetry was almost completely ignored. It is with Menendez Pelayo that modern appreciation of John's poetry really begins. He speaks of it as a heavenly poetry that does not seem to be of this world. In the wake of this confession, many modern critics have come to the same conclusion, at least about *The Dark Night*, *The Spiritual Canticle*, and *The Living Flame of Love*. Dámaso Alonso referred to John of the Cross as the loftiest poet of Spain.

The Carmelite friar considered his poetry to be a statement closer to his mystical experience than his commentaries. It represented an overflow in figures and similes from the abundance of God's spiritual communication. In his poetry John felt himself pouring out secrets and mysteries rather than rational explanations.[9]

Regarding his sources, it is worth remembering that in the sixteenth century the Church acknowledged certain writers as authoritative, and they could be appealed to in order to test new ideas or questionable claims. The past provided not merely source material but authority. Scripture especially carried much weight. A biblical passage was considered an authority from Scripture. To be sure, there was little concern at the time with accurate texts and critical scholarship, which we find so essential today. John may often be quoting from memory or from medieval compilations. Some of the works he quotes are now held to be spurious. It might be worth recalling, too, that since Dionysius, the pseudo-Areopagite, was thought to be a disciple of St. Paul, his works carried enormous weight. In sum, instead of historical scholarship, textual accuracy, and a healthy scepticism with regard to the received wisdom, John's world set high store by a tradition handed down through the centuries and mediated through sometimes corrupt texts.

A whole host of authors could have influenced the Carmelite mystic: Augustine, Gregory the Great, Bernard, the Victorines, the Rhineland mystics, Bonaventure, Aquinas, the Carmelites John Baconthorpe and Michael of Bologna, Lull, Osuna, Laredo, Teresa herself, and Luis de Leon. But any list calls for caution. Only in isolated phrases does John actually quote specific authors: Ovid, Boethius, Dionysius, Gregory, Augustine, Francis, Bernard, and Aquinas. The four times he quotes Dionysius explicitly, he refers to the same thing: Dionysius calls

---

9. See C. prol., 1–2.

GENERAL INTRODUCTION

contemplation a ray of darkness. Finally, John sometimes speaks in general of "what philosophers or theologians say."

One very definite source of his teaching, appearing on every page, is the Bible. John had the Bible with him constantly. One found him reading it everywhere: on his travels, on his outings, in his cell, in some corner of the monastery. The use of the Bible for one's spiritual life was very much a part of the Carmelite spirit. The Scriptures became so deeply planted in John's being that his memory was easily stirred by words that echoed or alluded to scriptural phrases and passages, which in turn would suggest other passages in the sacred books.

Through his interest in the spiritual meaning of the Scriptures, that deeper meaning that brings to light the significance of the text for one's spiritual life in the mystery of Jesus Christ, John saw God not only saving his people in times past but also saving them now. He does not say that the Holy Spirit "spoke" to us in Scripture, but that He "speaks" to us. In reading the Scriptures, John sometimes experienced in himself what the Word of God was declaring to him. At other times he felt that the words confirmed what he had already been given to know in his heart and expressed perfectly the experience he had of God's action. The prayerful emotions of the psalmist and others he recited as his own as rising out of his own heart.

With his purified soul, John reached a point in which he could feel with the Bible, feel the Bible as though it were a song springing spontaneously from his own soul. He has questions about those who do not accept such a possibility: "This spirit and life is perceived by souls who have ears to hear it, those souls, as I say that are cleansed and enamored. . . . Those who do not relish this language God speaks within them must not think on this account that others do not taste it; St. Peter tasted it in his soul when he said to Christ: *Lord, where shall we go; you have the words of eternal life* [Jn 6:69]. And the Samaritan woman forgot the water and the water pot because of the sweetness of God's words [Jn 4:28]."[10]

Thus, it is not surprising that when he came to write his works, John found the main support for his teaching in the Bible. He saw the Bible as a unique and inexhaustible source of our knowledge of God. In the Bible he uncovered the principles of God's activity and was able to apply them to the divine action in the spiritual life of individuals.

---

10. F. 1, 6.

GENERAL INTRODUCTION

To anyone claiming some new knowledge of God, new revelation in the sphere of the divine mystery or moral life, he replies that we can get sufficient guidance from reason and the message of the gospel. In fact, John insists that Christ is the fullness and culmination of God's revelation. We should no longer expect God to give us more truths. Everything is already revealed in Jesus Christ.[11] The Bible, then, contains all that God has said and will say of Himself. Any spiritual synthesis that traces out the way to be followed toward the divine encounter must have Sacred Scripture for its foundation.

John's extensive quotations from the Old Testament come from all the categories of books: historical, prophetical, and sapiential. His use of the New Testament reveals an ample and profound knowledge of those works as well. As for his recourse to a number of accommodations, we have to remember that the use of the accommodated sense was a custom among writers and preachers of that period. By it, they used the biblical words and images to describe persons and situations that had little or nothing in common with the original occasion of those words and images. The Bible was the book they all approached for examples to flesh out their ideas for the public. If John at times used this sense, it does not require us to reject his entire approach to Scripture.

To John it often seemed that the sacred author had an experience analogous to the one he is attempting to describe. His manner of discovering the depths of a soul revealed in the Bible is not usually followed in the commentaries of modern exegetes. But John considered the prophets saints and their writings expressions of an interior life consumed in charity. The spiritual life in its highest stages is nothing more than the unfolding of the life of grace into a strict union of the sanctified person with God, who is the source of sanctification. Before the coming of Christ, people walked in grace and along the paths of sanctity just as Christians were to do later. The sufferings of the prophets, of Job, and of David, their desolation in an irreligious environment, included interior sufferings. John, it seems, was attracted more by the personal histories of the great Old Testament personalities than by the universal history in germ of the people of Israel. As for the New Testament, only St. Paul leaves us some confidential personal confessions. Citing Old Testament experiences, then, above all in *The Dark Night*, John is more attentive to the somber and the tragic note of personal histories.

---

11. See A. 2, 22.

GENERAL INTRODUCTION

As for the Song of Songs, we must remember that it was the book most frequently commented on in the medieval cloisters. What these commentators saw in it above all was the desire for God, a pursuit of God that will reach its end only in eternity, but that also obtains fulfillment here by means of what might be called an obscure possession. This latter kind of possession only increases desire, which is the form love takes here below. The Song of Songs is a dialogue between the bridegroom and the bride seeking each other, calling to each other, growing nearer to each other, who find they are separated just when they believe they are finally about to be united. This is a text for contemplatives, which does not teach morality or prescribe good works to perform or precepts to observe. The medieval commentators found it to be more attuned than any other book in Sacred Scripture to loving, disinterested contemplation, and John read it in this sense and therefore fittingly asked on his death bed that it be read to him.[12]

Some of the key points of John's doctrine that he bases on Scripture may be stated as follows: The economy of salvation now carries with it a change in our manner of communing with God, for it is the economy of the Mediator, living and working in the Church, without a variety of visible divine interventions.[13] The night, the purification, is a demand of the gospel imposed on human history.[14] All the requirements and refinements of perfect charity are nothing but explicitations of the first commandment given in Deuteronomy (6:5).[15] The perfect union, the divinized activity that arises from it, is simply the full realization of what basic texts of the New Testament say about the divine adoption and the indwelling of the Holy Spirit.[16]

But what guarantee does John have that he is not using the Scriptures in a merely arbitrary way, in a kind of free interpretation? His reply to the question points to his ecclesial concept of the Bible. The Bible and the Church cannot be separated. Thus John states: "If I should misunderstand or be mistaken on some point, whether I deduce

---

12. For more on John's use of Scripture see Barnabas Ahern, "The Use of Scripture in the Spiritual Theology of St. John of the Cross," *Catholic Biblical Quarterly* 14 (January 1952): 6–17; Henri de Lubac, *Exégèse médiévale. Les quatre sens de l'écriture*, 4 vols. (Paris: Aubier, 1959–64), especially 4:500–05; Jean Vilnet, *Bible et mystique chez Saint Jean de la Croix* (Bruges, Belgium: Desclée de Brouwer, 1949).
13. See A. 2, 22.
14. See A. 2, 7.
15. See A. 2, 16, 1.
16. See C. 39, 4–6.

GENERAL INTRODUCTION

it from Scripture or not, my intention will not be to deviate from the true meaning of Sacred Scripture or from the doctrine of our Holy Mother the Catholic Church. If this should happen I submit entirely to the Church, or even to anyone who judges more competently about the matter than I."[17] We can see also how humility is required for the correct interpretation of Scripture. John teaches that a humble person does not dare deal with God independently or find complete satisfaction without human counsel and direction.

> God did not say where there is one alone, there I am; rather, He said: where there are at least two. Thus God announces that he does not want the soul to believe only by itself the communications it thinks are of divine origin, nor that anyone be assured or confirmed in them without the Church or her ministers. For God will not bring clarification and confirmation of the truth to the heart of one who is alone. Such a person would remain weak and cold in regard to truth.[18]

Then John goes on to give St. Paul as an example, and points out how Paul, after having preached the gospel for a long time and having heard it from God, could not resist going and conferring about it with St. Peter and the other Apostles.[19]

As John went out from himself and passed through the spiritual night, he entered through experience more and more into the substance of the Church, into God manifesting Himself in time. His experience is founded on a secret Presence offering Himself paradoxically through the visible body of the community of Christ. John, then, can rely on the judgment of others, on the judgment of the Church in matters concerning the expression of his experience and teaching. Moreover, Church life, doctrine, and prayer supply the context in which he reads and uses Scripture.

A central purpose of John's is to transmit the content of his mystical experience. That he is a mystic in no way prejudices his work as spiritual director or theologian. On the contrary, his experience enriches the other tasks. It favors theological reflection because the mystic enjoys a particularly enlightened perception of the mysteries of God,

---

17. A. prol., 2.
18. A. 2, 22, 11.
19. A. 2, 22, 12.

of the divine action, and of the life of grace in individuals. Mystical wisdom quickens one's penetration into the truths of faith and sensitizes one for discovering God's meaning in existence. The same holds true from the pastoral point of view. Through experience the mystic knows the goal, and is in a better position to delineate the way and evaluate the means.

In recent years the ancient term *mystagogy* has come again into use, and our attention has been drawn to the significance of this term in the life of the Church. The term has also been applied in reference to John of the Cross and other mystics. Today in spirituality it is used to refer to the gradual initiation of the believer into the mystery of the indwelling Christ by a master who is capable of communicating some experience of this mystery. A mystagogue, it may be said, is one who having had experience of God and His mystery accompanies another walking along the spiritual path. The art of the mystagogue lies in transmitting not one's own experience but, thanks to one's own experience, the mystery of the personal God who reveals Himself freely and gratuitously to those who seek Him. John transmits in veiled ways his own experience so as to awaken an experience in his listeners and readers. Instead of presenting the material so that it provides themes and problems appealing to intellectual curiosity and demanding intellectual keenness, he presents the mystery with the desire that others may be brought close to it and totally transformed by it.

According to Federico Ruiz, John of the Cross is perhaps the most original and vigorous of Spanish theologians.[20] If in the past this was not recognized, it was because of false criteria for discerning the true theologian, especially in a period of decadent Scholasticism; some chafed at the thought of John of the Cross being called a theologian. In his desire to penetrate into the mysteries of Christ and of God's communion with His people, John enters the most difficult and unexplored regions. His works reveal a kind of sublime theological daring. In his originality and creativity and in contrast to the habit of the theologians of his time to work within the restricted boundaries of the Scholastic system, he did not think it unsuitable to turn to the use of symbols as a most effective means of explaining and communicating a living knowledge of the mystery of God.

---

20. See the general introduction in *San Juan de la Cruz: Obras Completas*, introducciones y notas doctrinales Federico Ruiz Salvador (Madrid: Editorial de Espiritualidad 1981), p. 34.

GENERAL INTRODUCTION

In his theology he is not directly interested in legitimate attempts to define the nature of God, the person of Christ, grace, and so on. What he seeks is to teach and demonstrate how these realities are present and bring about the divinization of the human person. They are treated in their interrelationships rather than in isolation. In his academic studies, John learned the categories and theological priorities of his time. But at stake for him was the spiritual development of the human person, the creation of a doctrinal synthesis in which all these converging realities of the process of divinization would acquire unity and cohesion. Putting into order the basic underpinnings of all John's teachings can be helpful, for they may not be immediately evident in reading the works; but as one rereads they become more obvious, and the interconnection of themes comes into better focus.

Deification or divinization is the definitive *raison d'être* of human life. It calls for the union of two extremes infinitely distant: God and the human person. We have before us the absolute transcendence of God and the relative "nothingness" of the creature. Divinization, then, must be brought about on another level, by means of realities that are not "natural," but are built into nature.

In the realization of divinization there is necessarily produced a movement having both a negative side and a positive one. The negative factor relates to the elimination of all that is incompatible with God; the positive, to a kind of divine substitution for what is being eliminated.

By the same token, the two prime agents or protagonists are God and the human person. From the human viewpoint, in the measure that one of these holds sway, there will be either an active personal effort or a passively received divine action. The first tends, above all, to dispose us for the divine work, by means of the negation, emptiness, and nakedness of all that is not in conformity with God. The second fills this void with God's gifts, graces, and virtues, and uproots what humans are incapable of uprooting through their own efforts.

The final result is transformation, divinization, marriage, the human becoming divine insofar as possible in this life. This transformation in God is not merely a likeness of wills. What is divinely brought about by means of contemplation radically changes the human mode of functioning. That which is concrete and particular no longer plays the role of a determining stimulus on the cognitive and affective plane. What is substituted is general and unlimited, that which does not disfigure the absolute Good, whose communication we receive fully only in faith and contemplation.

GENERAL INTRODUCTION

As a consequence, in the natural relations, in the dynamics of knowing and loving, the interdependence of sense and spirit, and the prevalence of activity and passivity (of the "natural" and "supernatural"), a reversal in the customary order takes place.

Though he experienced these principles, John develops them doctrinally and presents them as objective and universal realities. Demonstrated by a rational process of argument, they serve him as premises for building his whole thought into a logical system.

Anthropology

In his structuring of human psychology, John makes use of a traditional heritage that was basically Aristotelian along with a residue of Platonic and Augustinian elements. In this tradition one comes to know the nature of a being by its activity, and in studying humans looks to the faculties and their operations for the parts that go to make up the multifaceted person.

John analyzes the various components of human psychology as the need arises for the presentation of his teaching. He never takes time to give a complete analysis of the whole complex. In the area of perception, there are first the five external senses: sight, hearing, smell, taste, and touch. Sight and hearing always come first on his list, although sometimes hearing precedes sight. Smell, taste, and touch appear last in that order. Sight and hearing are more suitable as symbols of certain sublime activities of the spirit.

Within this sensorial field, there are also the internal senses, the imagination, phantasy, and sense memory. But John is not much interested in the differences among them: "For our discussion there will be no need of differentiating between them."[21] They receive the material that comes from the external senses. It is impressed on the phantasy as on a mirror by which it is in turn presented to the intellect. The internal senses lie in a strategic place between the outer world and the intellect.

At the terminus of perception we find the intellect, the power of knowing in an immaterial way. John points out that the agent intellect has the function of working on the images in the phantasy, making them

---

21. A. 2, 12, 3.

actually intelligible to the possible or passive intellect. It is the passive intellect that receives the knowledge.

All that the external or internal senses perceive in our human mode of knowing John refers to as the "accident(s)," along with all that pertains to a determined way of knowing the truth, such as the circumstances of obscurity or inevidence, or even the very formulas or dogmatic articles.

"Substance" refers to that element or aspect which is most important or valuable in the consideration of something, or which is the truth of the thing. The word may also refer to that which is most inward or intimate to a way of being, to a problem or a question. In reference to our knowing, the substance for John is the truth known and loved, or, in other words, that which the inner, spiritual faculties receive, the truth known by the passive intellect and loved by the will. The substance may be the fruit of the natural process of knowing obtained by means of the senses or it may result from God's direct communication without mediation of the senses.

As often as the soul apprehends truth by means of sensible images or forms (the outer rind, the accident), there takes place an activity of the sense faculties with regard to the accidents and an activity of the spiritual faculties with regard to the truth, the substance. Whenever the soul knows the truth without the mediation of sensible forms and images, the activity of the senses is suppressed because they have no proper object, and there takes place an activity of the spiritual faculties, which apprehend the substance without the mediation of the senses. From the perspective of the natural activity of the sense faculties, the soul then is idle, doing nothing, although the substantial knowledge may at times overflow into the senses, activating them.

John also speaks of memory as a spiritual faculty. Despite all that has been written on the subject, there does not seem to be any clear solution as to whether he thought of the memory as being really distinct from the intellect.[22] The problem arises because St. Thomas allows for only two spiritual faculties, intellect and will, and commentators wonder if John deliberately chose to differ from Aquinas. John, with an interest more practical than theoretical, chose the traditional division of the three faculties and then related them to the three theological virtues. His concern centered about the objects proper to each faculty and the

---

22. Cf. André Bord, *Mémoire et espérance chez Jean de la Croix* (Paris: Beauchesne, 1971).

purification of each for the sake of union with God. His other concern is their interdependence and interaction.

The appetitive faculties do not receive as many subdivisions. Nonetheless, John's interest in the external senses has more to do with the repercussions the activity of the senses has on the appetites than with the knowledge it involves. In speaking of the passions, he follows Boethius, who divides the passions into four: joy, hope, fear, and sorrow. Because *The Ascent of Mount Carmel*, in which he began to expound his doctrine on the passions, is incomplete, however, John never develops this division to full effect.

The will, the inclination toward the good apprehended by the intellect, is the spiritual faculty that rules over and is responsible for the whole affective sector. John has the will in mind when he analyzes the appetites and passions.

He sometimes refers to the sensitive part (the external and internal senses) vertically as to the lower part, or, sometimes, horizontally as to the exterior part. Similarly, the spiritual part, the faculties of intellect, memory, and will, becomes the higher part or the interior part. The spiritual part may experience God's communications directly, yet in ways analogous to sense experiences. Thus he speaks of the spirit as seeing, hearing, being touched by God, and so on. The two parts, higher and lower, do not exist independently of each other. In their being and in their operations they form an indestructible unity, which is the *suppositum*, the person. In this sense there is no duality.

Accepting this structure from the philosophy of his time, John uses it only that it might serve him in a practical way for the exposition of his spiritual doctrine. The value of his religious message and the realities behind it do not rest on the medieval rational psychology that he uses.

On almost every page John speaks of sense and spirit. He experienced the antagonism existing between the two. It is difficult for humans to bring about harmony between them because each part gropes and twists to be in command. The biblical formulations of struggle between flesh and spirit, life and death, light and darkness, old man and new man, speak to John of this experience. Inner peace between the two comes about only gradually and with difficulty. The first phase is achieved when the senses "are accommodated and united to the spirit."[23] The spirit as a result is more likely to marvel in the discovery

---

23. N. 2, 3, 1.

of a new world that was previously eclipsed by the individual's undetached immersion in the life of the senses. The spirit now perceives beneath the rind (the accident) of things to which the senses cling new depths, the spirit, or truth, or substance of these things, which provide it with hitherto unknown joys. Through this superior perspective the sense life is enriched. Now it is the spirit that looks at things, through the senses, and not the senses independently of the spirit. "Each part of the soul can now in its own way receive nourishment from the same spiritual food and from the same dish of only one suppositum and subject. These two parts thus united and conformed are jointly prepared to suffer the rough and arduous purgation of the spirit which awaits them."[24]

The spirit is the part that bears relation to God; it is a capacity to perceive the divine object. The divine object itself is also called spirit. Yet the divine Reality to which the spirit is opened must not be looked on simply as pure object, for it is active and personal. In the presence of Pure Spirit, the human spirit adopts a deeper posture, not active but passive, the attitude of one who is receiving.

The most intimate depth of the spirit has both a psychological and a theological dimension. John often refers to it as the substance, another of the different ways he makes use of this term. When John speaks of fruition, joy, and delight, or of sadness, anguish, and desolation taking place in the substance of the soul, he is referring to that inmost capacity in the human psychological makeup for such experiences. Though this depth of the soul forms part of the human complex anterior to any mystical experience of God, it does not seem that there exists a way of activating it through human endeavor. What is needed is a nakedness and poverty of spirit that cannot be gained merely through an individual's own efforts.

Finally, John teaches that the center of the soul is God. By this he means that the capacity for the infinite is inherent in the human spirit, but unruly attachments of the heart keep humans from being aware of their immense capacities. They will never achieve true peace and satisfaction until they have attained the emptiness or poverty of spirit necessary for union with God.

---

24. Ibid.

GENERAL INTRODUCTION

Writings

Writing occupied only a secondary place in the life of St. John of the Cross. He seems to have known none of the concerns that occupy the minds of professional writers and academics. We get the idea at times that he focused more on masonry and carpentry work than on using his genius for writing about the spiritual life. The corpus of his written works is comparatively brief. It includes some dozen poems, some maxims and counsels, some short letters, and, more importantly, his larger book-length commentaries on three of his poems. All of it comes to no more than about a thousand pages.

Representing John's first years in Andalusia (1578–1582), we have the aphoristic writings destined for the immediate direction of his friars and nuns: sayings of light and love; maxims and counsels, precautions, the sketch of the mount of perfection, and so on. These fragments set the stage for the major works.

The major works were composed during John's years in Granada (1582–1587), and written at the urging of friends and disciples as commentaries on poems previously written: *The Spiritual Canticle, The Dark Night,* and *The Living Flame of Love.* The first work completed was *The Spiritual Canticle* (1584), later revised in a new redaction (1585–1586). While working on this first of his commentaries, John was simultaneously developing *The Ascent of Mount Carmel*, which he had begun as a commentary on *The Dark Night* before 1582 but which developed into a treatise of its own and was left incomplete while the author was still speaking of active purification. Setting aside the *Ascent*, he turned again to the poem *The Dark Night* and began a closer interpretation of it (1583–1585) from the viewpoint of passive purification, but never finished the work. The major writings were completed with his explanation of *The Living Flame of Love*, a work kept more carefully within the boundaries of a commentary. John composed it in one quick sweep sometime between 1585 and 1587 and then made some slight revisions in it during the last years of his life. As for his correspondence, only about thirty-five of his letters, or fragments of them, have been preserved or found, representing just the later years of his life.

In each of his major works, John gives the complete synthesis of his thought, but there is much difference in the extent to which he develops the various aspects of it. Since his works take their beginning from his poems, the symbols of the poetry give a certain thrust to his teaching. In selecting the writings for a volume suited to this series, The

GENERAL INTRODUCTION

Classics of Western Spirituality, I have chosen from John's major works, and those sections from each that adhere more closely to the central elements of the individual work. *The Ascent of Mount Carmel* and *The Dark Night* are influenced by the symbol "night," and concentrate on the purification that is wrought through various efforts and experiences symbolized by that term. The emphasis in *The Spiritual Canticle* is on love, a love whose key dimensions are presented under the symbolism of a loving exchange between bride and bridegroom. *The Living Flame of Love* raises the reader's attention to an exalted loving knowledge within the Blessed Trinity found at the peak of Christian mystical life. From these points of view the *Ascent* and *Night* lead into the *Canticle*, and the *Canticle* into the *Flame*.[25]

---

25. The best general introductions to St. John of the Cross are done in Spanish by Eulogio Pacho and Federico Ruiz Salvador, the former dwelling more on historical critical questions. See Eulogio (de la Virgen del Carmen) Pacho, *San Juan de La Cruz y Sus Escritos* (Madrid: Ediciones Cristiandad, 1969) and *Iniciación a S. Juan de la Cruz* (Burgos: Editorial Monte Carmelo, 1982); Federico Ruiz Salvador, *Introducción a San Juan de la Cruz* (Madrid: B.A.C., 1968). An older study in French still of interest is Jean Baruzi's *Saint Jean de la Croix et le problème de l'expérience mystique* (Paris: Felix Alcan, 1924); a more recent important study is Georges Morel's *Le Sens de l'existence selon S. Jean de la Croix*, 3 vols. (Paris: Aubier 1960–1961). In English there is the older general introduction by Bede Frost, *Saint John of the Cross: An Introduction to His Philosophy, Theology, and Spirituality* (New York: Harper & Bros. 1937); and the more recent work by E. W. Truman Dicken, *The Crucible of Love: A Study of the Mysticism of St. Teresa of Jesus and St. John of the Cross* (New York: Sheed & Ward, 1963).

The Ascent of Mount Carmel

Editor's Introduction

Four elements go to make up the works that have been referred to as a diptych: the poem "The Dark Night"; the sketch of the mount of perfection; the commentary called *The Ascent of Mount Carmel*; and the commentary called *The Dark Night*.

The poem consists of eight stanzas, and was written during the time John lived at El Calvario (1578–1579), after his escape from prison. The symbol "night" anchors the basic inspiration for the doctrine expounded throughout the *Ascent* and the *Night*, but it also gives a negative tone to the treatises. Yet the symbol implies much more than pure negation. God Himself and union with Him belong to this darkness; in it there is fullness of life.

The sketch of "the mount of perfection" has reached us through a notarized copy of an autograph drawn for Magdalena del Espíritu Santo. It offers a visual synthesis of the teaching John explains in his commentary. Though only one authenticated copy has come down to us, we know that John drew many such sketches both for friars and nuns on pieces of paper they could carry in their breviaries, and that not all the sketches were exactly alike. That this sketch was meant to be a part of his work is clear from his own words when he refers to "the drawing at the beginning of the book."

The treatise on the ascent of the mount, though it takes the poem as a starting point and is influenced by it in the distinctive style of the exposition, is not in the strict sense a commentary on the poem. The title of the treatise, *The Ascent of Mount Carmel*, comes from the sketch, and the exposition follows a structure and style of its own, largely independent of the poem, but colored by the synthesis presented in the sketch of the mount.

The work known as *The Dark Night* is the actual commentary on the poem and preserves in its style something of the poem's lyricism

SKETCH OF MOUNT CARMEL BY ST. JOHN OF THE CROSS.

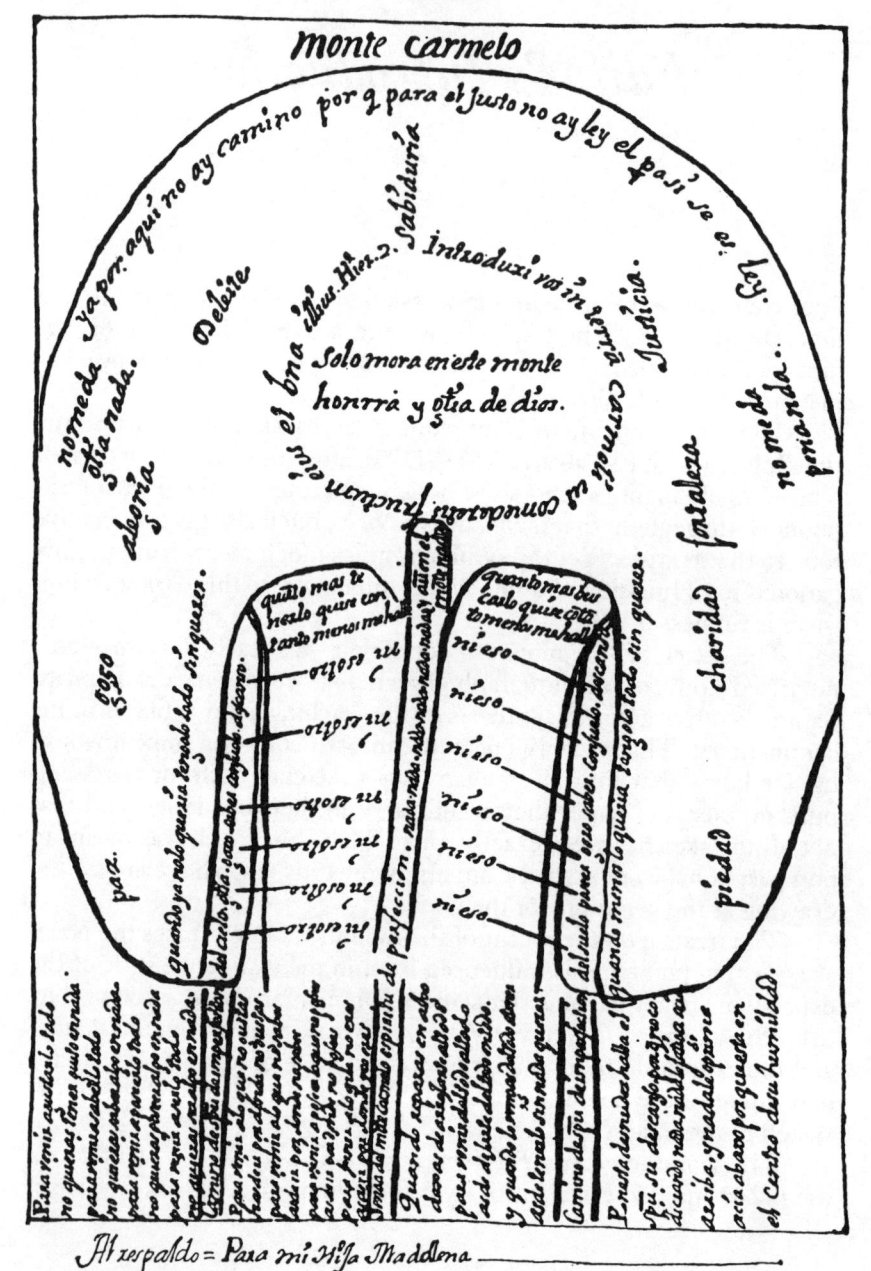

ENGLISH TRANSLATION OF TERMS USED IN ST. JOHN'S ORIGINAL DRAWING.

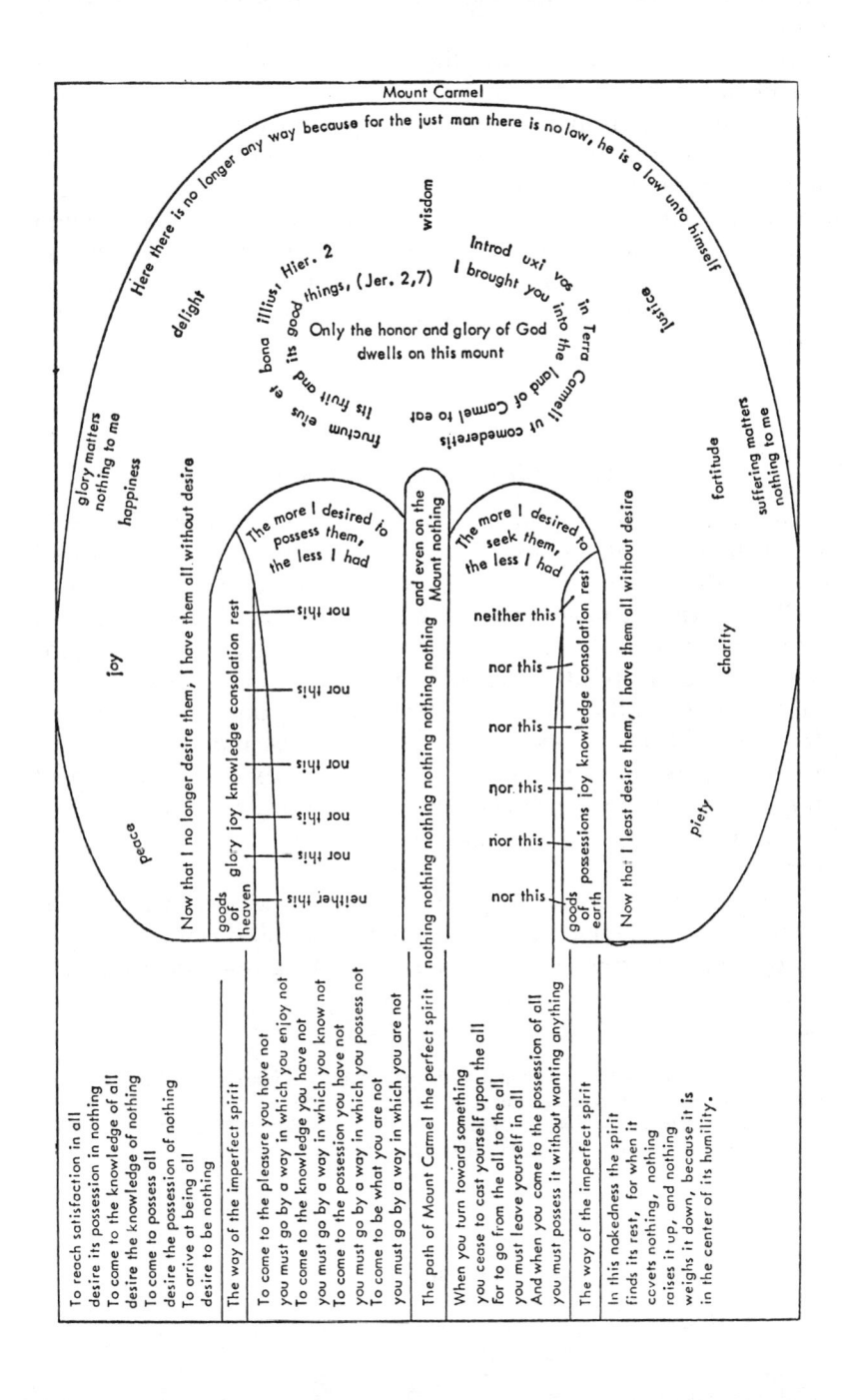

Mount Carmel

Here there is no longer any way because for the just man there is no law, he is a law unto himself

delight — wisdom — justice

Introd uxi vos in Terra Carmeli, ut comederetis fructum eius et bona illius, Hier. 2 (Jer. 2,7)
I brought you into the land of Carmel to eat its fruit and its good things

Only the honor and glory of God dwells on this mount

glory matters nothing to me
happiness

Now that I no longer desire them, I have them all without desire

joy — peace

The more I desired to possess them, the less I had
and even on the Mount nothing
The more I desired to seek them, the less I had

goods of heaven — glory joy knowledge consolation rest
neither this — nor this — nor this — nor this — nor this
nothing nothing nothing nothing nothing nothing
neither this — nor this — nor this — nor this — nor this
goods of earth — possessions joy knowledge consolation rest

The path of Mount Carmel the perfect spirit

Now that I least desire them, I have them all without desire

fortitude
suffering matters nothing to me

charity — piety

To reach satisfaction in all desire its possession in nothing
To come to the knowledge of all desire the knowledge of nothing
To come to possess all desire the possession of nothing
To arrive at being all desire to be nothing

The way of the imperfect spirit

To come to the pleasure you have not you must go by a way in which you enjoy not
To come to the knowledge you have not you must go by a way in which you know not
To come to the possession you have not you must go by a way in which you possess not
To come to be what you are not you must go by a way in which you are not

The way of the imperfect spirit

When you turn toward something you cease to cast yourself upon the all
For to go from the all to the all you must leave yourself in all
And when you come to the possession of all you must possess it without wanting anything

The way of the imperfect spirit

In this nakedness the spirit finds its rest, for when it covets nothing, nothing raises it up, and nothing weighs it down, because it is in the center of its humility.

and symbolic language. It has a character and literary style quite distinct from the heavy, scholastic, and conceptual mode of expression found in the *Ascent*. Its tone comes closer to that of *The Living Flame of Love*.[1]

Despite their differences, the two commentaries complement each other, the *Ascent* focusing more on the human initiative preceding the divine response, and the *Night*, on the divine initiative preceding the human response; or the former on the active night, the latter on the passive night. Many arguments have been brought forth and accepted by scholars to demonstrate how in John's mind these commentaries are parts of a unity.[2] Thus though the works come to us in separate manuscripts, one for the *Ascent* and the other for the *Night*, they are held together by the hinge of their thematic unity.

The Ascent of Mount Carmel

In a letter to Thomas Merton, a pastor of a Congregational Church in Massachusetts sought advice in his reading of St. John of the Cross.[3] Although the pastor felt drawn by the saint, he was at the same time repelled by the seeming harshness and almost superhuman demands that the spirituality seemed to call for. Could it have any meaning for people who are married and raising a family? The letter is a classic illustration of the difficulty people often run up against on first reading *The Ascent of Mount Carmel*. Undoubtedly a good number of readers have never persevered through the work. This difficulty has prompted editors to attempt various other ways of presenting the writings of St. John of the Cross so that one does not begin with *The Ascent of Mount Carmel*.

In his answer Merton suggested that John was speaking from the "other side" of attainment, from the fullness of fulfillment. In his picturesque way, Merton describes John as speaking from the experience

---
1. A. 1, 13, 10.
2. The arguments were carefully put forth by Juan de Jesús María in "El díptico Subida-Noche," in *Sanjuanistica* (Rome: Teresianum, 1943), pp. 27–83.
3. See *The Hidden Ground of Love: The Letters of Thomas Merton on Religious Experience and Social Concerns*, sel. and ed. William H. Shannon (New York: Farrar Straus Giroux, 1985), pp. 107–08.

of the completely *positive underside* of what appears to us to be a merely negative cloud of darkness.

From this other side, then, John knew the radical demands of union with God, which are involved in the main theme of the ascent: "the way that leads to the summit of the mount."[4] As a result, in much of his discussion he speaks strongly when explaining his theory on the nature of union and its demands. But in the practical realization of the journey there has to be flexibility. Why? Because to move from one extreme to the other, from sense to spirit, one must proceed according to the divine plan. In this plan, John insists, God adapts to the human condition and leads each one gently, with order, and according to the "mode" of each, that is, according to the individual's particular characteristics and life situation. Harsh procedure in practice goes contrary to God's method.[5] It is in addition important for the person and the spiritual director to observe how God is leading. If, for example, John insists on the rejection of revelations, he also points out pastorally to confessors that "not because we have greatly stressed the rejection of these communications . . . should directors show severity, displeasure, or scorn in dealing with these souls."[6] John goes on to observe that since God is leading these people by such means there is no reason for opposition, fear, or scandal; that the director should be kind and peaceful, giving encouragement and the opportunity to speak about one's experiences.

As implied previously, the negativity in the symbol of night is another reason for the apparent harshness. The symbol led John in the plan of his work to focus on the demands, the trials, the renunciation imposed by true love, leaving love itself in the shadows. In other works, however, he looks at things through the lens of love, observes the power of love's vital thrust toward its goal, the capacity it has to superabound in happiness.

At the outset of his work, John gives what appears to be a clear and simple division of the material. He will treat of the night or purification of the senses and of the spirit, of the senses in the first section of the book and of the spirit in the second and third sections.[7] But since, in reality, the experiences of the senses have their repercussions on the

---

4. A. theme.
5. See A. 2, 17, 1–6.
6. A. 2, 22, 19.
7. A. 1, 1, 1–3.

spirit and vice versa, there is no purification solely of the senses or of the spirit. This fact results in much overlapping of themes. A large amount of the material in the second and third sections deals with the purification of the senses. When John indeed came to speak of the theological virtues as the adequate means for the purification of the spiritual faculties and their union with God, he found that he had to take up again the question of the senses. To deal fully with the development of these virtues he was required to do so. In the concrete, life is not divided into sense and spirit. Taking into account, then, the true theological structure of the work, the first book is a kind of doctrinal introduction dealing with the notion, divisions, and necessity of the dark night. The second and third books deal with the life of the theological virtues as the means of purification and union with God.

In Chapter 4 of Book One of the *Ascent*, John speaks of God's transcendence over creatures. The distance between the being of God and the being of the created world is infinite. If the two were compared we would have to say that "all the being of creatures compared with the infinite being of God is nothing."[8] Illustrating this truth, John makes use of the biblical terms of light and darkness, God being the pure and simple light. God, then, is unique. Esteeming anything alongside Him, allowing it to dwell with Him, is to elevate it to the rank of idol. "God allows nothing else to dwell together with Him. We read, consequently, in the First Book of Kings that when the Philistines put the Ark of the Covenant in a temple with their idol, the idol was hurled to the ground at the dawn of each day and broken in pieces."[9] As transcendent, as unique, God alone must be the object of the entire appetitive activity of the human person.

The work of centering all the faculties on the transcendent God is essentially a negative activity, in that the unique One is attained only by the rejection of the many. In commenting on Deuteronomy 6:5, John teaches that the command "You shall love the Lord, your God, with all your heart, and with all your soul, and with all your strength" contains everything that a spiritual person must do and sums up all that there is to teach about how to reach union with God through charity.[10] In this precept of love, Deuteronomy underscores with the words "all your heart," "all your soul," and "all your strength," the totality with

---

8. A. 1, 4, 4.
9. A. 1, 5, 8.
10. A. 3, 16, 1.

which people must dedicate their entire being to God. They must respond to God's covenant with integrity and allow no room for any other divinity, any other value. All the religious duty owed by Israel to its God is comprised in this precept, and John remarked that the purification of the appetitive side of humans, of their affective and volitional life, could come about only through the complete practice of this commandment of love.

In what he says in Book One concerning the mortification of the appetites and in the second section of Book Three concerning the purification of the appetitive part through love, John teaches that the indulgence of the inordinate appetites is a form of idolatry. This may be deduced both from his descriptions and from the biblical texts he cites in this connection. Any appetite is potentially an idol. Insomuch as an appetite imposes a way of behavior contrary to the divine law, that appetite is a rival of God.

When John in turn speaks of the transcendence of God in relation to the intellect, he presents God not in the dimension of His uniqueness but in that of His incomprehensibility to the human mind. He insists that since the difference between God's being and the being of creatures is infinite, intellectual comprehension of God through creatures is impossible.

The apprehensions of the memory are in a class with those of the intellect, except that they belong and refer to the past. Thus, "if individuals bestow importance and attention on the apprehensions of the memory, they will find it impossible to remain free for the Incomprehensible, who is God."[11] Individuals in their journey to God must go not by comprehending but by not comprehending and "must exchange the mutable and comprehensible for the Immutable and Incomprehensible."[12]

Being incomprehensible, God is also incomparable: "Everything the intellect can understand, the will experience, and the imagination picture is most unlike and disproportioned to God."[13] Israel on Horeb, at the moment of the solemn encounter with God, saw no form or figure of the divine but only heard the voice. The original experience on Horeb became normative. Only the absence of any divine image would respect the inherent characteristic of Israel's God, that is, no image

---

11. A. 3, 5, 3.
12. Ibid.
13. A. 2, 8, 5.

could represent Him. As a result, the prescription that Israel should not have other gods or carve idols is closely bound up with the biblical idea of the divine transcendence.[14]

This commandment, though not quoted directly by John, prohibits any image of God. The true image of God conformable to him can be furnished only through faith and hope. Faith has as its object the divine revelation. Hope presents God in the dimension of the future. John treats of faith in Book Two of the *Ascent* and of hope in the first part of Book Three.

Faith, hope, and charity, which only with St. Paul appear formally as constituting the Christian life, are rooted in the center of salvific revelation, in the above two commandments.[15] Charity responds to the first commandment, to its obligation of a love for God that is total and undivided, He being unique and transcendent. Faith and hope correspond to the second, for only they can offer a true image of God.[16]

For John the journey in faith (faith in its broad sense, which includes hope and love), the principal subject matter of the *Ascent*, does not deal merely with the renunciation of idols and images. Through faith one moves, advances, journeys on a path to union with God.

In treating of faith John deals with its many aspects, sometimes identifying it with its objective dimension, sometimes with its subjective dimension. In itself the content of faith is simply the mystery of God revealed in Jesus Christ, who is the fount of all the particular dogmas.

The central moment in John's entire presentation of the journey in faith comes in Chapter 22 of Book Two. This chapter illumines all that precedes it and all that follows. In it John explains how Christ is the revelation of the Father, God's definitive word that leaves nothing else to reveal. "If I have already told you all things in My Word, My Son, and if I have no other word, what answer or revelation can I now make that would surpass this?"[17]

Since in Jesus Christ we find the full content of the divine revelation, we can take the next step by asserting that this object is personal

---

14. See Dt. 4:9–20, 5:6–10.
15. See Dt. 6:4–5, 5:6–7.
16. For further study of these ideas see Fabrizio Foresti, "Le radici bibliche della 'Salita del Monte Carmelo' di S. Giovanni della Croce," in *Carmelus* 28 (1981): 226–55; for an English version see *Sinai and Carmel: The Biblical Roots of the Spiritual Doctrine of St. John of the Cross* (privately printed by Darlington Carmel, England, 1981), pp. 1–38.
17. A. 2, 22, 5.

and not a matter of abstract ideas. The revelation given to us is our "brother, companion, master, ransom, and reward";[18] He offers Himself in fact as the soul's savior, beloved, and bridegroom.

At the same time the content of faith is a light so brilliant that the human intellect is dazzled and blinded. Though faith speaks truths to it (for example, of the hypostatic union of the human nature with the divine Word or of the three Persons in one God), the human intellect does not know how they are possible. Thus faith in giving us light also blinds us. It is a dark night for humans.[19]

But faith is nonetheless the light of the Godhead drawing people by its own power, imparting its own peace, empowering them to penetrate into its depths. John has frequent comments like the following: "Only by means of faith, in divine light exceeding all understanding, does God manifest Himself to the soul."[20] In fact the future vision, the light of glory, is germinally contained in faith, obscure though faith may be, faint subdued glimmer that it is. Using the example of the soldiers of Gideon who were carrying torches in clay jars so that the light could not be seen, John explains: "All of this darkness signifies the obscurity of faith with which the divinity is clothed. . . . Faith, represented by those clay jars, contains the divine light. When faith reaches its end and is shattered by the ending and breaking of this mortal life, the glory and light of the divinity, the content of faith, will at once begin to shine."[21]

The content of faith, the revelation of Jesus Christ, includes the law of Christ and the human and visible means He established in the Church and His ministers. As a result, one is drawn by faith to embrace their consequent values and demands. The person of faith seeks assurance and confirmation in the Church and her ministers. "For God will not bring clarification and confirmation of the truth to the heart of one who is alone."[22] Journeying by faith one also learns to remain within the boundaries of the ordinary and not to search for the divine in visions and revelations or other delightful spiritual feelings. One learns to es-

---

18. Ibid.
19. A. 2, 9, 1; C. 37, 1–3. For a theological discussion of this aspect of faith see Karol Wojtyla, *Faith According to Saint John of the Cross* (San Francisco: Ignatius Press, 1981); see also his "The Question of Faith in St. John of the Cross" in *Carmelite Studies* (Washington, D.C.: ICS Publications, 1982), pp. 223–73.
20. A. 2, 9, 1.
21. A. 2, 9, 3.
22. A. 2, 22, 11.

teem the use of reason in the solving of life's problems, for "to declare and strengthen truth on the basis of natural reason, He [God] draws near those who come together in an endeavor to know it."[23]

Though the content of faith is always the same, it is not always received in the same way. There is no end to the variety of shadings, the ways in which these truths may be illumined for individuals; dormant potentialities are awakened. Furthermore the journey toward union brings about at the same time a progress in human knowing: from the senses to the imagination to discursive thinking to intuition or contemplation.

Since Christ is the full revelation of the Father, John, speaking for the Father, advises: "Fasten your eyes on Him alone because in Him I have spoken and revealed all."[24] We are dealing in faith with one who awakens love, Christ the Father's Beloved Son in whom every good is given to us. If the object, indeed, is personal, the attitude on the part of the subject to what is being communicated in faith will be a personal one of listening, responding, and generous surrender.

The novice may begin in prayer by meditating on the life of Christ, who will exercise His attraction, calling forth love and the desire for imitation and likeness. He who is the end is also the way.[25] Through His life He reveals the radical renunciation, the death required before rising to the new happiness of full divinization. Only the love of Christ will enable seekers to disentangle themselves from the forces of their disordered appetites and reshape their lives. "A more intense enkindling of another, better love (love of one's heavenly bridegroom) is necessary for the vanquishing of the appetites."[26] To be sure, all of this brings us far beyond the situation of the beginner.

As the light of faith grows, there is a movement in prayer from sense to spirit, from ideas about Christ to an inner more personal relationship, an interiorization and simplification in the way of communing and being one with Him. The spiritual powers are drawn by faith in darkness to a presence within, to a receptive attitude of general loving attention. The new spiritual love may be felt and easily recognized; or it may be experienced as dryness and discerned through the persevering desire to be with the Other; or it may be recognized through the solic-

---

23. Ibid.
24. A. 2, 22, 5.
25. See A. 1, 13, 3–4; 14, 2; A. 2, 14, 2.
26. A. 2, 14, 2.

itude of love. God's self-communication in faith, the loving knowledge given to the spirit, is now more abundant since in this contemplation it need no longer be restricted by images and ideas.[27] As a consequence, in faith both the attraction to Christ and the dark sense of His presence grow stronger.[28]

But union with Christ through faith takes us a step further, which John developed in more detail in *The Spiritual Canticle*. It makes us sharers in His Sonship. In addition, all the bridegroom's mysteries are seen as reflections of the divine attributes, and union with Him brings us into union with the Father in the Holy Spirit.[29]

The *Ascent of Mount Carmel* may be divided as follows:

Book One
Chapters 1–3: Divisions and meaning of the night
Chapters 4–12: Necessity of the night of the mortification of the appetites
Chapter 13: Practical rules
Chapters 14–15: Commentary on the remaining verses of stanza 1

Book Two
Chapters 1–7: The night of the spirit, a journey in faith
Chapters 8–9: Faith, the only proximate means to union in the intellect
Chapter 10: The different kinds of apprehensions of which the intellect must be purified through faith
Chapters 11–16: Apprehensions through the senses
Chapters 17–22: The way of faith in God's dealings with His people
Chapters 23–32: Intellectual apprehensions received directly: visions, revelations, locutions, spiritual feelings

Book Three
Chapters 1–6: The purification of the memory through hope: of its natural apprehensions
Chapters 7–13: of its supernatural imaginative apprehensions
Chapter 14: of its spiritual apprehensions
Chapter 15: Practical rules

---

27. See the chapters on the signs of contemplation: A. 2, 13–15; N. 1, 8–10. For a more detailed explanation see my "Saint John of the Cross on Aridity and Contemplation," in *Spiritual Life* 8 (1962): 182–93.
28. See C. 12, 1–6.
29. See C. 36–39.

THE ASCENT OF MOUNT CARMEL

Chapter 16: The purification of the will through love of its inordinate feelings or passions
Chapters 17–45: The passion of joy arising from temporal, natural, sensory, moral, supernatural, and spiritual goods

Since John's autographs have been lost, editors must turn to those copies they judge most reliable. The copy of *The Ascent of Mount Carmel* considered the most trustworthy is the codex of *Alcaudete* preserved in the Silverio archives in Burgos. The handwriting of the copy is that of Padre Juan Evangelista, who besides being John's confessor was also his secretary and close companion. Another reliable copy of the *Ascent* used most often to help where there are deficiencies in *Alcaudete* is the codex of *Alba* (A) conserved by the Discalced Carmelite Friars in Alba de Tormes.

The Ascent of Mount Carmel

This treatise explains how to reach divine union quickly. It presents instruction and doctrine valuable for beginners and proficients alike that they may learn how to unburden themselves of all earthly things, avoid spiritual obstacles, and live in that complete nakedness and freedom of spirit necessary for divine union.

Theme

The following stanzas include all the doctrine I intend to discuss in this book, *The Ascent of Mount Carmel.* They describe the way that leads to the summit of the mount—that high state of perfection we here call union of a soul with God. Since these stanzas will serve as a basis for all I shall say, I want to cite them here in full that the reader may see in them a summary of the doctrine to be expounded. Yet I will quote each stanza again before its explanation and give the verses separately if the subject so requires.

> 5. O guiding night!
> O night more lovely than the dawn!
> O night that has united
> The lover with his beloved,
> Transforming the beloved in her lover.
>
> 6. Upon my flowering breast
> Which I kept wholly for him alone,

THE ASCENT OF MOUNT CARMEL

There he lay sleeping,
And I caressing him
There in a breeze from the fanning cedars.

7. When the breeze blew from the turret
Parting his hair,
He wounded my neck
With his gentle hand,
Suspending all my senses.

8. I abandoned and forgot myself
Laying my face on my beloved;
All things ceased; I went out from myself,
Leaving my cares
Forgotten among the lilies.

Stanzas

A song of the soul's happiness in having passed through the dark night of faith, in nakedness and purgation, to union with its Beloved.

1. One dark night,
Fired with love's urgent longings
—Ah, the sheer grace!—
I went out unseen,
My house being now all stilled;

2. In darkness and secure,
By the secret ladder, disguised,
—Ah, the sheer grace!—
In darkness and concealment,
My house being now all stilled;

3. On that glad night,
In secret, for no one saw me,
Nor did I look at anything,
With no other light or guide

THE ASCENT OF MOUNT CARMEL

Than the one that burned in my heart;

4. This guided me
More surely than the light of noon
To where he waited for me
—him I knew so well—
In a place where no one appeared.

Prologue

1. A deeper enlightenment and wider experience than mine is necessary to explain the dark night through which a soul journeys toward that divine light of perfect union with God that is achieved, insofar as possible in this life, through love. The darknesses and trials, spiritual and temporal, that fortunate souls ordinarily undergo on their way to the high state of perfection are so numerous and profound that human science cannot understand them adequately. Nor does experience of them equip one to explain them. Those who suffer them will know what this experience is like, but they will find themselves unable to describe it.

2. In discussing this dark night, therefore, I will not rely on experience or science, for these can fail and deceive us. Although I will not neglect whatever possible use I can make of them, my help in all that, with God's favor, I shall say, will be Sacred Scripture, at least in the most important matters, or those that are difficult to understand. Taking Scripture as our guide we do not err since the Holy Spirit speaks to us through it. Should I misunderstand or be mistaken on some point, whether I deduce it from Scripture or not, I will not be intending to deviate from the true meaning of Sacred Scripture or from the doctrine of our Holy Mother the Catholic Church. Should there be some mistake, I submit entirely to the Church, or even to anyone who judges more competently about the matter than I.

3. I am not undertaking this arduous task because of any particular confidence in my own abilities. Rather, I am confident that the Lord will help me explain this matter because it is extremely necessary to so many souls. Even though these souls have begun to walk along the road of virtue, and our Lord desires to place them in the dark night so that they may move on to the divine union, they do not advance. The reason is that sometimes they do not want to enter the dark night or allow

themselves to be placed in it, or that sometimes they misunderstand themselves and are without suitable and alert directors who will show them the way to the summit. God gives many souls the talent and grace for advancing, and should they desire to make the effort they would arrive at this high state. And so it is sad to see them continue in their lowly method of communion with God because they do not want or know how to advance, or because they receive no direction on breaking away from the methods of beginners. Even if our Lord finally comes to their aid to the extent of making them advance without these helps, they reach the summit much later, expend more effort, and gain less merit, because they do not willingly adapt themselves to God's work of placing them on the pure and reliable road leading to union. Although God does lead them—since He can do so without their cooperation—they do not accept His guidance. In resisting God who is conducting them, they make little progress and, as a result, must endure greater suffering. Some souls, instead of abandoning themselves to God and cooperating with Him, hamper Him by their indiscreet activity or by their resistance. They resemble children who kick and cry and struggle to walk by themselves when their mothers want to carry them; in walking by themselves they make no headway, or if they do it is at a child's pace.[1]

4. With God's help, then, we will propose doctrine and counsel for beginners and proficients that they may understand or at least know how to practice abandonment to God's guidance when He wants them to advance.[2]

Some spiritual directors are likely to be a hindrance and harm rather than a help to these souls that journey on this road. Such directors have neither enlightenment nor experience of these ways. They are like the builders of the tower of Babel [Gn 11:1–9]. When these builders were supposed to provide the proper materials for the project, they brought entirely different supplies because they failed to understand the language. And thus nothing was accomplished. Hence, it is arduous and difficult for a soul in these periods of the spiritual life when it cannot understand itself or find anyone else who understands it.

---

1. From what is being said and what follows, it may be deduced that John in this prologue is thinking mainly about what he plans to deal with in the passive night.

2. With regard to the spiritual journey, John accepts the traditional terminology of beginners, proficients, and the perfect. Here he is dealing only with the beginners and proficients because the perfect will already have reached the summit of the mount. In other passages he will use the equivalent terminology of the purgative, illuminative, and unitive ways.

THE ASCENT OF MOUNT CARMEL

It will happen to individuals that while they are being conducted by God along a sublime path of dark contemplation and aridity, in which they feel lost, they will meet someone in the midst of the fullness of their darknesses, trials, conflicts, and temptations who, in the style of Job's comforters [Jb 4:8–11], will proclaim that all of this is due to melancholia, depression, or temperament, or to some hidden wickedness, and that as a result God has forsaken them. Therefore the usual verdict is that these individuals must have lived an evil life since such trials afflict them.

5. Others will tell them that they are falling back since they find no satisfaction or consolation as they previously did in the things of God. Such talk only doubles the trial of a poor soul, because its greatest suffering is caused by the knowledge of its own miseries; that it is full of evil and sin is as clear as day, and even clearer, for, as we shall say presently, God is the author of this enlightenment in the night of contemplation. And when this soul finds someone who agrees with what it feels (that these trials are all its own fault), its suffering and distress grow without bounds. And this suffering usually becomes worse than death. Such a confessor is not satisfied with this but, in judging these trials to be the result of sin, he urges souls who endure them to go over their past and make many general confessions—which is another crucifixion. The director does not understand that now perhaps is not the time for such activity. Indeed, it is a period for leaving these persons alone in the purgation God is working in them, a time to give comfort and encouragement that they may desire to endure this suffering as long as God wills, for until then, no remedy—whatever the soul does, or the confessor says—is adequate.

6. We will discuss all this with the divine help: how individuals should behave; what method the confessor should use in dealing with them; the signs for the recognition of this purification of the soul, which we call the dark night; whether it is the purification of the senses or of the spirit; and how we can discern whether this affliction is caused by melancholia or some other deficiency of sense or spirit.

Some souls—or their confessors—may think that God is leading them along this road of the dark night of spiritual purgation, but perhaps this will not be so. What they suffer will owe its origin to one of these deficiencies. Likewise, many individuals think they are not praying, when, indeed, their prayer is intense. Others place high value on their prayer, while it is little more than nonexistent.

7. Some people—and it is sad to see them—work and tire them-

selves greatly, and yet go backward; they look for perfection in exercises that are of no profit to them, but rather a hindrance. Others continue to make fine progress in peace and tranquillity. Some individuals let themselves be encumbered by the very consolations and favors God bestows on them for the sake of their advancement, and they advance not at all.

We will also discuss many other experiences of those who walk along this road: joys, afflictions, hopes, and sorrows—some of these originating from the spirit of perfection, others from the spirit of imperfection. Our goal will be to explain, with God's help, all these points so that those who read this book will in some way discover the road they are walking along, and the one they ought to follow if they want to reach the summit of this mount.

8. Readers should not be surprised if this doctrine on the dark night—through which a soul advances toward God—appears somewhat obscure. This, I believe, will be the case as they begin to read, but as they read on they will understand it better since the latter parts will explain the former. Then, if they read this work a second time, the matter will seem clearer and the doctrine sounder.

But if some people still find difficulty in understanding this doctrine, it will be due to my deficient knowledge and awkward style, for the doctrine itself is good and very necessary. But I am inclined to believe that, even if it were presented with greater accuracy and polish, only a few would find profit in it, because we are not writing on pleasing and delightful themes addressed to the kind of spiritual people who like to approach God along sweet and satisfying paths. We are presenting a substantial and solid doctrine for all those who desire to reach this nakedness of spirit.

9. My main intention is not to address everyone, but only some of the persons of our holy order of the primitive observance of Mount Carmel, both friars and nuns, whom God favors by putting them on the path leading up this mount, since they are the ones who asked me to write this work. Because they are already detached to a great extent from the temporal things of this world, they will more easily grasp this doctrine on nakedness of spirit.[3]

---

3. The fact that John has particularly in mind the friars and nuns of the primitive observance of Mount Carmel does not negate his previous statement about his doctrine being good for all those wishing to make the journey to union with God. By reading and rereading,

Book One

Chapter One

Some remarks about the two different nights through which spiritual persons pass in both the lower and higher parts of their nature. A commentary on the first stanza.

First Stanza

One dark night,
Fired with love's urgent longings
—Ah, the sheer grace!—
I went out unseen,
My house being now all stilled;

1. The soul sings in this first stanza of its good luck and the grace it had in departing from its inordinate sensory appetites and imperfections.[4] To understand this departure one should know that a soul must ordinarily pass through two principal kinds of night—which spiritual persons call purgations or purifications of the soul—in order to reach the state of perfection. Here we will term these purgations "nights" because in both of them the soul journeys in darkness as though by night.

---

one will find that the doctrine will become clearer. A certain amount of detachment is also helpful in the attempt to grasp what he is saying.

4. In John's vocabulary the term "appetite," unless otherwise specified, refers to an inordinate impulse, an immoderate yearning, a desire not rightly ordered to the moral or spiritual good, in disaccord with or repugnant to right reason. It involves more than the simple inclination or natural passion that was meant by the term in Scholastic philosophy.

THE ASCENT OF MOUNT CARMEL

2. The first night or purgation, to which this stanza refers and which will be under discussion in the first section of this book, concerns the sensory part of the soul. The second night, to which the second stanza refers, concerns the spiritual part. We will deal with this second night, insofar as it is active, in the second and third sections of the book. In the fourth section we will discuss the night insofar as it is passive.[5]

3. This first night is the lot of beginners, at the time God commences to introduce them into the state of contemplation. It is a night in which their spirit also participates, as we will explain in due time. The second night or purification takes place in those who are already proficients, at the time God desires to lead them into the state of divine union. This purgation, of course, is more obscure, dark, and dreadful, as we will subsequently point out.

Commentary on the Stanza

4. In this stanza the soul desires to declare in summary fashion that it departed on a dark night, attracted by God and enkindled with love for Him alone. This dark night is a privation and purgation of all sensible appetites for the external things of the world, the delights of the flesh, and the gratifications of the will. All this deprivation is wrought in the purgation of sense. That is why the poem proclaims that the soul departed when its house was stilled, for the appetites of the sensory part were stilled and asleep in the soul, and the soul was stilled in them. One is not freed from the sufferings and anguish of the appetites until they are tempered and put to sleep. So it was a sheer grace, the soul declares, to have gone out unseen without encumbrance from the appetites of the flesh, or from anything else. It was also fortunate the departure took place at night; that is, that God took from the soul all these things through a privation that was a night to it.

5. It was a sheer grace to be placed by God in this night that occasioned so much good. The soul would not have succeeded in entering it, because souls are unable alone to empty themselves of all their appetites in order to reach God.

---

5. From this division comes the stereotype of the *Ascent*'s structure: active night of the senses in book one; active night of the spirit in books two and three; passive night of the spirit in book four. The first three books correspond to the *Ascent* and the last to the *Night*, which was not divided by John into two books. Sometimes John uses the term "section" instead of book. He presented this plan before he got into the actual developing of his work. Later he gives other outlines that do not fully match this one. He then superimposes them on this one or juxtaposes them to it.

THE ASCENT OF MOUNT CARMEL

6. Summarily, then, we have an explanation of the first stanza. Now we will expound on it verse by verse and explain whatever pertains to our subject. We will follow the method mentioned in the prologue: first cite each stanza and then the individual verses.[6]

Chapter Two

The nature of the dark night through which a soul journeys to divine union.

One Dark Night

1. We can offer three reasons for calling this journey toward union with God a night.

The first has to do with the point of departure because individuals must deprive themselves of their appetites for worldly possessions. This denial and privation is like a night for all their senses.

The second reason refers to the means or the road along which a person travels to this union. Now this road is faith, and for the intellect faith is also like a dark night.

The third reason pertains to the point of arrival, namely God. And God is also a dark night to the soul in this life. These three nights pass through a soul, or better, the soul passes through them in order to reach union with God.[7] . . .

Chapter Three

The first cause of this night—the privation of the appetite in all things. The reason for the use of the expression "night."

---

6. Actually John does not follow through on this promise. The *Ascent* becomes a treatise rather than a commentary. Only in the *Night* does he get back to a commentary on the poem.

7. This three-part division is different from the division into four parts given in the previous chapter. In using night here as a metaphor rather than a symbol, John makes the transition to a treatise. Just as in night there is a privation of light, so for three reasons there is a privation involved in the spiritual journey, and this journey can consequently be called a night. John then proceeds with his intention of explaining these three reasons for calling the spiritual journey a night.

THE ASCENT OF MOUNT CARMEL

1. We are using the expression "night" to signify a deprival of the gratification of the soul's appetites in all things. Just as night is nothing but the privation of light and, consequently, of all objects visible by means of the light—darkness and emptiness, then, for the faculty of sight—the mortification of the appetites can be called a night for the soul. To deprive oneself of the gratification of the appetites in all things is like living in darkness and in a void.[8] The eye feeds on its objects by means of light in such a way that when the light is extinguished the eye no longer sees them. Similarly do people by means of their faculties feed and pasture on worldly things that gratify their faculties. When the appetites are extinguished—or mortified—one no longer feeds on the pleasure of these things, but lives in a void and in darkness with respect to the appetites. . . .

4. We can easily affirm that if a soul denies whatever is perceptible through the senses, it lives in darkness and in a void since light can enter by no other natural means than these five senses. Now it is true that the sensory perceptions of hearing, sight, smell, taste, and touch are unavoidable; yet they will no more hinder a soul—if it denies them—than if they were not experienced. It is true also that those desiring to keep their eyes closed will live in darkness just like the blind.

David says on this subject: *Pauper sum ego, et in laboribus a juventute mea* (I am poor and in labors from my youth) [Ps 88:16]. Even though he was manifestly rich, he says he was poor because his will was not fixed on riches; and he thereby lived as though really poor. On the other hand, had he been actually poor, without his will being so, there would have been no true poverty, because the appetite of his soul would have been rich and full.

Hence, we call this nakedness a night for the soul. For we are not discussing the mere lack of things; this lack will not divest the soul if it craves for all these objects. We are dealing with the denudation of the soul's appetites and gratifications. This is what leaves it free and empty of all things, even though it possesses them. Since the things of the world cannot enter the soul, they are not in themselves an encumbrance

---

8. The use of the notions darkness and light may make us think more in terms of knowing since the scholastics spoke of understanding truth by means of the intellectual light. But John is speaking here on the affective level. What gives us a feeling of life and interest in things is the satisfaction that comes from them. When this satisfaction is gone, the mere material presence of these will not make up for the lack. This explains something of the depression that may be suffered in the passive night.

or harm to it; rather, it is the will and appetite dwelling within that cause the damage when set on these things.[9] . . .

Chapter Four

The necessity of truly passing through this dark night of sense (the mortification of the appetites) in order to journey to union with God.

1. The necessity of passing through this dark night (the mortification of the appetites and the denial of pleasure in all things) for the attainment of the divine union with God arises from the fact that all of a person's attachments to creatures are pure darkness in God's sight. Clothed in these affections, people will be incapable of the enlightenment and dominating fullness of God's pure and simple light; first they must reject them. There can be no concordance between light and darkness; as St. John says: *Tenebrae eam no comprehenderunt* (The darkness could not receive the light) [Jn 1:5].

2. The reason, as we learn in philosophy, is that two contraries cannot coexist in the same subject.[10] Darkness, an attachment to creatures, and light, which is God, are contraries and bear no likeness toward each other, as St. Paul teaches in his letter to the Corinthians: *Quae conventio lucis ad tenebras?* (What conformity is there between light and darkness?) [2 Cor 6:14]. Consequently, the light of divine union cannot be established in the soul until these affections are eradicated.

3. For a better proof of this, it ought to be kept in mind that an attachment to a creature makes a person equal to that creature; the stronger the attachment, the closer is the likeness to the creature and the greater the equality. For love effects a likeness between the lover and the loved.[11] As a result David said of those who set their hearts on

---

9. This clarification is basic to the understanding of John's doctrine.

10. This principle from Aristotelian-Scholastic philosophy is formulated and explained by Aristotle, *De sensu et sensato* 8.

11. This fundamental principle is basic in John's thought. It goes back to the Latin and Greek philosophers and poets and was taken over by Christian writers. John applies the principle to the human person's love for God. Despite God's transcendence on the ontological level, the human person can become like Him through love. Cf. C 38, 3; Aquinas *Summa Theologica* 2-2, 23, 1.

their idols: *Similis illis fiant qui faciunt ea, et omnes qui confidunt in eis* (Let all who set their hearts on them become like them) [Ps 115:8]. Anyone who loves a creature, then, is as low as that creature and in some way even lower because love not only equates but even subjects the lover to the loved creature. By the mere fact that a soul loves something, it becomes incapable of pure union and transformation in God; for the lowness of the creature is far less capable of the height of the Creator than is darkness of light.

All creatures of heaven and earth are nothing when compared to God, as Jeremiah points out: *Aspexi terram, et ecce vacua erat et nihil; et caelos, et non erat lux in eis* (I looked at the earth, and it was empty and nothing; and at the heavens, and I saw they had no light) [Jer 4:23]. By saying that he saw an empty earth, he meant that all its creatures were nothing and that the earth too was nothing. In stating that he looked up to the heavens and beheld no light, he meant that all the heavenly luminaries were pure darkness in comparison to God. All creatures considered in this way are nothing, and a person's attachments to them are less than nothing since these attachments are an impediment to and deprive the soul of transformation in God—just as darkness is nothing and less than nothing since it is a privation of light. One who is in darkness does not comprehend the light, so neither will a person attached to creatures be able to comprehend God. Until a soul is purged of its attachments it will be unable to possess God, neither here below through the pure transformation of love nor in heaven through the beatific vision. For the sake of greater clarity we will be more specific.

4. We just asserted that all the being of creatures compared to the infinite being of God is nothing and that, therefore, anyone attached to creatures is nothing in the sight of God, and even less than nothing because love causes equality and likeness and even brings the lover lower than the loved object. In no way, then, is such a person capable of union with the infinite being of God. There is no likeness between what is not and what is. To be particular, here are some examples.

All the beauty of creatures compared to the infinite beauty of God is the height of ugliness. As Solomon says in Proverbs: *Fallax gratia, et vana est pulchritudo* (Comeliness is deceiving and beauty vain) [Prv 31:30]. So a person attached to the beauty of any creature is extremely ugly in God's sight. A soul so unsightly is incapable of transformation into the beauty that is God because ugliness does not attain to beauty.

All the grace and elegance of creatures compared to God's grace is utter coarseness and crudity. That is why a person captivated by this grace and elegance of creatures becomes highly coarse and crude in God's sight. Someone like this is incapable of the infinite grace and beauty of God because of the extreme difference between the coarse and the infinitely elegant.

And all the goodness of the creatures of the world compared to the infinite goodness of God can be called wickedness. Nothing is good save God only [Lk 18:19]. Those who set their hearts on the good things of the world become extremely wicked in the sight of God. Since wickedness does not comprehend goodness, such persons will be incapable of union with God, who is supreme goodness.

5. All the world's wisdom and human ability compared to the infinite wisdom of God is pure and utter ignorance, as St. Paul writes to the Corinthians: *Sapientia hujus mundi stultitia est apud Deum* (The wisdom of this world is foolishness in God's sight) [1 Cor 3:19]. Those, therefore, who value their knowledge and ability as a means of reaching union with the wisdom of God are highly ignorant in God's sight and will be left behind, far away from this wisdom. Ignorance does not grasp what wisdom is; and in God's sight those who think they have some wisdom are very ignorant. For the Apostle says of them in writing to the Romans: *Dicentes enim se esse sapientes, stulti facti sunt* (Taking themselves for wise men, they became fools) [Rom 1:22].

Only those who set aside their own knowledge and walk in God's service like unlearned children receive wisdom from God. This is the wisdom about which St. Paul taught the Corinthians: *Si quis videtur inter vos sapiens esse in hoc saeculo, stultus fiat ut sit sapiens. Sapientia enim hujus mundi stultitia est apud Deum* (If anyone among you thinks he is wise, let him become ignorant so as to be wise. For the wisdom of this world is foolishness with God) [1 Cor 3:18–19]. Accordingly, to reach union with the wisdom of God, a person must advance by unknowing rather than by knowing.

6. All the sovereignty and freedom of the world compared to the freedom and sovereignty of the Spirit of God is utter slavery, anguish, and captivity. Those, then, who are attached to prelacies or to other such dignities and to freedom of their appetites will be considered and treated by God as base slaves and captives, not as His offspring. And this because of their not wanting to accept His holy teaching in which He instructs us that whoever wants to be the greater will be the least and that whoever wants to be the least will be the greater [Lk 22:26]. Thus, they will be unable to reach the royal freedom of spirit attained in divine union, for freedom has nothing to do with slavery. And free-

dom cannot abide in a heart dominated by desires, in a slave's heart. It abides in a liberated heart, in a filial heart. This is why Sarah told her husband Abraham to cast out the bondwoman and her son, declaring that the bondwoman's son should not be an heir together with the free son [Gn 21:10].

7. All the delights and satisfactions of the will in the things of the world compared to all the delight that is God are intense suffering, torment, and bitterness. Those who link their hearts to these delights, then, deserve in God's eyes intense suffering, torment, and bitterness. They will not be capable of attaining the delights of the embrace of union with God, since they merit suffering and bitterness.

All the wealth and glory of creation compared to the wealth that is God is utter poverty and misery in the Lord's sight. The person who loves and possesses these things is completely poor and miserable before God and will be unable to attain the richness and glory of transformation in God; the miserable and poor is extremely distant from the supremely rich and glorious.

8. Divine Wisdom, with pity for these souls that become ugly, abject, miserable, and poor on account of their love for worldly things, which in their opinion are rich and beautiful, exclaims in Proverbs: *O viri, ad vos clamito, et vox mea ad filios hominum. Intelligite, parvuli, astutiam, et insipientes, animadverte. Audite quia de rebus magnis locutura sum.* And further on: *Mecum sunt divitiae et gloria, opes superbae et justitia. Melior est fructus meus auro et lapide pretioso, et genimina mea argento electo. In viis justitiae ambulo, in medio semitarum judicii, ut ditem diligentes me, et thesauros eorum repleam.* The meaning of this passage is: O people, I cry to you, my voice is directed to the descendants of humanity. Be attentive, little ones, to cunning and sagacity; and you ignorant, be careful. Listen, because I want to speak of great things. Riches and glory are mine, high riches and justice. The fruit you will find in me is better than gold and precious stones; and my generations (what will be engendered of me in your souls) are better than choice silver. I walk along the ways of justice, in the midst of the paths of judgment, to enrich those who love me and to fill their treasures completely [Prv 8:4–6, 18–21].

Divine Wisdom speaks, here, to all those who are attached to the things of the world. She calls them little ones because they become as little as the things they love. She tells them, accordingly, to be cunning and careful, that She is dealing with great things, not small things, as they are; and that the riches and glory they love are with Her and in Her, not where they think; and that lofty riches and justice are present in Her. Although in their opinion the things of this world are riches, She tells them to bear in mind that Her riches are more precious, that the fruit found in them will be better than gold and precious stones, and that what She begets in souls has greater value than cherished silver, which signifies every kind of affection possible in this life.

Chapter Five

Continuation of the same matter. Proofs from passages and figures of Sacred Scripture for the necessity of journeying to God through this dark night, the mortification of the appetites.

1. We have some idea, from what was said, of the distance that lies between what creatures are in themselves and what God is in Himself, and, since love produces equality and likeness, of how souls attached to any of these creatures are just as distant from God. With a clear realization of this distance, St. Augustine addressed God in the *Soliloquies*: *Miserable man that I am, when will my pusillanimity and imperfection be able to conform with your righteousness? You indeed are good, and I evil; You are merciful, and I unmerciful; You are holy, and I miserable; You are just, and I unjust; You are light, and I blindness; You are life, and I death; You are medicine, and I sickness; You are supreme truth; and I utter vanity.*[12] These are the words of the saint.

2. They indeed are ignorant who think it is possible to reach this high state of union with God without first emptying their appetite of all the natural and supernatural things that can be a hindrance to them. For there is an extreme distance between such appetites and that which is given in this state, which is nothing less than transformation in God. Instructing us about this way, our Lord stated according to St. Luke: *Qui non renuntiat omnibus quae possidet, non potest meus esse discipulus* (The one who does not renounce all possessions cannot be my disciple) [Lk 14:33]. This statement is clear, for the doctrine the Son of Man came to teach is contempt of all things, that we may receive the gift of God's

---

12. The text is not from Augustine's *Soliloquies* but taken from an apocryphal work with the title *Liber soliloquiorum animae ad Deum* 3 (Migne PL 40, 866). A Spanish translation of it was available in John's time.

Spirit. As long as people fail to rid themselves of these possessions, they are incapable of receiving God's Spirit in pure transformation.

3. We have a figure of this in Exodus where we read that God did not give the children of Israel the heavenly manna until they exhausted the flour brought from Egypt [Ex 16:3–4, 15]. The meaning here is that first a total renunciation is needed, for this bread of angels is disagreeable to the palate of anyone desirous of tasting human food. Persons feeding on other strange tastes not only become incapable of the divine Spirit, but even greatly anger His divine Majesty because in their aspirations for spiritual food they are not satisfied with God alone, but intermingle with these aspirations a desire and affection for other things. This is likewise apparent in Sacred Scripture where it states that, discontented with that simple food, the people craved and requested meat, and seriously angered our Lord because of their desire to commingle a food so base and coarse with one so high and simple, which, even though simple, contained the savor and substance of all foods [Nm 11:4, 6:10]. Consequently, while morsels of manna were yet in their mouths, the wrath of God descended on them (as David also says: *Ira Dei descendit super eos* [Ps 78:31]), spouting fire from heaven and reducing thousands of them to ashes [Nm 11:1]. For God thought it shameful for them to crave other food while He was giving them heavenly food.

4. Oh, if spiritual persons knew how much spiritual good and abundance they lose by not attempting to raise their appetites above childish things, and if they knew to what extent, by not desiring the taste of these trifles, they would discover in this simple spiritual food the savor of all things! The Israelites did not perceive the taste, contained in the manna, of every other food, because their appetite was not restricted to this manna. They were unsuccessful in deriving from the manna all the taste and strength they were looking for because of their craving for other foods. Similarly, those who love something together with God undoubtedly make little of God, for they weigh in the balance with God an object far distant from God.

5. It is the common knowledge of experience that when the will is attached to an object, it esteems that object higher than any other, even though another, not as pleasing, may deserve higher admiration. And if people desire pleasure from two objects, they are necessarily offensive to the more deserving because through their desire for both they equate the two. Since nothing equals God, those who love and are at-

tached to something other than God, or together with Him, offend Him exceedingly. If this is true, what would happen if they loved something more than God?

6. This was also indicated when God ordered Moses to climb to the top of the mountain. He did this that Moses might be able to speak to Him. He commanded Moses not only to ascend and leave the children of Israel below, but to rule against the pasturing of beasts on the mountainside [Ex 34:3]. The meaning is that those who ascend this mount of perfection to converse with God must not only renounce all things by leaving them at the bottom, but also restrict their appetites (the beasts) from pasturing on the mountainside, on things that are not purely God. For in God, or in the state of perfection, all appetites cease.

The road and ascent to God, then, necessarily demands a habitual effort to renounce and mortify the appetites; the sooner this mortification is achieved, the sooner the soul reaches the top. But until the appetites are eliminated, one will not arrive no matter how much virtue one practices. For one will be failing to acquire perfect virtue, which lies in keeping the soul empty, naked, and purified of every appetite.

We also have a striking figure of this in Genesis. When the patriarch Jacob desired to ascend Mount Bethel to build an altar for the offering of sacrifice to God, he first ordered his people to do three things: to destroy all strange Gods; to purify themselves; and to change their garments [Gn 35:2].

7. Those desiring to climb to the summit of the mount in order to become an altar for the offering of a sacrifice of pure love and praise and reverence to God must first accomplish these three tasks perfectly. First, they must cast out strange Gods, all alien affections and attachments. Second, by denying these appetites and repenting of them—through the dark night of the senses—they must purify themselves of their residue. Third, in order to reach the top of this high mount, their garments must be changed. God, by means of the first two conditions, will substitute new vestments for the old. The soul will be clothed in God, in a new understanding of God (through the removal of the understanding of the old man) and in a new love of God in God, once the will is stripped of all the cravings and satisfactions of the old man. And God will vest the soul with new knowledge when the other old ideas and images are cast aside. He causes all that is of the old man, the abilities of one's natural being, to cease and attires all the faculties with new supernatural abilities. As a result, one's activities, once human, now

become divine. This is achieved in the state of union where the soul in which God alone dwells has no other function than that of an altar on which God is adored in praise and love.

God commanded that the altar of the Ark of the Covenant be empty and hollow [Ex 27:8] to remind the soul how void of all things God wishes it if it is to serve as His worthy dwelling. It was forbidden that the altar have any strange fire, or that its own go out; so much so that when Nadab and Abiu, the sons of the high priest, offered strange fire on our Lord's altar, God became angry and slew them there in front of the altar [Lv 10:1–2]. The lesson we derive here is that one's love for God must never fail or be mixed with alien loves if one wants to be a worthy altar of sacrifice.

8. God allows nothing else to dwell together with Him. We read, consequently, in the First Book of Kings that when the Philistines put the Ark of the Covenant in a temple with their idol, the idol was hurled to the ground at the dawn of each day and broken into pieces [1 Sm 5:2–4]. The only appetite God permits and wants in His dwelling place is the desire for the perfect fulfillment of His law and the carrying of His cross. Scripture does not teach that God ordered anything else to be placed in the Ark where the manna was; He wanted only the law and the rod of Moses (signifying the cross) to be placed there [Dt 31:26; Nm 17:10]. Those who have no other goal than the perfect observance of God's law and the carrying of the cross of Christ will be true arks, and they will bear within themselves the real manna, which signifies God, when they possess perfectly, without anything else, this law and this rod.

Chapter Six

The harm, privative as well as positive, that appetites cause in the soul.

1. For the sake of a clearer and fuller understanding of our assertions, it will be beneficial to explain here how these appetites cause harm in two principal ways within those in whom they dwell: They deprive them of God's Spirit; and they weary, torment, darken, defile, and weaken them. Jeremiah mentions this in Chapter 2: *Duo mala fecit populus meus: dereliquerunt fontem aquae vivae, et foderunt sibi cisternas dissipatas, quae continere non valent aquas* (They have forsaken Me, the

fountain of living water, and dug for themselves leaking cisterns that hold no water) [Jer 2:13]. . . .

* * *

Chapter Eleven

Proofs of how freedom from all appetites, even the smallest, is necessary to attain divine union.

1. The reader has apparently desired for quite a while to ask if the total mortification of all the appetites, large and small, is a requirement for the attainment of this high state of perfection, or if it is sufficient to mortify just some of them and leave the others, at least those that seem trifling. For it seems it would be an arduous task for individuals to attain such purity and nakedness that they would have no attachment to anything.

2. First, I respond that it is true that the appetites are not all equally detrimental, nor are all equally a hindrance to the soul. I am speaking of the voluntary appetites because the natural ones are little or no hindrance at all to the attainment of union, provided they do not receive one's consent or pass beyond the first movements, those stirrings in which the rational will does not take part either before or after. For to eradicate the natural appetites, that is, to mortify them entirely, is impossible in this life. Even though they are not entirely mortified, as I say, they are not such a hindrance as to prevent one from attaining divine union. A soul can easily experience them in its sensitive nature and yet be free of them in the rational part of its being. It will happen that while a person is experiencing an intense union of will in the prayer of quiet these appetites will be actually dwelling in the sensory part. Yet the superior part of the soul, which is in prayer, will be paying no attention to them.

But all the other voluntary appetites, whether they are the most serious, which involve mortal sin, or less grave in that they concern venial sin, or whether they be the least serious of all in that they only involve imperfections, must be mortified. A person must be liberated of them all, however slight they be, in order to arrive at this complete union. The reason is that in the state of divine union a person's will is so completely transformed into God's will that it excludes everything contrary to God's will, and in all and through all is motivated by the will of God.

3. Here we have the reason for stating that two wills become one. And this one will is God's will, which becomes also the soul's. If a person were to desire an imperfection unwanted by God, this one will of God would be undone because of the desire for what God does not will.

Clearly, for a soul to reach union with God through its will and love, it must first be freed from every appetite however slight. That is, one must not give consent of the will advertently and knowingly to an imperfection, and one must have the power and freedom to be able, upon advertence, to refuse this consent.

I say "knowingly," because one will fall into imperfections, venial sins, and the above-mentioned natural appetites without having advertence or knowledge or control in the matter. It is written of these semivoluntary and inadvertent sins that the just man will fall seven times a day and rise up again [Prv 24:16]. But any one of the voluntary appetites, even if trifling, is sufficient to impede the union, as I have said, if it is not mortified. I am referring here to habitual appetites because certain scattered acts of different desires are not such a hindrance to union when the habitual appetites are mortified. However, the soul must be liberated of these acts too, since they also proceed from habitual imperfection. Yet some habitual voluntary imperfections that are never completely mortified are an impediment not only to divine union but to spiritual progress as well. . . .

Chapter Twelve

The answer to another question. An explanation of the kinds of appetites that can bring this harm upon a soul.

1. We could explain this night of sense at greater length by mentioning everything relevant to the kind of damage the appetites cause, for they injure not merely in the ways described but in many others as well. What we have explained, however, is sufficient for our purpose. It has probably been understood how the mortification of the appetites can be called night and how suitable it is for people to enter this night in their approach to God. The only point that remains before we treat, in conclusion, the method of entering this night is a response to a doubt that may bother the reader concerning this matter.

THE ASCENT OF MOUNT CARMEL

2. First, can any appetite produce and cause the two evils mentioned above, namely: the privative, which removes the grace of God from the soul; and the positive, which causes the five cardinal kinds of harm we explained?

Second, is any appetite, however slight or of whatever kind, enough to produce all these types of damage together, or does each cause only a particular kind, in that one may produce torment, another weariness, another darkness, and so on?

3. To the first query, I answer that relevant to the privative evil, the loss of grace, only the voluntary appetites involving a matter of mortal sin can do this completely. For they deprive the soul of grace in this life and of glory, the possession of God, in the next.

To the second, my answer is that all these positive evils are together occasioned in the soul by each of these appetites. This is true whether the appetites concern mortal sin, venial sin, or imperfection. We call these evils positive, though in a certain fashion they are privative, because they correspond to a conversion to the creature, just as the privative evils correspond to the aversion from God.

Yet, there is this difference: The appetites for mortal sin produce total blindness, torment, filth, weakness, and so on; whereas the others do not cause these kinds of harm in a complete and absolute degree. For they do not deprive the soul of grace—a privation that would give them full possession, since the death of grace means life for the appetites. But these smaller appetites do cause this damage in a lesser degree according to the loss of grace they occasion. The extent of the torment, blindness, and weakness will correspond to the weakening of grace brought on by the appetites. . . .

5. The reason any act of a voluntary appetite gives rise to all these evils together is that it directly opposes the acts of virtue, which generate the contrary effects. An act of virtue produces in the soul mildness, peace, comfort, light, purity, and strength, just as an inordinate appetite brings about torment, fatigue, weariness, blindness, and weakness. Through the practice of one virtue all the virtues grow, and similarly, through an increase of one vice, all the vices and their effects grow.

These evils do not unmask themselves at the moment the appetite is being satisfied, since the pleasure of the moment is an obstacle to this. Yet sooner or later the harmful effects will certainly be felt. A good illustration of this is found in the Book of Revelation. An angel commanded St. John to eat the book, which was sweet to the mouth, but in the belly sour [Rv 10:9]. For the appetite when satisfied seems sweet and pleasant, but eventually the sour effect is felt. This truth will certainly be clear to those who allow themselves to be carried away by their appetites. I realize, however, that there are some so blind and unaware that they do not experience this bitter effect. Since they do not walk in God, they do not perceive what keeps them from Him.

6. I am not speaking here of the other natural, involuntary appetites, or of thoughts that do not pass beyond the first movements, or of other temptations in which there is no consent. These temptations do not give rise to any of the evils previously mentioned. Though the passion and disturbance they momentarily cause make it seem that one is being defiled and blinded, such is not the case; rather, they occasion the opposite good effects. Insofar as one resists them, one wins strength, purity, comfort, and many blessings, as our Lord told St. Paul: Virtue is made perfect in weakness [2 Cor. 12:9]. . . .

Chapter Thirteen

The manner and method of entering this night of sense.

1. Some counsels are in order now that the individual may both know the way of entering this night and be able to do so. It should be understood, consequently, that a person ordinarily enters this night of sense in two ways: active and passive.

The active way, which will be the subject of the following counsels, comprises what one can do and does by oneself to enter this night. The passive way is that in which one does nothing, but God accomplishes the work in the soul, while the soul acts as the recipient. This will be the subject of the fourth book where we will discuss beginners.[13] Since, with God's help, I will there give counsels pertinent to the numerous imperfections beginners ordinarily possess on this road, I will not take the time to offer many here. Nor is this the proper place to give them, since presently we are dealing only with the reasons for calling this journey a night, and with the nature and divisions of this night.[14]

---

13. John never got to this fourth book as promised; however he did deal in *The Dark Night* with what he mentions here.

14. This passage demonstrates how little is the attention John gives in this first book to the active night of the senses. In fact what he says about it could almost be reduced to the counsels he gives in this chapter.

THE ASCENT OF MOUNT CARMEL

Nevertheless, if we do not offer some immediate remedy or counsel, this part would seem very short and less helpful. Therefore I want to set down the following abridged method. And I will do the same at the end of my discussion of each of the next two parts (or reasons for the use of the term "night") which, with God's help, will follow.[15]

2. Though these counsels for the conquering of the appetites are brief and few in number, I believe they are as profitable and efficacious as they are concise. A person who sincerely wants to practice them will need no others since all the others are included in these.

3. First, have a habitual desire to imitate Christ in all your deeds by bringing your life into conformity with His. You must then study His life in order to know how to imitate Him and behave in all events as He would.

4. Second, in order to be successful in this imitation, renounce and remain empty of any sensory satisfaction that is not purely for the honor and glory of God. Do this out of love for Jesus Christ. In His life He had no other gratification, nor desired any other, than the fulfillment of His Father's will, which He called His meat and food [Jn 4:34]. . . .

5. Many blessings flow from the harmony and tranquillity of the four natural passions: joy, hope, fear, and sorrow. The following maxims contain a complete remedy for mortifying and pacifying the passions. If put into practice these maxims will give rise to abundant merit and great virtues.

6. Endeavor to be inclined always:

> not to the easiest, but to the most difficult;
> not to the most delightful, but to the harshest;
> not to the most gratifying, but to the less pleasant;
> not to what means rest for you, but to hard work;
> not to the consoling, but to the unconsoling;
> not to the most, but to the least;
> not to the highest and most precious, but to the lowest and most despised;
> not to wanting something, but to wanting nothing;
> do not go about looking for the best of temporal things, but for

---

15. He did not follow through on this promise.

THE ASCENT OF MOUNT CARMEL

the worst, and desire to enter for Christ into complete nudity, emptiness, and poverty in everything in the world.

7. You should embrace these practices earnestly and try to overcome the repugnance of your will toward them. If you sincerely put them into practice with order and discretion, you will discover in them great delight and consolation. . . .

10. As a conclusion to these counsels and rules it would be appropriate to repeat the verses in "The Ascent of Mount Carmel" (the drawing at the beginning of the book), which are instructions for climbing to the summit, the high state of union.[16] Although in the drawing we admittedly refer to the spiritual and interior aspect, we also deal with the spirit of imperfection existent in the sensory and exterior part of the soul, as is evident by the two roads, one on each side of that path that leads to perfection. Consequently, these verses will here bear reference to the sensory part. Afterward, in the second division of this night, they may be interpreted in relationship to the spiritual part.

11. The verses are as follows:

> To reach satisfaction in all
>   desire its possession in nothing.
> To come to possess all
>   desire the possession of nothing.
> To arrive at being all
>   desire to be nothing.
> To come to the knowledge of all
>   desire the knowledge of nothing.
> To come to the pleasure you have not
>   you must go by a way in which you enjoy not.
> To come to the knowledge you have not
>   you must go by a way in which you know not.
> To come to the possession you have not
>   you must go by a way in which you possess not.
> To come to be what you are not
>   you must go by a way in which you are not.

---

16. He copies only those verses that are at the bottom of the sketch of the mount. They are not applicable solely to the night of the senses but to the other stages of purification as well. They apply to the whole journey. Cf. A 3, 15, 1.

When you turn toward something
>   you cease to cast yourself upon the all.
For to go from all to the all
>   you must deny yourself of all in all.
And when you come to the possession of the all
>   you must possess it without wanting anything.
Because if you desire to have something in all
>   your treasure in God is not purely your all.

12. In this nakedness the spirit finds its quietude and rest. For in coveting nothing, nothing raises it up and nothing weighs it down, because it is in the center of its humility. When it covets something, in this very desire it is wearied.

Chapter Fourteen

An explanation of verse 2 of the first stanza.

Fired With Love's Urgent Longings

1. Now that we have explained the night of sense, to which the first verse of this stanza refers, and have discussed the nature of this night, the reason for calling it night, and the method of actively entering it, we should logically continue with an explanation of the admirable properties and effects contained in the remaining stanzas. I will explain these verses, as promised in the prologue, by merely touching on them, and then proceed to Book Two, a treatise on the remaining, or spiritual, part of this night.

2. The soul, then, states that "fired with love's urgent longings" it passed through this night of sense to union with the beloved. A love of pleasure, and attachment to it, usually fires the will toward the enjoyment of things that give pleasure. A more intense enkindling of another, better love (love of one's heavenly bridegroom) is necessary for the vanquishing of the appetites and the denial of this pleasure. By finding satisfaction and strength in this love, one will have the courage and constancy to deny readily all other appetites.[17] The love of one's spouse

---

17. One does not begin, then, with negation but with love. The renunciation of one love implies the preexistence of another love. In going on to speak of an enkindling with longings of love, John uses terminology more characteristic of that which he uses for later stages along the spiritual journey.

is not the only requisite for conquering the strength of the sensitive appetites; an enkindling with longings of love is also necessary. For the sensory appetites are moved and attracted toward sensory objects with such cravings that if the spiritual part of the soul is not fired with other more urgent longings for spiritual things, the soul will be able neither to overcome the yoke of nature nor enter the night of sense; nor will it have the courage to live in the darkness of all things by denying its appetites for them.

3. This is not the appropriate section for a description—nor would this be possible—of the nature of these longings of love or of the numerous ways they occur at the outset of the journey to union. Neither is it the place for a discussion of the diligence and ingenuity of persons in departing from their house (self-will) into the night of the mortification of their senses, or of how easy, sweet, and delightful these longings for their spouse make all the trials and dangers of this night seem. It is better to experience all of this and meditate on it than to write of it. . . .

* * *

Book Two

This book is a treatise on faith, the proximate means of ascent to union with God. It consequently considers the second part of this night, the night of spirit to which the following stanza refers.[1]

Chapter One

The Second Stanza

In darkness and secure,
By the secret ladder, disguised,
—Ah, the sheer grace!—
In darkness and concealment,
My house being now all stilled;

1. This second stanza tells in song of the sheer grace that was the soul's in divesting the spirit of all its imperfections and appetites for spiritual possessions. This grace is far greater here because of the greater hardship involved in quieting the house of one's spiritual nature and entering this interior darkness (the spiritual nudity of all sensory and immaterial things), leaning on pure faith alone, in an ascent by it to God.

The secret ladder represents faith, because all the rungs or articles of faith are secret to and hidden from both the senses and the intellect. Accordingly the soul lived in darkness, without the light of the senses and intellect, and went out beyond every natural and rational boundary

---

1. John gives an explanation of the second stanza in this chapter, but then never returns to it until his work *The Dark Night*. There he interprets it from a different perspective and also explains the stanza verse by verse.

to climb the divine ladder of faith that leads up to and penetrates the deep things of God [1 Cor 2:10].

The soul declares that it was disguised because in the ascent through faith its garments, apparel, and capacities were changed from natural to divine. On account of this disguise, neither the devil, nor temporal, nor rational things recognized or detained it. None of these can do harm to the one who walks in faith.

The soul's advance, moreover, was so concealed, hidden, and withdrawn from all the wiles of the devil that it indeed involved darkness and concealment. That is, the soul was hidden from the devil, to whom the light of faith is worse than darkness. We can say as a result that a person who walks in faith is concealed and hidden from the devil; this will be more evident as we proceed. . . .

* * *

Chapter Three

Arguments, passages, and figures from Scripture in proof that faith is a dark night for the soul.

1. Faith, the theologians say, is a certain and obscure habit of soul. It is an obscure habit because it brings us to believe divinely revealed truths that transcend every natural light and infinitely exceed all human understanding. As a result the excessive light of faith bestowed on a soul is darkness for it; a brighter light will eclipse and suppress a dimmer one. The sun so obscures all other lights that they do not seem to be lights at all when it is shining, and instead of affording vision to the eyes, it overwhelms, blinds, and deprives them of vision since its light is excessive and unproportioned to the visual faculty. Similarly, the light of faith in its abundance suppresses and overwhelms that of the intellect. For the intellect, by its own power, comprehends only natural knowledge, though it has the potency to be raised to a supernatural act whenever our Lord wishes.[2]

---

2. John does not intend to give a complete definition of faith here. For the classic Scholastic thinking on the nature of faith, see Aquinas, *Summa Theologica* 2-2, 1-4; 2-2, 6, 1; *Contra Gentiles* 3, 40; *De veritate* 14, 1.

2. The intellect knows only in the natural way, that is, by means of the senses. If one is to know in this natural way, the phantasms and species of objects will have to be present either in themselves or in their likenesses; otherwise one will be incapable of knowing naturally. As the scholastic philosophers say: *Ab ojecto et potentia paritur notitia* (Knowledge arises in the soul from both the faculty and the object at hand).[3] If we were told of objects we had never known or seen resemblances of, we would in the end have no more knowledge than before.

For example, if we were informed that on a certain island there was an animal whose like or kind we had never seen, we would then have no more idea or image of that animal in our mind than previously, no matter how much we were told.

Another clearer example will shed more light on this subject: If those born blind were told about the nature of the color white or yellow, they would understand absolutely nothing no matter how much instruction they received. Since they never saw these colors nor their like, they would not have the means to form a judgment about them. Only the names of these colors would be grasped since the names are perceptible through hearing; but never their form or image, because these colors were never seen by those born blind.

3. Such is faith to the soul; it informs us of matters we have never seen or known, either in themselves or in their likenesses. In fact, nothing like them exists. The light of natural knowledge does not show us the object of faith, since this object is unproportioned to any of the senses. Yet, we come to know it through hearing, by believing what faith teaches us, blinding our natural light and bringing it into submission. St. Paul states: *Fides ex auditu* [Rom 10:17]. This amounts to saying that faith is not a knowledge derived from the senses but an assent of the soul to what enters through hearing.

4. Faith, moreover, far exceeds what these examples teach us. Not only does it fail to produce knowledge and science but, as we said, it deprives and blinds people of any other knowledge by which they may judge it. Other knowledge is acquired by the light of the intellect, but not the knowledge of faith. Faith nullifies the light of the intellect; and if this light is not darkened, the knowledge of faith is lost. Accordingly, Isaiah said: *Si no credideritis, non intelligetis* (If you do not believe, you will not understand) [Is 7:9].

---

3. The axiom stems from Aristotle, *De anima* 1, 2; 3, 8.

THE ASCENT OF MOUNT CARMEL

Faith, manifestly, is a dark night for souls, but in this way it gives them light. The more darkness it brings on them, the more light it sheds. For by blinding, it illumines them, according to those words of Isaiah that if you do not believe you will not understand; that is, you will not have light [Is 7:9].

Faith was foreshadowed in that cloud which separated the children of Israel, just before their entry into the Red Sea, from the Egyptians [Ex 14:19–20]. Scripture says of the cloud: *Erat nubes tenebrosa et illuminans noctem* (The cloud was dark and illuminated the night) [Ex 14:20].

5. How wonderful it was: A cloud, dark in itself, could illumine the night! This was related to illustrate how faith, a dark and obscure cloud to souls (also a night in that it blinds and deprives them of their natural light), illumines and pours light into their darkness by means of its own darkness. This is fitting so that the disciple may be like the master.

A person in darkness does not receive adequate enlightenment save by another darkness, according to David's teaching: *Dies diei eructat verbum et nox nocti indicat scientiam* (The day brims over and breathes speech to the day, and the night manifests knowledge to the night) [Ps 19:3]. Expressed more clearly, this means: The day, which is God (in bliss where it is day), communicates and pronounces the Word, His Son, to the angels and blessed souls, who are now day; and this He does that they may have knowledge and enjoyment of Him. And the night, which is the faith, present in the Church Militant where it is still night, manifests knowledge to the Church and, consequently, to every soul. This knowledge is night to souls because they do not yet possess the clear beatific wisdom, and because faith blinds them as to their own natural light.

6. Our deduction is that since faith is a dark night, it illumines the soul that is in darkness. We verify, then, David's assertion on this matter: *Et nox illuminatio in deliciis meis* (Night will be my illumination in the midst of my delights) [Ps 138:11]. This amounts to saying: The night of faith will be my guide in the delights of my pure contemplation and union with God. By this passage David clearly informs us of the darkness demanded on this road if a soul is to receive light.

THE ASCENT OF MOUNT CARMEL

Chapter Four

A general discussion of how the soul with respect to its own efforts must remain in darkness so as to be well guided by faith to supreme contemplation.

1. I believe you are learning how faith is a dark night for the soul and how the soul as well must be dark—or in darkness as to its own light—that it may allow itself to be guided by faith to this high goal of union. But for knowledge of how to do this, a somewhat more detailed explanation of the darkness required for entering this abyss of faith will be beneficial. In this chapter I will deal with this darkness generally. Further on I will present, with God's help, a more detailed explanation of the behavior necessary for obviating error in faith and any encumbrance to its guidance.

2. I affirm, then, that if people take faith as a good guide to this state, not only must they live in darkness in the sensory and lower part of their nature (concerning creatures and temporal things), which we have already discussed, but they must also darken and blind themselves in that part of their nature that bears relation to God and spiritual things. This latter part, which we are now discussing, is the rational and higher part of their nature.

The attainment of supernatural transformation manifestly demands a darkening of the soul and an elevation above all the sensory and rational parts of nature. For the word "supernatural" indicates that which is above nature; nature, consequently, remains beneath.

Since this transformation and union is something that falls beyond the reach of the senses and of human capability, the soul must empty itself perfectly and voluntarily—I mean in its affection and will—of all the earthly and heavenly things it can grasp. It must through its own efforts empty itself insofar as it can. As for God, who will stop Him from accomplishing His desires in the soul that is resigned, annihilated, and despoiled?

Insofar as they are capable, people must void themselves of all, so that however many supernatural communications they receive they will continually live as though denuded of them and in darkness. Like the blind, they must lean on dark faith, accept it for their guide and light, and rest on nothing of what they understand, taste, feel, or imagine. All these perceptions are a darkness that will lead them astray. Faith lies beyond all this understanding, taste, feeling, and imagining.

THE ASCENT OF MOUNT CARMEL

If they do not blind themselves in these things and abide in total darkness, they will not reach what is greater: the teaching of faith.

3. Those who are not yet entirely blind will not allow a good guide to lead them. Still able to perceive a little, they think that the road they see is the best, for they are unable to see other and better ones. And because they are the ones giving the orders, they will consequently lead astray their young guide who has better vision. Similarly, if the soul in traveling this road leans on any elements of its own knowledge or experience of God, it will easily go astray or be detained for not having desired to abide in complete blindness, in faith which is its guide. For, however impressive may be one's knowledge or feeling of God, that knowledge or feeling will have no resemblance to God and amount to very little.

4. St. Paul also meant this in his assertion: *Accedentem ad Deum oportet credere quod est* (The one who would approach union with God should believe in His existence) [Heb 11:6]. This is like saying: Those who want to reach union with God should advance neither by understanding, nor by the support of their own experience, nor by feeling or imagination, but by belief in God's being. For God's being cannot be grasped by the intellect, appetite, imagination, or any other sense; nor can it be known in this life. The most that can be felt and tasted of God in this life is infinitely distant from God and the pure possession of Him. Isaiah and St. Paul affirm: *Nec oculus videt, nec auris audivit, nec in cor hominis ascendit quae praeparavit Deus iis qui diligunt illum* (No eye has ever seen, nor ear heard, nor has the human heart or thought ever grasped what God has prepared for those who love Him) [Is 64:4; 1 Cor 2:9].

Now souls may be striving for a perfect union in this life through grace with that to which through glory they will be united in the next (with what St. Paul says eye has not seen nor ear heard, nor the human, fleshly heart grasped). But, manifestly, the perfect union in this life through grace and love demands that they live in darkness to all the objects of sight, hearing, imagination, and everything comprehensible to the heart—that is, to the soul.

Those are decidedly hindered, then, from attainment of this high state of union with God who are attached to any understanding, feeling, imagining, opinion, desire, or way of their own, or to any other of their works or affairs, and know not how to detach and denude themselves of these impediments. Their goal transcends all of this, even the loftiest object that can be known or experienced. Consequently, they must pass beyond everything to unknowing.

5. As regards this road to union, entering on the road means leaving one's own road; or better, moving on to the goal. And turning from one's own mode implies entry into what has no mode; that is, God. People who reach this state no longer have any modes or methods, still less are they—nor can they be—attached to them. I am referring to modes of understanding, tasting, and feeling. Within themselves, though, they possess all methods, like one who though having nothing yet possesses all things [2 Cor 6:10]. By being courageous enough to pass beyond the interior and exterior limits of their own nature, they enter within supernatural bounds—bounds that have no mode, yet in substance possess all modes. To reach these supernatural bounds, souls must depart from their natural bounds and leave self far off in respect to their interior and exterior limits in order to mount from a low state to the highest.

6. Passing beyond all that is naturally and spiritually intelligible or comprehensible, souls ought to desire with all their might to attain what in this life is unknowable and unimaginable. And parting company with all they can or do taste and feel, temporally and spiritually, they must ardently long to acquire what surpasses all taste and feeling. To be empty and free for the achievement of this, they should by no means seize on what they receive spiritually or sensitively (as we shall explain in our particular discussion of this matter), but consider it of little import. The higher rank and esteem they give to all this knowledge, experience, and imagining (whether spiritual or not), the more they subtract from the Supreme Good and the more they delay in their journey toward Him. And the less they esteem what they can possess—however estimable it may be relative to the Supreme Good—the more they value and prize Him, and, consequently, the closer they come to Him. In this way, in obscurity, souls approach union swiftly by means of faith, which is also dark. And in this way faith gives them wondrous light. Obviously, if they should desire to see, they would be in darkness as regards God more quickly than if they opened their eyes to the blinding brightness of the sun.

7. By blinding one's faculties along this road, one will see light, as the Savior proclaims in the Gospel: *In judicium veni in hunc mundum: ut qui non vident videant, et qui vident caeci fiant* (I have come into this world for judgment, that they who see not, may see, and that they who see

may become blind) [Jn 9:39]. In reference to the spiritual road, these words should be understood literally, that is: Those who both live in darkness and blind themselves of all their natural lights will have supernatural vision, and those who want to lean on some light of their own will become blind and be held back on this road leading to union.

8. That we may continue less confusedly, I believe it will be necessary in the following chapter to explain this reality we call union with God. Since an understanding of the nature of union will shed more light on the subsequent doctrine, I think this is the suitable place for a discussion of it. Although our thread of thought will be interrupted, we will not be digressing, because an explanation of this union will serve in illustration of the matter we are treating. The following chapter will be like a parenthesis within the same enthymeme since in this second night we plan to treat of the relationship of the three faculties of the soul to the three theological virtues.

Chapter Five

Explanation of the nature of union with God.
An illustration.

1. In our previous discussion, we have already given some indication of the meaning of the phrase "union of the soul with God." Thus our teaching here about the nature of this union will be more understandable.

It is not my intention now to discuss the divisions and parts of this union. Indeed, I would never finish were I to begin explaining the union of the intellect, or that of the will, or that of the memory, or try to expound the nature of the transitory and the permanent union in each of these faculties, or the significance of the total, the transitory, or the permanent union wrought in these three faculties together. We will discuss all this frequently in the course of our treatise. But such an exposition is unnecessary for an understanding of what we now wish to state about these different unions. A better explanation of them will be given in sections dealing with the subject, and then we shall have a concrete example to go with the actual teaching. In those sections the reader will note and understand the union being discussed and will form a better judgment of it.

2. Here I intend to discuss only this total and permanent union in the substance and faculties of the soul.[4] And I shall be speaking of the obscure habit of union, for we will explain later, with God's help, how a permanent actual union of the faculties in this life is impossible; such a union can only be transient.

3. To understand the nature of this union, one should first know that God sustains every soul and dwells in it substantially, even though it may be that of the greatest sinner in the world. This union between God and creatures always exists. By it He conserves their being so that if the union should end they would immediately be annihilated and cease to exist.

Consequently, in discussing union with God, we are not discussing the substantial union that is always existing but the soul's union with and transformation in God. This union is not always existing, but we find it only where there is likeness of love. We will call it "the union of likeness"; and the former, "the essential or substantial union." The union of likeness is supernatural; the other, natural. The supernatural union exists when God's will and the soul's are in conformity, so that nothing in the one is repugnant to the other. When the soul rids itself completely of what is repugnant and unconformed to the divine will, it rests transformed in God through love.

4. The lack of conformity with God's will can be had not only in one's acts but in one's habits as well. Not only must actual voluntary imperfections cease, but habitual imperfections must be annihilated too.

No creature, none of its actions and abilities, can reach or express God's nature. Consequently, a soul must strip itself of all creatures and of its actions and abilities (of its understanding, taste, and feeling) so that when everything unlike and unconformed to God is cast out, it may receive the likeness of God. And the soul will receive this likeness because nothing contrary to the will of God will be left in it. Thus it will be transformed in God.

It is true that God is ever present in the soul, as we said, and thereby bestows and preserves its natural being by His sustaining pres-

---

4. This chapter is basic to the understanding of John's thought. His exposition here is an essentialist one and can be completed with his descriptions of union elsewhere in his writings. He makes distinctions that he holds to throughout the rest of his works: the union in the substance of the soul and in the faculties; the union insofar as it is an act or a habit, or the transitory and permanent union.

ence. Yet He does not always communicate supernatural being to it. He communicates supernatural being only through love and grace, which not all souls possess. And those who do, do not possess them in the same degree. Some have attained higher degrees of love, others remain in lower degrees. To that soul which is more advanced in love, more conformed to the divine will, God communicates Himself more. A person who has reached complete conformity and likeness of will has attained total supernatural union and transformation in God.

Manifestly, then, the more that individuals through attachment and habit are clothed with their own abilities and with creatures, the less disposed they are for this union. For they do not afford God full opportunity to transform their souls into the supernatural. As a result, individuals have nothing more to do than to strip their souls of these natural contraries and dissimilarities so that God, who is naturally communicating Himself to them through nature, may do so supernaturally through grace.

5. This is what St. John meant when he said: *Qui non ex sanguinibus, neque ex voluntate carnis, neque ex voluntate viri, sed ex Deo nati sunt* [Jn 1:13], which can be interpreted: He gives power for becoming the children of God (for being transformed in God) only to those who are not born of blood (of natural complexion and humors), or of the will of the flesh (the free will included in one's natural aptitude and capacity), or even less of the human will (which includes every mode and manner by which the intellect judges and understands). To none of these has He conferred the power of becoming the children of God; only to those who are born of God (those who, in their rebirth through grace and death to everything of the old man, rise above themselves to the supernatural and receive from God this rebirth and relationship as His child, which transcends everything imaginable).

St. John affirms elsewhere: *Nisi quis renatus fuerit ex aqua et spiritu Sancto non potest videre regnum Dei* (The one who is not reborn in the Holy Spirit will be unable to see the kingdom of God, which is the state of perfection) [Jn 3:5]. To be reborn in the Holy Spirit during this life is to become most like God in purity, without any mixture of imperfection. Accordingly, pure transformation can be effected—although not essentially—through the participation of union.

6. Here is an example that will provide a better understanding of this explanation. A ray of sunlight shining on a smudgy window is unable to illumine that window completely and transform it into its own light. It could do this if the window were cleaned and polished. The

less the film and stain are wiped away, the less the window will be illumined; and the cleaner the window is, the brighter will be its illumination. The extent of illumination is not dependent on the ray of sunlight but on the window. If the window is totally clean and pure, the sunlight will so transform and illumine it that to all appearances the window will be identical with the ray of sunlight and shine just as the sun's ray. Although obviously the nature of the window is distinct from that of the sun's ray (even if the two seem identical), we can assert that the window is the ray or light of the sun by participation.

The soul on which the divine light of God's being is ever shining, or better, in which it is ever dwelling by nature, is like this window, as we have affirmed.

7. A soul makes room for God by wiping away all the smudges and smears of creatures, by uniting its will perfectly to God's; for to love is to labor to divest and deprive oneself for God of all that is not God. When this is done the soul will be illumined by and transformed in God. And God will so communicate His supernatural being to it that it will appear to be God Himself and will possess what God Himself possesses.

When God grants this supernatural favor to the soul, so great a union is caused that all the things of both God and the soul become one in participant transformation, and the soul appears to be God more than a soul. Indeed, it is God by participation. Yet truly, its being (even though transformed) is naturally as distinct from God's as it was before, just as the window, although illumined by the ray, has being distinct from the ray's.[5]

8. Consequently, we understand with greater clarity that the preparation for this union, as we said, is not an understanding by the soul, nor the taste, feeling, or imagining of God or of any other object, but purity and love, the stripping off and perfect renunciation of all such experiences for God alone. Also we clearly see how perfect transformation is impossible without perfect purity, and how the illumination of the soul and its union with God correspond to the measure of its purity. The illumination will not be perfect until the soul is entirely cleansed, clear, and perfect.

---

5. However deep and intimate the union, the difference between the human person and God remains. The transformation, as a participation in the divine life, is situated on a plane distinct from the ontological. John, nonetheless, will speak in daring ways of this union. Cf. C 38, 3–4.

9. The following example will also shed light on the nature of this union. Let us imagine a perfect painting with many finely wrought details and delicate, subtle adornments, including some so delicate and subtle that they are not wholly discernible. Now one whose sense of sight is not too clear and refined will discover less detail and delicacy in the painting; one whose vision is somewhat purer will discover more details and perfections; and another with yet clearer vision will find still more perfection; finally, the one who possesses the clearest faculty will discern the greatest number of excellent qualities and perfections. There is so much to behold in the painting that no matter how much one sees in it, still more remains unseen.

10. We can make the same application to souls in their relationship with God in this illumination and transformation. Although individuals may have truly reached union, this union will be proportioned to their lesser or greater capacity, for not all souls attain an identical degree of union. This depends on what the Lord wishes to grant each one. Here we have a resemblance to the saints' vision of God in heaven: Some see more, others less, but all see Him and are happy owing to the satisfaction of their capacity.

11. In this life we may encounter individuals who are in the state of perfection and enjoying equal peace and tranquillity, and the capacity of each will be satisfied, yet one may be many degrees higher than the other. Those who do not reach purity in the measure of their capacity never achieve true peace and satisfaction; they have not attained in their faculties the nakedness and emptiness required for the simple union.[6]

Chapter Six

The theological virtues perfect the faculties of the soul and produce emptiness and darkness in them.

1. We must discuss the method of leading the three faculties (intellect, memory, and will) into this spiritual night, the means to divine union.

---

6. John will return to this important idea, especially in the *Night*. Within the state of union there is room for differences, not with regard to the nature of the union but with regard to the degree of union or the capacity of the individual. The intensity of the experiences of purification and union will bear relation to the degree of union to which a person is called.

THE ASCENT OF MOUNT CARMEL

But we must first explain how the theological virtues (faith, hope, and charity, related to these faculties as their proper supernatural objects, and through which the soul is united with God) cause the same emptiness and darkness in their respective faculties: faith in the intellect, hope in the memory, and charity in the will. Then we shall explain how in order to journey to God the intellect must be perfected in the darkness of faith, the memory in the emptiness of hope, and the will in the nakedness and absence of every affection.

As a result, the necessity of the soul's journey through this dark night with the support of these three virtues will be manifest. They darken and empty it of all things that its advancement along this spiritual road may be more secure. As we said, the soul is not united with God in this life through understanding, or through enjoyment, or through imagination, or through any other sense; but only faith, hope, and charity (according to the intellect, memory, and will) can unite the soul with God in this life. . . .

Chapter Seven

The extreme narrowness of the path leading to eternal life. The denudation and freedom required of those who tread it. The nakedness of the intellect.

1. I would need greater knowledge and perfection than I possess to treat of the denudation and purity of the three faculties of the soul. For I desire to give clear instructions to spiritual persons on the narrowness of the way leading to eternal life—that narrowness of which our Savior spoke—so that convinced of this they will not marvel at the emptiness and nakedness in which we must leave the faculties of the soul in this night.

2. We ought to note carefully the words our Savior spoke in St. Matthew's Gospel, chapter seven, about this road: *Quam angusta porta et arcta via est quae ducit ad vitam! Et pauci sunt qui inveniunt eam* (How narrow is the gate and constricting the way that leads to life! And few there are who find it) [Mt 7:14]. We should note particularly in this passage the exaggeration and hyperbolism conveyed by the word *quam*. Considering the emphatic use of *quam*, the phrase could be reworded: Indeed the gate is very narrow, more so than you think.

We must also note that first He says the gate is narrow to teach that entrance through this gate of Christ (the beginning of the journey) involves a divestment and narrowing of the will in relation to all sensible and temporal objects by loving God more than all of them. This task belongs to the night of sense, as we have said.[7] Next He asserts that the way (of perfection) is constricting to teach that the journey along this way includes entry through the narrow gate, a void of sense objects, and also a constricting of oneself through the dispossession and removal of obstacles in matters relating to the spiritual part of the soul.

3. We can apply, then, what Christ says about the narrow gate to the sensitive part of the human person, and what He says about the constricting way to the spiritual or rational part. Since He proclaims that few find it, we ought to note the cause: Few there are with the knowledge and desire to enter on this supreme nakedness and emptiness of spirit. As this path on the high mount of perfection is narrow and steep, it demands travelers who are neither weighed down by the lower part of their nature nor burdened in the higher part. This is a venture in which God alone is sought and gained, thus only God ought to be sought and gained.

4. Obviously one's journey must not only exclude the hindrance of creatures but also embody a dispossession and annihilation in the spiritual part of one's nature. Our Lord, for our instruction and guidance along this road, imparted that wonderful teaching—I think it is possible to affirm that the more necessary the doctrine the less it is practiced by spiritual persons—that I will quote fully and explain in its genuine and spiritual sense because of its importance and relevance to our subject. He states in the eighth chapter of St. Mark: *Si quis vult me sequi, deneget semetipsum et tollat crucem suam et sequatur me. Qui enim voluerit animam suam salvam facere, perdet eam; qui autem perdiderit animam suam propter me . . . salvam faciet eam* (They who wish to follow my way should deny themselves, take up their cross and follow me. For those who save their soul shall lose it, but the one who loses it for me shall gain it) [Mk 8:34–35].

5. Oh, who can make this counsel of our Savior understandable,

---

7. A. 1, 13, 3–4. In this chapter John sets down the general message of the gospel as the following of Christ and the sharing in His cross. He presents a scriptural basis for the journey to the summit of the mount as presented in the sketch of the mount and for his teaching on the purification of the senses and the spirit through the theological virtues.

and practicable, and attractive that spiritual persons might become aware of the difference between the method many of them think is good and that which ought to be used in traveling this road! They are of the opinion that any kind of withdrawal from the world or reformation of life suffices. Some are content with a certain degree of virtue, perseverance in prayer, and mortification but never achieve the nakedness, poverty, selflessness, or spiritual purity (which are all the same) about which the Lord counsels us here. For they still feed and clothe their natural selves with spiritual feelings and consolations instead of divesting and denying themselves of these for God's sake. They think a denial of self in worldly matters is sufficient without an annihilation and purification of spiritual possessions. It happens that, when some of this solid, perfect food (the annihilation of all sweetness in God—the pure spiritual cross and nakedness of Christ's poverty of spirit) is offered them in dryness, distaste, and trial, they run from it as from death and wander about in search only of sweetness and delightful communications from God. Such an attitude is not the hallmark of self-denial and nakedness of spirit but the indication of a spiritual sweet tooth. Through this kind of conduct they become, spiritually speaking, enemies of the cross of Christ [Phil 3:18].

A genuine spirit seeks the distasteful in God rather than the delectable, leans more toward suffering than toward consolation, more toward going without everything for God than toward possession. It prefers dryness and affliction to sweet consolation. It knows that this is the significance of following Christ and denying self, that the other method is perhaps a seeking of self in God—something entirely contrary to love. Seeking oneself in God is the same as looking for the caresses and consolations of God. Seeking God in oneself entails not only the desire of doing without these consolations for God's sake but also the inclination to choose for love of Christ all that is most distasteful whether in God or in the world; and this is what loving God means.

6. Oh, who can explain the extent of the denial our Lord wishes of us! This negation must be similar to a temporal, natural, and spiritual death in all things, that is, with regard to the esteem the will has for them. It is in the will that all negation takes place. Our Savior referred to this when He declared: *They who wish to save their life shall lose it* (Anyone who wants to possess something, or seeks it for self, will lose it); *and they who lose their soul for my sake, the same shall gain it* [Mt 16:25; Lk 9:24]. This latter means: Those who renounce for Christ all that their

wills can both desire and enjoy by choosing what bears closer resemblance to the cross—which our Lord in St. John terms hating one's own soul [Jn 22:25]—these same will gain it.

His Majesty taught this to those two disciples who came to ask Him for places at His right and left. Without responding to their request for glory, He offered them the chalice He was about to drink as something safer and more precious on this earth than enjoyment [Mt 20:22].

7. This chalice means death to one's natural self through denudation and annihilation. As a result of this death, one is able to walk along the narrow path in the sensitive part of the soul, as we said, and in the spiritual part (in one's understanding, joy, and feeling). Accordingly, one can attain to dispossession in both parts of the soul. Not only this, but even in the spirit one will be unhindered in one's journey on the narrow road. For on this road there is room only for self-denial (as our Savior asserts) and the cross. The cross is a supporting staff and greatly lightens and eases the journey.

Our Lord proclaimed through St. Matthew: *My yoke is sweet and my burden (the cross) light* [Mt 11:30]. If individuals resolutely submit to the carrying of the cross, if they decidedly want to find and endure trial in all things for God, they will discover in all of them great relief and sweetness. This will be so because they will be traveling the road denuded of all and with no desire for anything. If they aim after the possession of something, from God or elsewhere, their journey will not be one of nakedness and detachment from all things, and consequently there will be no room for them on this narrow path nor will they be able to climb it.

8. I should like to persuade spiritual persons that the road leading to God does not entail a multiplicity of considerations, methods, manners, and experiences—though in their own way these may be a requirement for beginners—but demands only the one thing necessary: true self-denial, exterior and interior, through surrender of self both to suffering for Christ and to annihilation in all things. In the exercise of this self-denial everything else, and even more, is discovered and accomplished. If one fails in this exercise, the root and sum total of all the virtues, the other methods would amount to no more than going about in circles without any progress, even if they result in considerations and communications as lofty as those of the angels. A person makes progress only by imitating Christ, who is the Way, the Truth, and the Life. No one goes to the Father but through Him, as He states Himself in

THE ASCENT OF MOUNT CARMEL

St. John [Jn 14:6]. Elsewhere He says: *I am the door, anyone who enters by Me shall be saved* [Jn 10:9]. Accordingly, I would not consider any spirituality worthwhile that wants to walk in sweetness and ease and run from the imitation of Christ.

9. Because I have said that Christ is the Way and that this Way is a death to our natural selves in the sensory and spiritual parts of the soul, I would like to demonstrate how this death is patterned on Christ's. For He is our model and light.

10. First, during His life He died spiritually to the sensitive part, and at His death He died naturally. He proclaimed during His life that He had no place whereon to lay His head [Mt 8:20]. And at His death He had less.

11. Second, at the moment of His death he was certainly annihilated in His soul, without any consolation or relief, since the Father had left Him that way in innermost aridity in the lower part. He was thereby compelled to cry out: *My God, My God, why have You forsaken me?* [Mt 27:46]. This was the most extreme abandonment, sensitively, that He had suffered in His life. And by it He accomplished the most marvelous work of His whole life surpassing all the works and deeds and miracles that He had ever performed on earth or in heaven. That is, He brought about the reconciliation and union of the human race with God through grace. The Lord achieved this, as I say, at the moment in which He was most annihilated in all things: in His reputation before people, since in beholding Him die they mocked Him instead of esteeming Him; in His human nature, by dying; and in spiritual help and consolation from His Father, for He was forsaken by His Father at that time so as to pay the debt fully and bring people to union with God. David says of Him: *Ad nihilum redactus sum et nescivi*[8] [Ps 72:22], that those who are truly spiritual might understand the mystery of the door and way (which is Christ) leading to union with God, and that they might realize that their union with God and the greatness of the work they accomplish will be measured by their annihilation of themselves for God in the sensory and spiritual parts of their souls. When they are brought to nothing, the highest degree of humility, the spiritual union between their souls and God will be effected. This union is the most noble and sublime state attainable in this life. The journey, then, does not consist in recreations, experiences, and spiritual feelings,

---

8. I was brought to nothing and did not understand.

but in the living, sensory and spiritual, exterior and interior, death of the cross.

12. I will not enlarge on this, though I would like to continue discussing the matter because from my observations Christ is little known by those who consider themselves His friends. For we see them going about seeking in Him their own consolations and satisfactions, loving themselves very much; but not seeking His bitter trials and deaths, loving Him very much.

I am referring to those who believe themselves His friends; not to those who live withdrawn and far away from Him; people of extensive learning and high repute, and many others living yonder with the world, anxious about their pretensions and rank. These people, we can affirm, do not know Christ. However prosperous the end of their lives may seem, it will be in fact most bitter to them. On judgment day they will be spoken of, for they are the ones to whom we should first speak this word of God [Acts 13:46]. Because of their learning and higher state, they are the ones whom God intended as the target for this doctrine.

13. Let us address the intellects of spiritual people, particularly of those whom God has favored with the state of contemplation, for as I asserted, I am now speaking especially to these people. We shall discuss the direction of self to God through faith, and the purification of what is contrary to faith so that the soul by limiting itself may enter on the narrow path of obscure contemplation.

Chapter Eight

No creature or knowledge comprehensible to the intellect can serve it as a proximate means for the divine union with God.

1. Before dealing with faith, the proper and adequate means of union with God, we should prove how nothing created or imagined can serve the intellect as a proper means for union with God, and how all that can be grasped by the intellect would serve as an obstacle rather than a means if a person were to become attached to it.

This chapter will contain a general proof of this; afterward we will discuss in particular the knowledge that the intellect can receive through the interior or exterior senses. We will also deal with the difficulty and harm occasioned by these exterior and interior ideas, for because of them the intellect does not advance with the support of faith, which is the proper means.

2. Let it be recalled, then, that according to a philosophical axiom all means must be proportionate to their end.[9] That is, they must manifest a certain accord with and likeness to the end so that through them the desired end may be attained.

For example, those who want to reach a city must necessarily take the road, the means, that leads to the city. As another example: If fire is to be united with a log of wood, it is necessary for heat, the means, to prepare the log first, through so many degrees of heat, with a certain likeness and proportion to the fire. Now if anyone wanted to prepare the log by an inadequate means, such as air, water, or earth, there would be no possibility of union between the log and the fire, just as it would be impossible to reach the city without taking the proper road that connects with it.

If the intellect, then, is to reach union with God in this life, insofar as is possible, it must take that means which bears a proximate likeness to God and unites with Him.

3. It is noteworthy that among all creatures both superior and inferior none bears a likeness to God's being or unites proximately with Him. Although truly, as theologians say, all creatures carry with them a certain relation to God and a trace of Him (greater or lesser according to the perfection of their being), yet God has no relation or essential likeness to them. Rather the difference that lies between His divine being and their being is infinite. Consequently, intellectual comprehension of God through heavenly or earthly creatures is impossible; there is no proportion of likeness.

David proclaims in reference to heavenly creatures: *There is none among the gods like You, O Lord!* [Ps 85:8]. This was equivalent to saying that the way of approach to you, O God, is a holy way, namely, purity of faith. For what god can be great enough (that is, what angel so elevated in being, or saint in glory) to serve as an adequate and sufficient approach to you?

David also proclaims of earthly and heavenly things: "The Lord is high up and looks at low things, and the high things He knows from

---

9. Cf. Aristotle, *Metaphysica* 2, 1; Aquinas, *Summa Theologica* 1-2, 96; 1-2, 102, 1; 1-2, 114, 2.

afar" [Ps 137:6]. In other words: High in His own being, He looks at the being of objects here below as exceedingly low in comparison with His high being; and the high things, the heavenly creatures, He knows to be far distant from His own being. Thus, no creature can serve the intellect as a proportionate means to the attainment of God.

4. Nothing that could be imagined or comprehended in this life can be a proximate means of union with God. In our natural way of knowing, the intellect can only grasp an object through the forms and phantasms of things perceived by the bodily senses. Since these objects cannot serve as a means, the intellect cannot profit from its natural knowing. As for the supernatural way of knowing, the intellect according to the possibilities of its ordinary power is neither capable nor prepared, while in the prison of this body, for the reception of the clear knowledge of God. Such knowledge does not belong to this state, since death is a necessary condition for possessing it.

God told Moses, who had asked for this clear knowledge, that no one would be able to see Him: *No one shall see Me and remain alive* [Ex 33:20]. St. John says: *No one has ever seen God or anything like Him* [Jn 1:18]. And St. Paul with Isaiah says: *Eye has not seen, nor ear heard, nor has it entered the human heart* [1 Cor 2:9; Is 64:4]. This is why Moses, as affirmed in the Acts of the Apostles, dared not look at the bush while God was present. He thought his intellect was powerless to look at God in a way that conformed to what he felt about Him [Acts 7:30–32]. It is told of our Father Elijah that on the mount he covered his face (blinded his intellect) in the presence of God [1 Kgs 19:11–13]. He did this because, in his lowliness, he did not dare gaze on something so lofty, and he realized that anything he might behold or understand particularly would be far distant from God and most unlike Him.

5. In this mortal life no supernatural knowledge or apprehension can serve as a proximate means for the high union with God through love. Everything the intellect can understand, the will experience, and the imagination picture is most unlike and disproportioned to God, as we have said. . . .

In order to draw nearer the divine ray the intellect must advance by unknowing rather than by the desire to know, and by blinding itself and remaining in darkness rather than by opening its eyes.

6. Contemplation, consequently, by which the intellect has a higher knowledge of God, is called mystical theology, meaning the secret wisdom of God. For this wisdom is secret to the very intellect that receives it. St. Dionysius on this account refers to contemplation as a

ray of darkness.[10] The prophet Baruch declares of this wisdom: *There is no one who knows its way or can think of its paths* [Bar 3:25]. To reach union with God the intellect must obviously blind itself to all the paths along which it can travel. Aristotle teaches that just as the sun is total darkness to the eyes of a bat, so the brightest light in God is complete darkness to our intellect. And he teaches in addition that the loftier and clearer the things of God are in themselves, the more unknown and obscure they are to us.[11] The Apostle also affirms this teaching: That which is highest in God is least known by humans [Rom 11:33].

7. We would never finish if we continued to quote passages and present arguments as proof that there is no ladder among all created, knowable things by which the intellect can reach this high Lord. Rather, it should be known that if the intellect desired to use all or any of these objects as a proximate means to this union, it would be encumbered by them. Not only this but they would become an occasion of many errors and deceptions in the ascent of this mount.

Chapter Nine

Faith is the proximate and proportionate means to the intellect for the attainment of the divine union of love. Proofs from passages and figures of sacred Scripture.

1. We can gather from what has been said that to be prepared for this divine union the intellect must be cleansed and emptied of everything relating to sense, divested and liberated of everything clearly apprehensible, inwardly pacified and silenced, and supported by faith alone, which is the only proximate and proportionate means to union with God. For the likeness between faith and God is so close that no other difference exists than that between believing in God and seeing Him. Just as God is infinite, faith proposes Him to us as infinite. Just as there are three Persons in one God, it presents Him to us in this way. And just as God is darkness to our intellect, so faith dazzles and blinds us. Only by means of faith, in divine light exceeding all understanding,

---

10. Cf. Dionysius the Pseudo-Areopagite, *De Mystica theologia* 1, 1 (Migne PG 3, 999). John here identifies contemplation with mystical theology.

11. Aristotle, *Metaphysica* 2, 1.

does God manifest Himself to the soul. The greater one's faith the closer is one's union with God.

St. Paul indicated this in the passage cited above: *The one who would be united with God must believe* [Heb 11:6]. This means that people must walk by faith in their journey to God. The intellect must be blind and dark, and abide in faith alone, because it is joined with God under the cloud: *He set darkness under His feet. And he rose above the cherubim and flew on the wings of the wind. He made darkness and the dark water His hiding place* [Ps 17:10–12].

2. This darkness under God's feet and of His hiding place and the dark water of His dwelling denote the obscurity of faith in which He is enclosed. The verse stating that He rose above the cherubim and flew on the wings of the wind alludes to how God soars above all understanding. The cherubim refer to those who understand or contemplate; the wings of the wind signify the subtle ideas and lofty concepts of the spirit. Above these is His being, which no one can reach through human effort.

3. In Scripture we read figuratively of this that when Solomon had completed the temple, God descended in darkness and filled it so that the children of Israel were unable to see. Solomon then said: *The Lord has promised to dwell in darkness* [1 Kgs 8:12]. God was also covered with darkness when He appeared to Moses on the mount [Ex 24:16]. And as often as God communicated at length with someone, He appeared in darkness. This is evident in the Book of Job, where Scripture asserts that God spoke to Job from the dark air [Jb 38:1, 40:1].

All of this darkness signifies the obscurity of faith with which the divinity is clothed while communicating itself to the soul. This darkness will be dispelled when, as St. Paul states, that which is in part (this darkness of faith) is taken away, and that which is perfect (the divine light) comes [1 Cor 13:10]. We also find a fairly good figure of this obscurity of faith in the scriptural narration about the militia of Gideon. According to the account, all the soldiers held lamps in their hands, yet did not see the light because the lamps were hidden in darkness within earthenware jars. But when these jars were broken, the soldiers immediately beheld the shining light [Jgs 7:16–20]. Faith, represented by those clay jars, contains the divine light. When faith reaches its end and is shattered by the ending and breaking of this mortal life, the glory and light of the divinity, the content of faith, will at once begin to shine.

4. Manifestly, then, union with God in this life, and direct communication with Him, demands that we be united with the darkness in

which, as Solomon said [1 Kgs 8:12], God promised to dwell, and that we approach the dark air in which God was pleased to reveal His secrets to Job. Individuals must take in darkness the earthenware jars of Gideon and hold in their hands (the works of their wills) the lamp (the union of love, though in the darkness of faith), so that when the clay jar of this life, which is all that impedes the light of faith, is broken, they may see God face to face in glory.

5. We must discuss now in particular all the concepts and apprehensions of the intellect, the hindrance and harm they cause along the road of faith, and the conduct that is proper for the soul. We do this so that the soul may profit rather than suffer harm from either sensory or spiritual apprehensions.

Chapter Ten

A division of all apprehensions and ideas comprehensible to the intellect.

1. To discuss in particular both the advantage and the harm that intellectual concepts and apprehensions cause to the soul's faith, which is the means to divine union, we need to set up a division of all the natural and supernatural apprehensions of the intellect. Later, then, in a more logical order, we shall be able to guide the intellect through them into the night and darkness of faith. Our division will be as concise as possible.

2. It is noteworthy that the intellect can get ideas and concepts in two ways, naturally and supernaturally. Natural knowledge includes everything the intellect can understand by way of the bodily senses or through reflection. Supernatural knowledge comprises everything imparted to the intellect in a way transcending the intellect's natural ability and capacity.[12]

3. This supernatural knowledge is subdivided into corporal and spiritual. The corporal is made up of two kinds: knowledge received

---

12. John in his writings distinguishes the natural and the supernatural in the sense that the latter refers to knowledge or experiences that go beyond one's natural ability. Thus he identifies "supernatural" with "passive." Supernatural in his usage need not mean that the knowledge or experience is from God or beyond what in modern psychology is known as the unconscious. Such factors must be discerned from the context.

from the exterior bodily senses; and knowledge received from the interior bodily senses, including all that the imagination can apprehend, form, or fashion.

4. The spiritual is also made up of two kinds: distinct and particular knowledge; and vague, dark, and general knowledge.

The particular knowledge includes four kinds of distinct apprehensions communicated to the spirit without the means of the bodily senses: visions, revelations, locutions, and spiritual feelings.

The dark and general knowledge (contemplation, which is imparted in faith) is of one kind only. We have to lead the soul to this contemplation by guiding it through all these other apprehensions and divesting it of them, beginning with the first.

Chapter Eleven

The impediment and harm caused by intellectual apprehensions arising from objects supernaturally represented to the exterior senses. The proper conduct of the soul in their regard.

1. The first kind of knowledge referred to in the preceding chapter is that which originates naturally. Since we already discussed this kind of knowledge in the first book where we guided the soul through the night of sense, we will have nothing to say of it here. There we presented appropriate doctrine about this knowledge.

Our discussion in this chapter will deal only with the supernatural knowledge that reaches the intellect by way of the exterior bodily senses (sight, hearing, smell, taste, and touch). Through these senses, spiritual persons can, and usually do, perceive supernatural representations and objects.

As for sight, they are wont to have visions of images and persons from the other life: of saints, of the good and bad angels, and of unusual lights and splendors.

Through hearing they apprehend certain extraordinary words, sometimes from the vision, and at other times without seeing the one who speaks.

With the sense of smell they sometimes notice sensibly the sweetest fragrances without knowledge of their origin.

Also it happens with regard to taste that they experience very exquisite savors.

And concerning touch they feel extreme delight, at times so intense that all the bones and marrow rejoice, flourish, and bathe in it. This delight is usually termed spiritual unction because in pure souls it passes from the spirit to the senses. And it is common with spiritual persons. It is an overflow from the affection and devotion of the sensible spirit, which individuals receive in their own way. . . .

12. Manifestly, these visions and sense apprehensions cannot serve as a means for union since they bear no proportion to God. This was one of the reasons for Christ's not wanting Mary Magdalene or St. Thomas to touch Him [Jn 20:17, 27–29].

The devil is most pleased when he sees that people desire to admit revelations, for then he has an excellent opportunity to inject errors and disparage faith. As I have declared, people desiring these apprehensions become coarse in their faith and even expose themselves to many temptations and follies. . . .

Chapter Twelve

The nature of natural imaginative apprehensions. Proofs that they are inadequate means for the attainment of union with God. The harm caused from attachment to them.

1. Before discussing the imaginative visions, which are usually imparted supernaturally to the interior sense (imaginative power and phantasy), a discussion of the natural apprehensions of this interior corporal sense is in order. As a result we can proceed logically and progress from the lesser to the greater and from the more exterior to the more interior until reaching the ultimate perfection in which the soul is united with God. We have been following this very method: first we discussed the divesting of the exterior senses of their natural apprehensions, and, consequently, of the natural strength of the appetites. This we did in Book One where we spoke of the night of sense. Then we began to divest these senses of the supernatural exterior apprehensions and to lead the soul into the night of the spirit, as in the preceding chapter.

2. The first point to consider in this second book concerns the interior corporal sense (the imaginative power and phantasy). We must also empty this sense of every imaginative form and apprehension that

can be naturally grasped by it and demonstrate the impossibility of union with God before the activity relating to these apprehensions ceases. Such apprehensions are incapable of being the proper and proximate means of this union.

3. We are speaking of two interior bodily senses: the imagination and the phantasy. They are of service to each other in due order because the one is discursive with the images and the other forms them. For our discussion there will be no need of differentiating between them. This should be remembered if we do not mention them both explicitly.

All that these senses, then, can receive and construct are termed imaginations and phantasms. These are forms represented to the interior senses through material images and figures.

There are two kinds: supernatural and natural. The supernatural are represented passively without the work of the senses. These we call supernatural imaginative visions; we will discuss them afterward. The natural are those the soul can actively construct by its own power through forms, figures, and images.

Meditation is the work of these two faculties since it is a discursive act built on forms, figures, and images, imagined and fashioned by these senses. For example: the imagining of Christ crucified or at the pillar or in some other scene; or of God seated on a throne with resplendent majesty; or the imagining and considering of glory as a beautiful light, and so on; or, in similar fashion, of any other human or divine object imaginable.

The soul will have to empty itself of these images and leave this sense in darkness if it is to reach divine union. For these images, just as the corporal objects of the exterior senses, cannot be an adequate, proximate means to God.[13]

4. The reason is that the imagination cannot fashion or imagine anything beyond what it has experienced through the exterior senses, that is, seen with the eyes, heard with the ears, and so on. At the most it can compose resemblances of these objects that are seen, heard, or felt. But such resemblances do not reach a greater entity or even as

---

13. In speaking of a contemplative simplification in this chapter, John is stressing communion in contradistinction to reflection. If he advises against attempting to reflect on the life of Christ with the help of images formed in the imagination, he is not with that opposing the simple gaze of faith and personal communion with Jesus Christ. His teaching does not contradict St. Teresa's with respect to not abandoning the humanity of Christ in the higher stages of the spiritual life. There is a contemplative form of being present to Christ in His humanity. Cf. A. 2, 22, 5–6; *Interior Castle* VI, 7, 9–13.

much entity as that of other sense objects. Even though individuals may imagine palaces of pearls and mountains of gold—for they have seen gold and pearls—all of this imagination will indeed be less than the essence of a little gold or of a pearl. And this, even though in the imagination there is a larger quantity and more excellent structure. Since created things, as has been said, have no proportion to God's being, all imaginings fashioned from the likenesses of creatures are incapable of serving as proximate means toward union with God. Rather, as we said, they serve for much less.

5. Those who imagine God through some of these figures (as an imposing fire or as brightness, or through any other forms) and think that He is somewhat like them are very far from Him. These considerations, forms, and methods of meditation are necessary to beginners that the soul may be enamored and fed through the senses, as we shall point out later. They are suitable as the remote means to union with God, which beginners must ordinarily use for the attainment of their goal and the abode of spiritual repose. Yet these means must not be so used that one always employs them and never advances, for then one would never achieve the goal, which is unlike the remote means and unproportioned to it—just as none of the steps on a flight of stairs has any resemblance to the goal at the top toward which they are the means. If in climbing them we do not leave each one behind until there are no more, or should want to stay on one of them, we would never reach the level and peaceful room at the top.

Consequently, a person who wants to arrive at union with the Supreme Repose and Good in this life must climb all the steps, which are considerations, forms, and concepts, and leave them behind, since they are dissimilar and unproportioned to the goal toward which they lead. And this goal is God. Accordingly, St. Paul teaches in the Acts of the Apostles: *Non debemus aestimare auro vel argento, aut lapidi sculpturae artis, et cogitationis hominis divinum esse simile* (We should not consider or esteem the divinity to be like gold or silver, or stone sculptured by the artist, or like anything a person can fashion with the imagination) [Acts 17:29].

6. Many spiritual persons, after having exercised themselves in approaching God through images, forms, and meditations suitable for beginners, err greatly if they do not determine, dare, or know how to detach themselves from these palpable methods. For God then wishes to lead them to more spiritual, interior, and invisible graces by removing the gratification derived from discursive meditation. They still try

THE ASCENT OF MOUNT CARMEL

to hold on to these methods, desiring to travel the road of consideration and meditation, using images as before. They think they must always act in this way. Striving hard to meditate, they draw out little satisfaction, or none at all. Rather the aridity, fatigue, and restlessness of soul increases the more they strive through meditation for that former sweetness, now unobtainable. They will no longer taste that sensible food, as we said, but rather will enjoy another food, more delicate, interior, and spiritual. Not by working with the imagination will they acquire this spiritual nourishment but by pacifying the soul, by leaving it to its more spiritual quiet and repose.

The more spiritual they are, the more they discontinue trying to make particular acts with their faculties, for they become more engrossed in one general, pure act. Once the faculties reach the end of their journey, they cease to work, just as we cease to walk when we reach the end of our journey. If everything consisted in going, one would never arrive; and if everywhere we found means, when and where could we enjoy the end and goal?

7. It is sad to see many disturb their soul when it desires to abide in this calm and repose of interior quietude, where it is filled with the peace and refreshment of God. Desiring to make it retrace its steps and turn back from the goal in which it now reposes, they draw their soul out to more exterior activity, to considerations, which are the means. This they do, not without strong repugnance and reluctance in the soul. The soul would want to remain in that peace, which it does not understand, as in its right place. People suffer if, after laboring to reach their place of rest, they are forced to return to their labors.

Since these individuals do not understand the mystery of that new experience, they imagine themselves to be idle and doing nothing. Thus, in their struggle with considerations and discursive meditations they disturb their quietude. They become filled with aridity and trial because of efforts to get satisfaction by means no longer apt. We can say that the more intense their efforts, the less will be their gain. The more they persist at meditation, the worse their state becomes because they drag the soul further away from spiritual peace. They resemble one who abandons the greater for the lesser, turns back on a road already covered and wants to redo what is already done.

8. The advice proper for these individuals is that they must learn to abide in that quietude with a loving attentiveness to God and pay no

heed to the imagination and its work.[14] At this stage, as was said, the faculties are at rest and do not work actively but passively, by receiving what God is effecting in them. If at times the soul puts the faculties to work, excessive efforts or studied reasonings should not be used, but it should do so with gentleness of love, moved more by God than by its own abilities, as we will explain later.

This explanation should be sufficient at present for those wanting to make progress. They will understand the appropriateness and necessity of detaching oneself at the required time and season from all these methods, ways, and uses of the imagination.

9. To explain just when this practice must be employed, we will describe in the following chapter some signs that spiritual persons must notice in themselves. These signs will indicate that the time and season has come when they can freely make use of that loving attentiveness and discontinue their journey along the way of reasoning and imagination.

Chapter Thirteen

The signs for recognizing in spiritual persons when they should discontinue discursive meditation and pass on to the state of contemplation.

1. To avoid obscurity in this doctrine it will be opportune to point out in this chapter when one ought to discontinue discursive meditation (a work through images, forms, and figures) so that the practice will not be abandoned sooner or later than required by the spirit. Just as it should be abandoned at the proper time that it may not be a hindrance in the journey to God, this imaginative meditation should not be abandoned before the due time so that there be no regression. For though the apprehensions of these faculties are not a proximate means toward union for proficients, they are a remote means for beginners. By these sensitive means beginners dispose their spirit and habituate it to spiritual things, and at the same time they void their senses of all other base, temporal, secular, and natural forms and images.

---

14. This loving attention gradually takes the place of discursive meditation. Thus we have the transition to a new attitude in which a passivity or receptivity before God takes the place of human effort.

THE ASCENT OF MOUNT CARMEL

Hence we will delineate some signs and indications by which one can judge whether or not it is the opportune time for the spiritual person to discontinue meditation.[15]

2. The first is the realization that one cannot make discursive meditation or receive satisfaction from it as before. Dryness is now the outcome of fixing the senses on subjects that formerly provided satisfaction. As long as one can, however, make discursive meditation and draw out satisfaction, one must not abandon this method. Meditation must be discontinued only when the soul is placed in that peace and quietude to be spoken of in the third sign.

3. The second sign is an awareness of a disinclination to fix the imagination or sense faculties on other particular objects, exterior or interior. I am not affirming that the imagination will cease to come and go (even in deep recollection it usually wanders freely), but that the person is disinclined to fix it purposely on extraneous things.[16]

4. The third and surest sign is that a person likes to remain alone in loving awareness of God, without particular considerations, in interior peace and quiet and repose, and without the acts and exercises (at least discursive, those in which one progresses from point to point) of the intellect, memory, and will. Such a one prefers to remain only in the general, loving awareness and knowledge we mentioned, without any particular knowledge or understanding.

5. To leave safely the state of meditation and sense and enter that of contemplation and spirit, spiritual persons must observe within themselves at least these three signs together.

6. It is insufficient to possess the first without the second. It could be that the inability to imagine and meditate derives from one's dissipation and lack of diligence. The second sign, the disinclination and absence of desire to think about extraneous things, must be present. When this inability to concentrate the imagination and sense faculties on the things of God proceeds from dissipation and tepidity, there is then a yearning to dwell on other things and an inclination to give up the meditation.

Neither is the realization of the first and second sign sufficient if the third sign is not observed together with them. When one is incapable of

---

15. He speaks of these signs from a different perspective again in N. 1, 9.
16. The fact that the imagination will wander to and fro in the prayer of recollection or quiet was a source of affliction to St. Teresa until she was enlightened on the matter by a learned man (perhaps John himself). See *Interior Castle* IV, 1, 8–9; *Life* 17, 7.

making discursive meditation on the things of God and disinclined to consider subjects extraneous to God, the cause could be melancholia or some other kind of humor in the heart or brain capable of producing a certain stupefaction and suspension of the sense faculties. This anomaly would be the explanation for want of thought or of desire and inclination for thought. It would foster in a person the desire to remain in the delightful ravishment. Because of this danger, the third sign, the loving knowledge and awareness in peace, and so on, is necessary.

7. Actually, at the beginning of this state the loving knowledge is almost unnoticeable. There are two reasons for this: First, the loving knowledge initially is likely to be extremely subtle and delicate, and almost imperceptible; second, a person who is habituated to the exercise of meditation, which is wholly sensible, hardly perceives or feels this new insensible, purely spiritual experience. This is especially so when through failure to understand it one does not permit oneself any quietude but strives after the other more sensory experience. Although the interior peace is more abundant, the individual allows no room for its experience and enjoyment. But the more habituated persons become to this calm, the more their experience of this general, loving knowledge of God will increase. This knowledge is more enjoyable than all other things because without the soul's labor it affords peace, rest, savor, and delight.

8. For greater clarity we will expound in the following chapter some reasons showing the necessity for these three signs in order to journey on the road of spirit.

Chapter Fourteen

Proves the appropriateness of these three signs and explains why their presence is necessary in order that one advance.

1. As for the first sign it should be known that there are two reasons almost comprised in one for requiring spiritual persons to give up the imaginative way or sensory meditation when they are unable to meditate or derive satisfaction from it and enter the way of the spirit, which is the contemplative way.

First, because these persons have been granted all the spiritual good obtainable through discursive meditation on the things of God.

THE ASCENT OF MOUNT CARMEL

An indication of this is their inability to make discursive meditation as before or derive from it any new satisfaction or pleasure. For previously they had not yet arrived at the spirituality that was in store for them.

Ordinarily, as often as individuals receive some profitable grace, they experience—at least spiritually—gratification in the means through which the grace is obtained. If this is not received, there will rarely be profit, neither will they find in the cause of that former gratification the support and satisfaction they did before when they received grace through that means. This agrees with what the philosophers hold: *Quod sapit, nutrit* (What is savory nourishes and fattens).[17] Hence holy Job asks: *Numquid poterit comedi insulsum, quod non est sale conditum?* (Could one perchance eat the unsavory that is not seasoned with salt?) [Jb 6:6]. Here we have the cause of the person's inability to consider and meditate as before: the lack of savor and benefit derived by the spirit from this exercise.

2. The second reason is that these persons have now acquired the substantial and habitual spirit of meditation. It should be known that the purpose of discursive meditation on divine subjects is the acquisition of some knowledge and love of God. Each time individuals procure through meditation some of this knowledge and love they do so by an act. Many acts, in no matter what area, will engender a habit. Similarly, the repetition of many particular acts of this loving knowledge becomes so continuous that a habit is formed in the soul. God, too, is wont to effect this habit in many souls, without the precedence of at least many of these acts as means.

What the soul, therefore, was periodically acquiring through the labor of meditation on particular ideas has now, as we said, been converted into the habitual and substantial, general and loving knowledge. This knowledge is neither distinct nor particular, as the previous. Accordingly the moment prayer begins, the soul, as one with a store of water, drinks peaceably without the labor and the need of fetching the water through the channels of past considerations, forms, and figures. At the moment it recollects itself in the presence of God, it enters on an act of general, loving, peaceful, and tranquil knowledge, drinking wisdom and love and delight.

3. This is why people experience difficulty and displeasure when, despite the calm they are enjoying, they meet others who want to make

---

17. Cf. Aristotle, *De anima* 3, 28; Aquinas, *Summa Theologica* 2-2, 141, 5.

them meditate and work with particular concepts. Their experience resembles that of the suckling child. It finds that the breast is taken away just when it is beginning to taste the milk that was gathered there for it. As a result it is forced to renew its efforts. Or their experience is like that of a person who, while enjoying the substance of the fruit, once the rind is peeled, is forced to stop and begin again to remove the rind from the fruit even though the fruit has already been peeled. In such an instance the person would fail to find the rind and cease enjoying the substance of the fruit that is at hand. Or this is like turning away from the captured prey to go hunting for another.

4. Many behave similarly at the beginning of this state. They are of the opinion that the whole matter consists in understanding particular ideas and reasoning through images and forms (the rind of the spirit). Since they do not encounter these images in that loving, substantial quietude, where nothing is understood particularly and in which they like to rest, they believe they are wasting time and straying from the right road; and they turn back to search for the rind of images and reasoning. They are unsuccessful in their search because the rind has already been removed. There is no enjoyment of the substance nor ability to meditate, and they become disturbed with the thought of backsliding and going astray. Indeed they are getting lost, but not in the way they imagine, for they are losing the exercise of their own senses and first mode of experience. This loss indicates that they are approaching the spirit being imparted to them, in which the less they understand the further they penetrate into the night of the spirit—the subject of this book. They must pass through this night to a union with God beyond all knowing.

5. There is little to be said about the second sign, for it is obvious that these persons at this time necessarily find worldly images dissatisfying. Even those that concern God, which are more conformable to their state, fail to satisfy them, as we explained. Nevertheless, as we mentioned above, the imagination usually wanders back and forth during this recollection. But these individuals do not desire or find delight in this; rather, they are troubled about it on account of the disturbance it brings to that gratifying peace.

6. Nor do I believe it is necessary to indicate here why the third sign (the loving, general knowledge or awareness of God) is a requirement for discontinuing meditation. Some doctrine has already been expounded about this sign in our explanation of the first one, and afterward in the proper place we will have a special discussion of this

when dealing with the general, obscure knowledge.[18] This matter will be taken up after our treatise on the distinct, intellectual apprehensions. We will, however, state one reason that manifests how this loving, general knowledge and awareness of God in the soul is required before discontinuing discursive meditation.

If people do not have this knowledge or attentiveness to God, they would, as a consequence, be neither doing anything nor receiving anything. Having left the discursive meditation of the sensitive faculties and still lacking contemplation (the general knowledge in which the spiritual faculties—memory, intellect, and will—are actuated and united in this passive, prepared knowledge), they would have no activity whatsoever relative to God. For a person can neither conceive nor receive knowledge already prepared save through either the sensitive or spiritual faculties. With the sensory faculties, as we affirmed, one can make discursive meditation, seek out and form knowledge from the objects; and with the spiritual faculties one can enjoy the knowledge received without any further activity of the senses.

7. The difference between the functions of these two groups of faculties resembles that existing between toil and the enjoyment of the fruits of this toil; between the drudgery of the journey and the rest and quiet gladdening its end; or again, between cooking a meal and eating without effort what has already been cooked and prepared; it is like the difference between receiving a gift and profiting by it.

If the sensitive faculties are idle as to their work of discursive meditation, and the spiritual faculties as to the contemplation and knowledge received and formed in them, there is no basis for asserting that the soul is occupied. This knowledge is necessary, then, in order to leave the way of discursive meditation.

8. It is noteworthy that this general knowledge is at times so recondite and delicate (especially when purer, simpler, and more perfect), spiritual, and interior that the soul does not perceive or feel it, even though employed with it. This is especially so when, as we affirmed, this knowledge is clearer, simpler, and more perfect. And then this knowledge is still less perceptible when it shines on a purer soul, one freer from the particular ideas and concepts apprehensible by the senses or intellect. Since one lacks the feelings of the sensitive part of the soul,

---

18. John never deals directly with this subject as promised here, although he does speak of it in various parts of his work, especially in *The Dark Night*.

THE ASCENT OF MOUNT CARMEL

by not possessing these particular ideas and concepts, which the senses and intellect are accustomed to act on, one does not perceive this knowledge.

For this reason the purer, simpler, and more perfect the general knowledge is, the darker it seems to be and the less the intellect perceives. On the other hand, the less pure and simple the knowledge is in itself, although it enlightens the intellect, the clearer and more important it appears to the individual, since it is clothed, wrapped, or commingled with some intelligible forms apprehensible to the intellect or the senses.

9. The following example is a clear illustration of this. In observing a ray of sunlight stream through the window, we notice that the more it is pervaded with particles of dust, the clearer and more palpable and sensible it appears to the senses. Yet obviously the sun ray in itself is less pure, clear, simple, and perfect in that it is full of so many specks of dust. We also notice that when it is more purified of these specks of dust it seems more obscure and impalpable to the material eye. And the purer it is, the more obscure and inapprehensible it seems to be. If the ray of sunlight should be entirely cleansed and purified of all dust particles, even the most minute, it would appear totally obscure and incomprehensible to the eye since visible things, the object of the sense of sight, would be absent. Thus the eye would find no images on which to rest, because light is not the proper object of sight but only the means by which visible things are seen. If there is nothing visible off which the ray of light can reflect, nothing will be seen. If the ray, then, were to enter through one window and go out another without striking any quantitative object, it would be invisible. Yet the ray of sunlight would be purer and cleaner than when, on account of being filled with visible objects, it is more manifestly perceived.

10. The spiritual light has a similar relationship to the intellect, the eye of the soul. This supernatural, general knowledge and light shines so purely and simply in the intellect and is so divested and freed of all intelligible forms (the objects of the intellect) that it is imperceptible to the soul. This knowledge, when purer, is even at times the cause of darkness because it dispossesses the intellect of its customary lights, forms, and phantasies and effects a noticeable darkness.

When this divine light does not strike so forcibly, individuals apprehend neither darkness, nor light, nor anything at all from heavenly or earthly sources. Thus they will sometimes remain in deep oblivion and afterward will not realize where they were, or what occurred, or how the time passed. As a result it can and does happen that a person will spend many hours in this oblivion, yet on returning to self think that only a moment or no time at all has passed.

11. The purity and simplicity of the knowledge is the cause of this oblivion. While occupying a person's soul, it renders that soul simple, pure, and clear of all the apprehensions and forms through which the senses and memory were acting when conscious of time. And thus it leaves the soul in oblivion and unaware of time.

Although as we asserted, the prayer lasts a long while, it seems of short duration to these souls since they have been united with pure knowledge which is independent of time. This is the short prayer that, it is said, pierces the heavens [Sir 35:17]. It is short because it is not subject to time, and it pierces the heavens because the soul is united with heavenly knowledge. When these persons return to themselves they observe the effects this knowledge produced in them without their having been aware of it. These effects are: an elevation of the mind to heavenly knowledge and a withdrawal and abstraction from all objects, forms, and figures and from the remembrance of them.

David declares that such was his experience on returning to himself after this oblivion: *Vigilavi, et factus sum sicut passer solitarius in tecto* (I became conscious and discovered that I was like the solitary sparrow on the housetop) [Ps 101:8]. By solitary he refers to the withdrawal and abstraction from all things; by the housetop, to the mind elevated on high. The soul remains, in consequence, as though ignorant of all things since it only knows God without knowing how it knows Him. For this reason the bride in the Song of Songs, when she states that she went down to Him, numbers unknowing among the effects this sleep and oblivion produced in her, saying: *Nescivi* (I knew not) [Sg 6:12].

As we mentioned, it seems to individuals when occupied with this knowledge that they are idle because they do not work with their senses or faculties. Nevertheless they must believe that they are not wasting time, for even though the harmonious interaction of their sensory and spiritual faculties ceases, the soul is occupied with knowledge in the way we explained. This is why, also, in the Song of Songs, the wise bride responded to one of her doubts: *Ego dormio et cor meum vigilat* [Sg 5:2]. This was like saying: Though I (according to what I am) sleep, naturally, by ceasing to work, my heart watches, supernaturally, in its elevation to supernatural knowledge.

12. But one should not think this knowledge, if it is to be all we said it was, will necessarily cause oblivion. This forgetfulness occurs

only when God abstracts the soul from the exercise of all the natural and spiritual faculties. Because such knowledge does not always occupy the entire soul, this forgetfulness is less frequent. The knowledge we are discussing only requires abstraction of the intellect from any particular, temporal, or spiritual knowledge and an unwillingness to think of either, as we have said. For then we have a sign that the soul is occupied.

This sign is necessary for recognizing this knowledge when it is applied and communicated only to the intellect. For then sometimes it is imperceptible. When, however, there is also a communication to the will, as there almost always is, people will not fail to understand more or less their being occupied with this knowledge if they want to discern this. For they will be aware of the delight of love, without particular knowledge of what they love. As a result they will call it a general, loving knowledge.

This communication, consequently, is called a general loving knowledge, for just as it is imparted obscurely to the intellect, so too a vague delight and love is given to the will without distinct knowledge of the object loved.

13. This explanation is sufficient at present to understand the need for this knowledge before leaving the way of discursive meditation and for the assurance that, despite the apparent idleness, the soul is well employed if these three signs are noticeable. It is also sufficient for an understanding of how the representation of this light in a more comprehensible and palpable way is not a sign of its greater purity, sublimity, and clarity, as was demonstrated through the example of the ray of sunlight permeated with dust particles and thereby perceptible to the eye. Evidently, as Aristotle and the theologians assert, the higher and more sublime the divine light, the darker it is to our intellect.[19]

14. A great deal can be said about this divine knowledge, as to both its nature and the effects it produces in the soul. We are reserving this discussion for its proper place.[20] There was no reason for such a lengthy treatment of it here, except that we were undesirous of leaving this doctrine somewhat more vague than it is. Certainly, I admit that it is very obscure. To the fact that this knowledge is a subject seldom dealt with in this style, in word or in writing, since in itself it is supernatural and

---

19. *Metaphysica* 2, 1.
20. See note 18 from no. 6 of this chapter.

obscure, can be added that of my unpolished style and lack of knowledge. Doubtful of my ability to make myself understood, I am often aware of exceeding the limits required for a sufficient presentation of this doctrine. I confess that I sometimes do so intentionally because what is not understandable with one reason may become so by others. Also I think that such procedure will give more clarification to later explanations.

15. In conclusion, I think a question concerning the duration of this knowledge should be answered. I will do so briefly in the following chapter.

Chapter Fifteen

Proficients, at the beginning of their entry into this general knowledge of contemplation, must at times practice discursive meditation and work with the natural faculties.

1. A question may arise about our teaching. Are proficients (those whom God begins to place in this supernatural knowledge of contemplation), because they are beginning to experience contemplation, never again to practice discursive meditation and work with natural forms?

We did not mean that those beginning to have this general, loving knowledge should never again try to meditate. In the beginning of this state the habit of contemplation is not so perfect that one can at will enter into this act, neither is one so remote from discursive meditation as to be always incapable of it. One can at times in a natural way meditate discursively as before and discover something new in this. Indeed, at the outset, on judging through the signs mentioned above that the soul is not occupied in repose and knowledge, individuals will need to make use of meditation. This need will continue until they acquire the habit of contemplation in a certain perfect degree. The indication of this will be that every time they intend to meditate, they will immediately notice this knowledge and peace as well as their own lack of power or desire to meditate, as we said. Until reaching this stage (of those already proficient in contemplation), people will sometimes contemplate and sometimes meditate.

2. They will often find that they are experiencing this loving or

peaceful awareness passively without having first engaged in any active work (regarding particular acts) with their faculties. But on the other hand they will frequently find it necessary to aid themselves gently and moderately with meditation in order to enter this state.

But once they have been placed in it, as we already pointed out, they do not work with the faculties. It is more exact to say that the work is then done in the soul and the knowledge and delight is already produced than that the soul does anything, besides attentively loving God and refraining from the desire to feel or see anything. In this loving awareness the soul receives God's communication passively, just as those who without doing anything else but keep their eyes open receive light passively. This reception of the light infused supernaturally into the soul is passive knowing. It is affirmed that these individuals do nothing, not because they fail to understand but because they understand by dint of no effort other than the receiving of what is bestowed. This process is similar to God's illuminations and inspirations, although here the person freely receives this general, obscure knowledge.

3. One should not commingle other more palpable lights of forms, concepts, or figures of meditative discourse, if one wants to receive this divine light in greater simplicity and abundance. For none of these tangible lights are like that serene, limpid light. If individuals were to desire to consider and understand particular things, however spiritual these things may be, they would hinder the general, limpid, and simple light of the spirit. They would be interfering by their cloudy thoughts. When an obstruction is placed in front of the eyes, one is impeded from seeing the light and the view before one.

4. What clearly follows is that when people have finished purifying and voiding themselves of all forms and apprehensible images, they will abide in this pure and simple light and be perfectly transformed in it. This light is never lacking to the soul, but because of creature forms and veils weighing on and covering it, the light is never infused. If individuals would eliminate these impediments and veils and live in pure nakedness and poverty of spirit, as we shall explain later, their soul in its simplicity and purity would then be immediately transformed into simple and pure Wisdom, the Son of God. As soon as natural things are driven out of the enamored soul, the divine are naturally and supernaturally infused since there can be no void in nature.

5. When spiritual persons cannot meditate, they should learn to remain in God's presence with a loving attention and a tranquil intellect, even though they seem to themselves to be idle. For little by little

and very soon the divine calm and peace with a wondrous, sublime knowledge of God, enveloped in divine love, will be infused into their souls. They should not interfere with forms or discursive meditations and imaginings. Otherwise the soul will be disquieted and drawn out of its peaceful contentment to distaste and repugnance. And if, as we said, scruples about their inactivity arise, they should remember that pacification of the soul (making it calm and peaceful, inactive and desireless) is no small accomplishment. This, indeed, is what our Lord asks of us through David: *Vacate et videte quoniam ego sum Deus* [Ps 46:11]. This would be like saying: Learn to be empty of all things—interiorly and exteriorly—and you will behold that I am God.

Chapter Sixteen

The imaginative apprehensions represented supernaturally to the phantasy are incapable of serving as a proximate means to union with God.

1. Now that we have discussed the natural apprehensions that the phantasy and imagination receive and work with through discursive meditation it is fitting that we discuss the supernatural apprehensions, called imaginative visions. These visions pertain to the phantasy just as natural apprehensions do because they belong to the category of image, form, and figure. . . .

3. It is noteworthy that as the five exterior senses send the images and species of their objects to these interior senses, so God and the devil can supernaturally represent to these faculties—without the exterior senses—the same images and species. In fact, they can effect this in a more beautiful and perfect way. . . .

13. A question, though, may arise concerning this subject: If it is true that God in giving supernatural visions does not want one thereby to desire, lean on, or pay attention to them, why does He give them at all? Through them an individual can fall into numerous dangers and errors, or at least encounter the many impediments to further progress described here. Furthermore, why would God do this if He can communicate to the soul substantially and spiritually what he bestows on it through the sensible communication of these visions and forms?

14. We will explain our answer to this question in the following

chapter. There we will present for spiritual persons and their teachers doctrine that, in my opinion, is both important and necessary. We will expound God's method and purpose—of which many are ignorant—in bestowing these visions. As a result of their ignorance about visions, many are unenlightened on how to behave and how to guide themselves or others through them to union. They think that, because of their awareness of the genuineness and divine origin of these visions, it is advantageous to admit and trust them. They do not reflect that, as with worldly goods, failure to deny them can be a hindrance, and cause attachment and possessiveness concerning them. They consider it beneficial to admit some visions as true and reject others as false. In this way they subject themselves and other souls to the considerable labor and danger of discerning the truth or falsity of these visions. God does not impose this task on them, nor does He desire the exposure of simple and unlearned people to this dangerous endeavor, for these persons have faith, the sound and safe doctrine by which they can advance.

15. There is no advancing in faith without the closing of one's eyes to everything pertaining to the senses and to clear, particular knowledge. Though St. Peter was truly certain of his vision of Christ's glory in the transfiguration, yet, after relating the fact in his second canonical epistle, he did not want anyone to take this as the chief testimony for certitude. But leading them on to faith, he declared: *Et habemus firmiorem propheticum sermonem: cui benefacitis attendentes, quasi lucernae lucenti in caliginoso loco, donec dies elucescat* (We have a more certain testimony than this vision of Tabor: the sayings and words of the prophets bearing testimony to Christ, of which you must make good use as of a candle shining in a dark place) [2 Pt 1:16–18].

Reflecting on this comparison, we discover the doctrine taught here. Telling us to behold the faith spoken of by the prophets as we would a candle shining in a dark place, he asserts that we should live in darkness, with our eyes closed to all other lights, and that in this darkness faith alone—which is dark also—should be the light we use. If we want to employ these other bright lights of distinct knowledge, we cease to make use of faith, the dark light, and we cease to be enlightened in the dark place mentioned by St. Peter. This place (the intellect—the holder on which the candle of faith is placed) must remain in darkness until the day, in the next life, when the clear vision of God dawns on the soul; and in this life, until the daybreak of transformation in God and union with Him, the goal of a person's journey.

Chapter Seventeen

An answer to the proposed question. God's procedure and purpose in communicating spiritual goods by means of the senses.

1. A great deal may be said about God's intention (the elevation of a soul from its low state to divine union) and method of procedure in bestowing these goods.[21] All spiritual books deal with these points, and in our explanation we will also consider them. Accordingly, in this chapter I will do no more than offer a sufficient solution to our question, which is: Since there is so much danger and hindrance to progress in these supernatural visions, as we said, why does God, who is all wise and in favor of removing obstacles and snares, communicate them?

2. An answer to this requires the establishment of three fundamental principles.

The first is taken from St. Paul's Epistle to the Romans: *Quae autem sunt, a Deo ordinata sunt* (The works that are done are well ordered by God) [Rm 13:1].[22]

The second comes from the Holy Spirit in the Book of Wisdom: *Disponit omnia suaviter*. This is similar to stating: God's wisdom, though it touches from one end to the other (from one extreme to the other), disposes all things gently [Wis 7:30, 8:1].

The third originates with the theologians who say: *Omnia movet secundum modum eorum* (God moves each thing according to its mode).[23]

3. In order that God lift the soul from the extreme of its low state to the other extreme of the high state of divine union, He must obviously, in view of these fundamental principles, do so with order, gently, and according to the mode of the soul. Since the order followed in the process of knowing involves the forms and images of created things, and since knowledge is acquired through the senses, God, to

---

21. This important chapter deals with the general principles God follows in leading persons to union with Himself. It is interesting to note that in John's teaching the element of passivity or receptivity is present from the beginning, that God is instructing souls also through their discursive meditation; they do not receive from Him only in contemplation. But when the senses are used as means, God's communication comes only in morsels; cf. nos. 5, 8.

22. In this passage Paul is speaking of civil authorities established by God. John says *ordinata* instead of *ordinatae*. His principles do not depend for their value on the texts cited here.

23. This frequently quoted axiom may be found in Aquinas, *De veritate* 12, 6.

achieve His work gently and to lift the soul to supreme knowledge, must begin by touching the low state and extreme of the senses. And from there He must gradually bring the soul after its own manner to the other end, spiritual wisdom, which is incomprehensible to the senses. Thus, naturally or supernaturally, He brings people to the supreme spirit of God by first instructing them through discursive meditation and through forms, images, and sensible means, according to each individual's own manner of acquiring knowledge.

4. This is the reason God gives a person visions, forms, images, and other sensitive and spiritual knowledge—not because He does not desire to give spiritual wisdom immediately, in the first act. He would do this if the two extremes (human and divine, sense and spirit) could through the ordinary process be united by only one act, and if He could exclude the many preparatory acts, which are so connected in gentle and orderly fashion that, as is the case with natural agents, each is the foundation and preparation for the next. The first preparative acts serve the second; the second, the third, and so on. Therefore God perfects people gradually, according to their human nature, and proceeds from the lowest and most exterior to the highest and most interior.

He first perfects the corporal senses, moving one to make use of natural exterior objects that are good, such as: hearing sermons and Masses, looking upon holy objects, mortifying the palate at meals, and disciplining the sense of touch through penance and holy rigor.

When these senses are somewhat disposed, He is wont to perfect them more by granting some supernatural favors and gifts to confirm them further in good. These supernatural communications are, for example: corporal visions of saints or holy things, very sweet odors, locutions, and extreme delight in the sense of touch. The senses are greatly confirmed in virtue through these communications and the appetites withdrawn from evil objects.

Besides this, the interior bodily senses, such as the imagination and phantasy, are gradually perfected and accustomed to good through considerations, meditations, and holy reasonings, and the spirit is instructed.

When through this natural exercise they are prepared, God may enlighten and spiritualize them further with some supernatural imaginative visions from which the spirit, as we affirmed, at the same time profits notably. This natural and supernatural exercise of the interior sense gradually reforms and refines the spirit.

This is God's method of bringing a soul step by step to the innermost good, although it may not always be necessary for Him to keep so mathematically to this order, for sometimes God bestows one kind of communication without the other, or a less interior one by means of a more interior one, or both together. The process depends on what God judges expedient for the soul, or on the favor He wants to confer. But His ordinary procedure conforms with our explanation.

5. By this method, then, God instructs people and makes them spiritual. He begins by communicating spirituality, in accord with their littleness or small capacity, through elements that are exterior, palpable, and accommodated to sense. He does this so that by means of the rind of those sensible things, in themselves good, the spirit, making progress in particular acts and receiving morsels of spiritual communication, may form a habit in spiritual things and reach the actual substance of spirit foreign to all sense. Individuals obtain this only little by little, after their own manner, and by means of the senses to which they have always been attached.

In the measure that people approach spirit in their dealings with God, they divest and empty themselves of the ways of the senses, of discursive and imaginative meditation. When they have completely attained spiritual communion with God, they will be voided of all sensory apprehensions concerning God. The more an object approaches one extreme, the further it retreats from the other; on complete attainment of the one extreme, it will be wholly separated from the other. There is a frequently quoted spiritual axiom that runs: *Gustato spiritu, desipit omnis caro* (Once the taste and savor of the spirit is experienced, everything carnal is insipid).[24] The ways of the flesh (which refer to the use of the senses in spiritual things) afford neither profit nor delight. This is obvious. If something is spiritual, it is incomprehensible to the senses; but if the senses can grasp it, it is no longer purely spiritual. The more knowledge the senses and natural apprehensions have about it, the less spiritual and supernatural it will be, as we explained above.

6. As a result the perfect spirit pays no attention to the senses. It neither receives anything through them, nor uses them principally, nor judges them to be requisite in its relationship with God, as it did before its spiritual growth.

A passage from St. Paul's epistle to the Corinthians bears this

---

24. This spiritual saying has been traced back to St. Bernard, *Epistola* 111 (Migne PL 182, 2588).

meaning: *Cum essem parvulus, loquebar ut parvulus, sapiebam ut parvulus, cogitabam ut parvulus. Quando autem factus sum vir, evacuavi quae erant parvuli* (When I was a child, I spoke as a child, I knew as a child, I thought as a child. But when I became a man, I put away childish things) [1 Cor 13:11].

We have already explained how sensible things and the knowledge the spirit can abstract from them are the work of a child. Those who are always attached to them and never become detached will never stop being like a little child, or speaking of God as a child, or knowing and thinking of God as a child. In their attachment to the rind of sense (the child), they will never reach the substance of spirit (the perfect person). For the sake of their own spiritual growth, therefore, persons should not admit these revelations, even though God is the author of them, just as a child must be weaned in order to accustom its palate to a hardier and more substantial diet.

7. Is it necessary, you ask, for the soul while it is a child to accept these sensible things and then set them aside when grown, just as an infant must be nourished at the breast until, when grown older, it can be weaned?

I reply in regard to discursive meditation, in which individuals begin their quest for God, that it is true that they must not turn away from the breast of the senses for their nourishment until they arrive at the time and season suitable for so doing—that is, when God brings the soul to a more spiritual converse, to contemplation, of which we spoke in Chapter 11 of this book.[25]

But when there is question of imaginative visions or other supernatural communications apprehensible by the senses and independent of one's free will, I affirm that at whatever time or season they occur (in the state of perfection or one less perfect) individuals must not desire to admit them, even though they come from God. And this for two reasons:

First, because God, as we said, produces His effect in the soul without its being able to hinder this, although it can impede the vision—which often happens. Consequently, the effect to be communicated becomes more substantial even though it is given differently. As we said, people cannot hinder the goods God desires to impart, nor in

---

25. In the present state of the text, the reference is to Chapter 13. The apparent inaccuracy is due to the fact that initially the opening explanation of the second stanza was not counted as a chapter and Chapters 11 and 12 were joined.

fact do they do so except by some imperfection or possessiveness. And there is no imperfection or possessiveness if they renounce these apprehensions with humility and misgivings.

Second, by so doing individuals free themselves from the task and danger of discerning the true visions from the false ones and deciding whether their visions come from an angel of light or of darkness. Such an effort is profitless, a waste of time, a hindrance to the soul, an occasion of many imperfections as well as of spiritual stagnancy, since a person is not then employed with the more important things and disencumbered of the trifles of particular apprehensions and knowledge. This was mentioned regarding the corporal visions, and it will be asserted later in respect to imaginative visions.

8. One can be sure that if our Lord did not have to lead a soul according to its own manner of being, He would never communicate the abundance of His Spirit through these aqueducts of forms, figures, and particular knowledge by which He sustains the soul with crumbs. This is why David said: *Mittit crystallum suam sicut bucellas*, which is as much as to say, He sent His wisdom in morsels [147:17]. It is extremely regrettable that a soul having as it were an infinite capacity should be fed, because of its limited spirituality and sensory incapacity, with morsels for the senses.

St. Paul, too, when writing to the Corinthians grieved over this littleness and limited preparation for the reception of spirituality: "When I came to you brethren I could not speak as to spiritual persons, but only as to carnal, because you were unable to receive it, nor can you now." *Tamquam parvulis in Christo lac potum vobis dedi, non escam* (As to infants in Christ I gave you milk to drink and not solid food to eat) [1 Cor 3:1–2].

9. In conclusion, people must not fix the eyes of their souls on that rind of the figure and object supernaturally accorded to the exterior senses, such as locutions and words to the sense of hearing: visions of saints and beautifully resplendent lights to the sense of sight; fragrance to the sense of smell; delightful tastes to the palate; and other pleasures, usually derived from the spirit, to the sense of touch, as is more commonly the case with spiritual persons. Neither must they place their eyes on interior imaginative visions. They must instead renounce all these things.

They must fasten the eyes of their souls only on the valuable spirituality these experiences cause, and endeavor to preserve it by putting into practice and properly carrying out whatever is for the service of

God, and pay no attention to those representations, nor desire any sensible gratification.

With this attitude, individuals take from these apprehensions only what God wants them to take, that is, the spirit of devotion, since God gives these sense experiences for no other principal reason. And they reject the sensory element, which would not have been imparted had they possessed the capacity for receiving spirituality without the apprehensions and exercises of the senses.

*   *   *

Chapter Twenty-Two

The answer to a question concerning the reason for the illicitness in the law of grace of a practice permissible in the old law, that of petitioning God through supernatural means. Proof from St. Paul.

1. Questions keep springing up so that we are unable to make the rapid progress we would like. Since we raise them, we necessarily have the obligation of answering them, that the truth of the doctrine will remain clear and vigorous. These questions have this advantage that, although they slow up our progress, they are still an aid to greater clarity and to further explanations about our subject. Such is the case with this question.

2. In the last chapter we affirmed that God was unwilling that souls desire the supernatural communication of distinct knowledge from visions and locutions, and so on. On the other hand, in the proofs from Scripture, we saw that this kind of communication with God was lawful and made use of in the old law. Not only was this licit, but God commanded it. When the people did not comply, God reproved them. An example of this is seen in Isaiah when the children of Israel desired to descend into Egypt without first asking God; and He thus reprehended them: *Et os meum non interrogastis* (You did not first ask from My mouth what was suitable) [Is 30:2]. We also read in Joshua that when the children of Israel were deceived by the Gabaonites, the Holy Spirit reminded them of this fault: *Susceperunt ergo de cibariis eorum, et os Domini non interrogaverunt* (They took their food without consulting the mouth of the Lord) [Jos 9:2–14].

THE ASCENT OF MOUNT CARMEL

We observe in Sacred Scripture that Moses, King David, the kings of Israel, in their wars and necessities, and the priests and ancients always questioned God, and that He replied and spoke to them without becoming angry. And they had done well if they questioned Him, but if they failed to do so, they were at fault. And if this is true, why, then, in the new law of grace is it different than it was previously?

3. In answer to this, the chief reason why in the old law the inquiries made of God were licit, and the prophets and priests appropriately desired visions and revelations from Him, was that at that time faith was not yet perfectly established, nor was the gospel law inaugurated. It was necessary for them to question God, and that He respond sometimes by words, sometimes through visions and revelations, now in figures and types, now through many other kinds of signs. All His answers, locutions, and revelations concerned mysteries of our faith or matters touching on or leading up to it, since the truths of faith are not derived from other humans but from the mouth of God. He therefore reproved them because in their affairs they did not seek counsel from His mouth, that He might answer and direct them toward the unknown and as yet unfounded faith.

But now that the faith is established through Christ, and the gospel law made manifest in this era of grace, there is no reason for inquiring of Him in this way, or expecting him to answer as before. In giving us His Son, His only Word (for He possesses no other), He spoke everything to us at once in this sole Word—and He has no more to say.

4. This is the meaning of that passage where St. Paul tries to persuade the Hebrews to turn from communion with God through the old ways of the Mosaic law and instead fix their eyes on Christ: *Multifariam multisque modis olim Deus loquens patribus in prophetis: novissime autem diebus istis locutus est nobis in Filio* (That which God formerly spoke to our fathers through the prophets in many ways and manners, now, finally, in these days He has spoken to us all at once in His Son) [Heb 1:1–2]. The Apostle indicates that God has become as it were mute, with no more to say, because what He spoke before to the prophets in parts, He has now spoken all at once by giving us the All, who is His Son.

5. Those who desire to question God or receive some vision or revelation are guilty not only of foolish behavior but also of offending Him, by not fixing their eyes entirely on Christ and by living with the desire for some other novelty.

God could reason as follows: If I have already told you all things

THE ASCENT OF MOUNT CARMEL

in My Word, My Son, and if I have no other word, what answer or revelation can I now make that would surpass this? Fasten your eyes on Him alone because in Him I have spoken and revealed all and in Him you will discover even more than you ask for and desire. You are making an appeal for locutions and revelations that are incomplete, but if you turn your eyes to Him you will find them complete. For he is My entire locution and response, vision and revelation, which I have already spoken, answered, manifested, and revealed to you by giving Him to you as a brother, companion, master, ransom, and reward. On that day when I descended on Him with my Spirit on Mount Tabor proclaiming: *Hic est filius meus dilectus in quo mihi bene complacui, ipsum audite* (This is my Beloved Son in whom I am well pleased, hear Him) [Mt 17:5], I gave up these methods of answering and teaching and presented them to Him. Hear Him because I have no more faith to reveal or truths to manifest. If I spoke before, it was to promise Christ. If they questioned me, their inquiries were related to their petitions and longings for Christ in whom they were to obtain every good, as is now explained in all the doctrine of the evangelists and apostles. But now those who might ask me in that way and desire that I speak and reveal something to them would somehow be requesting Christ again and more faith, yet they would be failing in faith because Christ has already been given. Accordingly, they would offend my Beloved Son deeply because they would not merely be lacking faith in Him, but obliging Him to become incarnate and undergo His life and death again. You will not find anything to ask or desire through revelations and visions. Behold Him well, for in Him you will uncover all these revelations already made, and many more.

6. If you desire me to answer with a word of comfort, behold my Son subject to me and to others out of love for me, and you will see how much He answers. If you desire me to declare some secret truths or events to you, fix your eyes on Him and you will discern hidden in Him the most secret mysteries, and wisdom, and the wonders of God, as my Apostle proclaims: *In quo sunt omnes thesauri sapientiae et scientiae Dei absconditi* (In the Son of God are hidden all the treasures of the wisdom and knowledge of God) [Col 2:3]. These treasures of wisdom and knowledge will be far more sublime, delightful, and advantageous than what you want to know. The Apostle, therefore, gloried, affirming that he had acted as though he knew no other than Jesus Christ and Him crucified [1 Cor 2:2]. And if you should seek other divine or corporal

visions and revelations, behold Him, become human, and you will encounter more than you imagine. For the Apostle also says: *In ipso habitat omnis plenitudo Divinitatis corporaliter* (In Christ all the fullness of the divinity dwells bodily) [Col 2:9].

7. One should not, then, inquire of God in this manner, nor is it necessary for God to speak any more. Since He has finished revealing the faith through Christ, there is no more faith to reveal, nor will there ever be. Anyone wanting to get something in a supernatural way, as we stated, would as it were be accusing God of not having given us in His Son all that is required. Although in such endeavors one presupposes the faith and believes in it, still, one's curiosity displays a lack of faith. Hence there is no reason to hope for doctrine or anything else through supernatural means.

When Christ dying on the cross exclaimed: *Consummatum est* (It is consummated) [Jn 19:30], He consummated not these ways alone, but all the other ceremonies and rites of the old law. We must be guided humanly and visibly in all by the law of Christ who was human and that of His Church and of His ministers. This is the method of remedying our spiritual ignorances and weaknesses. Here we shall find abundant medicine for them all. Any departure from this road is not only curiosity but extraordinary boldness. One should not believe anything coming in a supernatural way, but believe only the teaching of Christ, who became human, as I say, and of His ministers who are human. So true is this that St. Paul insists: *Quod si angelus de coelo evangelizaverit, praeterquam quod evangelizavimus vobis, anathema sit* (If an angel from heaven should preach to you any gospel other than that which we humans have preached, let him be accursed and excommunicated) [Gal 1:8].

8. Since it is true that one must ever adhere to Christ's teaching, and that everything unconformed to it is nothing and worthy of disbelief, anyone who desires to commune with God after the manner of the old law is walking in vain.

We see even more how true this is when we recall that it was not lawful at that time for everyone to question God; nor did God give an answer to everyone but only to the priests and prophets from whom the common people were to learn the law and doctrine. Those eager to know something from God did not ask by themselves but through a prophet or priest. If David sometimes asked of himself, it was because he was a prophet. But even then he did not do so without being clothed in priestly vestments, as is evident in the First Book of Samuel when he said to Ahimelech the priest: *Applica ad me Ephod* [1 Sm 23:9].[26] The ephod was the most dignified of the priest's vestments, and David wore it for consultation with God. At other times he consulted God through the prophet Nathan or through other prophets. And the people were to believe that God spoke to them through the mouth of these prophets and priests and not through their own opinion.

9. What God said at that time did not have the authority or force to induce complete belief unless approved by the priests and prophets. God is so content that the rule and direction of humans be through other humans and that a person be governed by natural reason that He definitely does not want us to bestow entire credence on His supernatural communications, or be confirmed in their strength and security, until they pass through this human channel of the mouth of another human person. As often as He reveals something to individuals, He confers on them a kind of inclination to manifest this to the appropriate person. Until people do this, they usually go without complete satisfaction, for they have not received this knowledge from another human like themselves.

In Judges we see that this happened to the captain Gideon. Though God had often told him that he would be conqueror of the Midianites, Gideon nonetheless remained doubtful and cowardly since God had left him in that weakness until through the mouth of other humans he had heard what God had revealed to him. Since God saw that he was weak, He declared: *Rise up and go down to the camp; . . . et cum audieris quid loquantur, tunc confortabuntur manus tuas, et securior ad hostium castra descendes* (When you hear what the men are saying there, you shall get strength from what I have told you, and you will descend more securely to the enemy host) [Jgs 7:9–11]. And it happened that when Gideon heard of a Midianite's dream about the future victory, he was deeply strengthened; and full of gladness he prepared for the battle [Jgs 7:13–15]. Evidently, then, God did not want Gideon to receive assurance through supernatural means alone, for until Gideon had certitude through natural means, God did not bestow on him a feeling of security.

10. And still more wondrous is what happened in a similar instance to Moses. In spite of the fact that God had commanded him with many persuasive arguments to go and bring about the liberation of the chil-

---

26. Bring forward the Ephod.

dren of Israel, and had confirmed these arguments with signs from the rod, which was changed into a serpent, and from the leprous hand [Ex 4:2–4, 6–10], he was so weak and doubtful about this mission that, in spite of God's anger [Ex 4:14], he did not possess the courage to give strong credence to the mission until heartened by God through his brother Aaron: *Aaron frater tuus Levites, scio quo eloquens sit: ecce ipse egredietur in occursum tuum, vidensque te, laetabitur corde. Loquere ad eum, et pone verba mea in ore ejus, et ego ero in ore tuo, et in ore illius* (I know that your brother Aaron is an eloquent man: behold he will go to meet you and at sight of you sincerely rejoice. Speak and tell him all my words, and I will be in your mouth and in his so that each of you will receive certitude through the mouth of the other) [Ex 4:14–15].

11. At these words Moses was immediately encouraged in the hope of the comfort he was to obtain from his brother's counsel [Ex 4:18]. This is the trait of humble people: They do not dare deal with God independently, nor can they be completely satisfied without human counsel and direction. God wants this, for to declare and strengthen truth on the basis of natural reason, He draws near those who come together in an endeavor to know it. He indicated this by asserting that He would be in the mouth of both Aaron and Moses when they were together for consultation.

This is why He also affirmed in the Gospel: *Ubi fuerint duo vel tres congregati in nomine meo, ibi sum ego in medio eorum* (Where two or three are gathered to consider what is for the greater honor and glory of my name, there I am in the midst of them—that is, clarifying and confirming truths in their hearts) [Mt 18:20]. It is noteworthy that He did not say: Where there is one alone, there I am; rather, He said: where there are at least two. Thus God announces that He does not want the soul to believe only by itself the communications it thinks are of divine origin, or anyone to be assured or confirmed in them without the Church or her ministers. God will not bring clarification and confirmation of the truth to the heart of one who is alone. Such a person would remain weak and cold in regard to truth.

12. This is what Ecclesiastes extols: *Vae soli, quia cum ceciderit, non habet sublevantem se. Si dormierint duo, favebuntur mutuo: unus quomodo calefiet? et si quispiam praevaluerit contra unum, duo resistent ei* [Eccl 4:10–12]. This means: Woe to those who are alone, for when they fall they have no one to lift them up. If two sleep together, the one shall give warmth (the warmth of God who is in their midst) to the other; how shall one alone be warm? How shall one alone stop being cold in the things of

THE ASCENT OF MOUNT CARMEL

God? And if one prevails and overcomes the other (that is, if the devil prevails and overcomes anyone who may desire to remain alone in the things of God), two together will resist the devil. And these are the disciple and the master who come together to know the truth and practice it. Until consulting another, one will usually experience only tepidity and weakness in the truth, no matter how much may have been heard from God. This is so true that after St. Paul had for a long time been preaching the gospel, which he heard not from humans but from God [Gal 1:12], he could not resist going and conferring about it with St. Peter and the apostles: *ne forte in vacuum currerem aut cucurrissem* (lest he should run or might have run in vain) [Gal 2:2]. He did not feel secure until he had received assurance from other humans. This, then, seems remarkable, O Paul! Could not He who revealed the gospel to you also give security from any error you might make in preaching its truth?

13. This text clearly teaches that there is no assurance in God's revelations save through the means we are describing. Even though individuals have certitude that the revelation is of divine origin—as St. Paul had of his gospel, since he had already begun to preach it—they can still err in regard to the object of the revelation or its circumstances. Even though God reveals one factor, He does not always manifest the other. Often He will reveal something without telling how to accomplish it. He usually does not effect or reveal to people that which through human effort or counsel can be arrived at, even though He may frequently and affably commune with them. St. Paul understood this clearly since, as we are saying, he went to confer about the gospel in spite of his knowledge that it was divinely revealed. . . .

16. I deduce in concluding this part that whatever is received through supernatural means (in whatever manner) should immediately be told clearly, integrally, and simply to one's spiritual director. It may appear that there is no reason for a manifestation to one's spiritual director, or that doing so would be a waste of time since as we pointed out one is safe by not wanting these communications, by rejecting and paying no attention to them, especially in this matter of visions or revelations or other supernatural communications since either they are clear or it matters little if they are not. Yet it is always necessary to manifest the entire communication even though there is no apparent reason for so doing. This requirement is based on three reasons:

First, the effect, light, strength, and security of many divine communications are not completely confirmed in a soul, as we stated, until it discusses them with one whom God has destined to be spiritual judge over it, who has power to bind, loose, approve, and reprove. We have established this principle through the texts cited above, and through experience we see it verified each day. We witness humble recipients of these experiences obtain new satisfaction, strength, light, and security after consulting about them with the proper person. This is so true that to some it seems that these communications neither take root nor belong to them until they confer about them and that the communications are then seemingly imparted anew.

17. Second, a soul ordinarily needs instruction pertinent to its experience in order to be guided through the dark night to spiritual denudation and poverty. Without this instruction a person would unknowingly become hardened in the way of the spirit and habituated to that of the senses, in which these communications are partly experienced.

18. Third, for the sake of humility, submission, and mortification, individuals should give a complete account to their director, even if the director disregards or shows no esteem for these communications. Because these communications are seemingly of little importance, or because of concern about the director's possible reaction, some may dread to tell their director about them. This indicates a lack of humility, and for that very reason one should submit to the ordeal. Others feel abashed about manifesting these favors lest they appear to be saints on account of these experiences, and because of other difficulties they feel in speaking about them. They think that because they themselves pay no attention to these experiences, a manifestation of them to their director is unnecessary. But because of this very hardship they ought to mortify themselves and manifest it all to their director, and thereby become humble, simple, meek, and prompt in relating these communications. And from then on they will always do so easily.

19. It ought to be noted in this regard that not because we have greatly stressed the rejection of these communications and the duty of confessors to forbid souls from making them a topic of conversation should directors show severity, displeasure, or scorn in dealing with these souls. With such an attitude they would make them cower and shrink from a manifestation of these experiences, would close the door to these souls, and cause them many difficulties. Since God is leading them by this means, there is no reason for opposing it or becoming frightened or scandalized over it. The director should instead be kind and peaceful. He should give these souls encouragement and the opportunity of speaking about their experiences, and, if necessary, oblige

them to do so, for at times everything is needful on account of the hardship some find in discussing these matters.

Spiritual directors should guide them in the way of faith by giving them good instructions on how to turn their eyes from all these things and on their obligation to denude their appetite and spirit of these communications. They should explain how one act done in charity is more precious in God's sight than all the visions and communications possible—since they imply neither merit nor demerit—and how many who have not received these experiences are incomparably more advanced than others who have had many.

Chapter Twenty-Three

Begins the discussion of the intellectual apprehensions that come in a purely spiritual way. Tells what they are.

1. Though our doctrine on the intellectual apprehensions that are derived from the senses is somewhat brief in comparison with what it ought to be, I have not wanted to enlarge on the matter any more. I believe, rather, that my explanation has been longer than necessary in view of the goal I have in mind, which is to liberate the intellect from these apprehensions and direct it to the night of faith.

Now we will embark on a discussion of those other four kinds of intellectual apprehensions: visions, revelations, locutions, and spiritual feelings. We call these apprehensions purely spiritual because they are not communicated to the intellect through the corporal senses as are imaginative corporal visions. They are clearly, distinctly, and supernaturally imparted to the intellect without the intervention of the exterior or interior bodily senses; and this is done passively, that is, the soul posits no act, at least through its own effort.

2. Let it be known that in a broad sense these four kinds of apprehensions can all be titled visions of the soul because we also call the understanding of the soul its vision. And insofar as all these apprehensions are intelligible, they are called spiritually visible. Accordingly, the understanding formed from them in the intellect can be termed an intellectual vision. The objects of the other senses (of sight, hearing, smell, taste, and touch) are objects of the intellect insofar as they bear relation to the notion of truth or falsehood. And all that is intelligible

to the intellect, the spiritual eye of the soul, causes spiritual vision. For, as we said, understanding an object is seeing it. Thus, speaking generally, we can call these four apprehensions visions. This could not be done with the other senses, because none of them is capable of perceiving the object as such of any of the others.

3. But since these apprehensions reach the soul in ways similar to those of the other senses, we can, properly and specifically speaking, apply the term "vision" to whatever the intellect receives in a manner resembling sight because the intellect can see objects spiritually just as the eyes can corporally. And the new truth the intellect gains as though by learning and understanding (just as the ears in hearing what has never before been heard), we call revelation. A locution signifies whatever is received in a way similar to that of hearing. And we apply the term "spiritual feelings" to whatever is perceived after the manner of the other senses, such as the supernaturally enjoyable experience of a sweet spiritual fragrance, savor, or delight.[27] The intellect derives knowledge or spiritual vision from all these communications, without the apprehension of any form, image, or figure of the imagination or natural phantasy. For these experiences are communicated immediately to the soul through a supernatural work and through a supernatural means.

4. As was the case with the imaginative corporal apprehensions, we must disencumber the intellect of these spiritual apprehensions by guiding and directing it past them into the spiritual night of faith, to the divine and substantial union with God, lest the solitude and denudation concerning all things, which is a requisite for this union, be impeded by the hindrance and weakness these apprehensions occasion. These apprehensions are nobler, safer, and more advantageous than the imaginative corporal visions because they are already interior, purely spiritual, and less exposed to the devil's meddlesomeness. They are more purely and delicately communicated to the soul and involve none of its own work—at least active. Nonetheless, through lack of caution and by treading such a path, the intellect might be not merely encumbered but highly deceived.

5. As a general conclusion, we could give the same counsel for

---

27. Traditionally, spiritual writers going back as far as Origen spoke of the spiritual senses recognizing that one could speak of spiritual experience in ways analogous to sense experience. Here John speaks of four senses. He omits touch, although he does speak of the spiritual touch in other parts of his writings. Cf. A. 2, 26, 5–10.

these four kinds of apprehensions that we accorded for the others: that they be the object of neither our aims nor our desires. Yet it would be worthwhile to discuss these apprehensions in particular in order to explain some points about each of them and shed more light on the practice of this counsel. And thus we will deal with the first kind, which are the spiritual or intellectual visions.

* * *

Chapter Twenty-Six

The two kinds of knowledge of naked truths. The proper conduct of the soul in their regard.

1. For an adequate exposition of this subject (the knowledge of naked truths), God would have to move my hand and pen. For you should know, beloved reader, that what they in themselves are for the soul is beyond words. Since, however, I intentionally speak of these only so as to impart instruction and guide the soul through them to the divine union, let me discuss them in a brief and restricted way, which will be sufficient for our purpose.

2. . . . . This intellectual vision is not like the vision of corporal objects, but rather consists in an intellectual understanding or vision of truths about God, or to a vision of present, past, or future events, which bears great resemblance to the spirit of prophecy, as we shall perhaps explain later.

3. This type of knowledge is divided into two kinds: The object of the one kind is the Creator; and that of the other is the creature, as we said. Both kinds bring intense delight to the soul. Yet those of God produce an incomparable delight; there are no words or terms to describe them, for they are the knowledge and delight of God Himself. And as David says: *There is nothing like unto Him* [Ps 40:6]. God is the direct object of this knowledge in that one of His attributes (His omnipotence, fortitude, goodness, sweetness, and so on) is sublimely experienced. And as often as this experience occurs, it remains fixed in the soul. Since this communication is pure contemplation, the soul clearly understands that it is ineffable. People are capable of describing it only through general expressions—expressions caused by the abundance of

the delight and good of these experiences. But they realize the impossibility of explaining with these expressions what they tasted and felt in this communication.

4. David, after having received a similar experience, spoke in these unprecise terms: *Judicia Domini vera, justificata in semetipsa. Desiderabilia super aurum et lapidem pretiosum multum, et dulciora super mel et favum* (God's judgments—the virtues and attributes we experience in God—are true, in themselves justified, more desirable than gold and extremely precious stone, and sweeter than the honey and the honeycomb) [Ps 19:11].

We read that Moses spoke only in general terms of the lofty knowledge that God, while passing by, gave him. And it happened that when the Lord passed before him in that knowledge, Moses quickly prostrated himself, crying: *Dominator Domine Deus, misericors et clemens, patiens, et multae miserationis, ac verax. Qui custodis misericordiam in millia*, and so on (Sovereign Lord God, merciful and clement, patient, and of great compassion, and true. You guard the mercy that you promise to thousands) [Ex 34:6–7]. Evidently, since Moses could not express with one concept what he knew in God, he did so through an overflow of words.

Although at times individuals use words in reference to this knowledge, they clearly realize that they have said nothing of what they experienced, for no term can give adequate expression to it. And thus when St. Paul experienced that lofty knowledge of God, he did not care to say anything else than that it was not licit for humans to speak of it [2 Cor 12:4].

5. This divine knowledge of God never deals with particular things, since its object is the Supreme Principle. Consequently one cannot express it in particular terms, unless a truth about something less than God is seen together with this knowledge of Him. But in no way can anything be said of that divine knowledge.

This sublime knowledge can be received only by a person who has arrived at union with God, for it is itself that very union. It consists in a certain touch of the divinity produced in the soul, and thus it is God Himself who is experienced and tasted there.[28] Although the touch of

---

28. Although the general topic in this book deals with the purification of the spiritual faculties, John speaks here of experiences of actual union, substantial touches, proper to the state of transformation in God and to one already purified.

knowledge and delight that penetrates the substance of the soul is not manifest and clear, as in glory, it is so sublime and lofty that the devil is unable to meddle or produce anything similar (for there is no experience similar or comparable to it), or infuse a savor and delight like it. This knowledge savors of the divine essence and of eternal life, and the devil cannot counterfeit anything so lofty.

6. He could, nevertheless, ape that experience by presenting to the soul some very sensible feelings of grandeur and fulfillment, trying to persuade it that these are from God. But this attempt of the devil does not enter the substance of the soul and suddenly renew and fill it with love as does a divine touch. Some of these divine touches produced in the substance of the soul are so enriching that one of them would be sufficient not only to remove definitively all the imperfections that the soul would have been unable to eradicate throughout its entire life, but also to fill it with virtues and blessings from God.

7. These touches engender such sweetness and intimate delight in the soul that one of them would more than compensate for all the trials suffered in life, even though innumerable. Through these touches individuals become so courageous and so resolved to suffer many things for Christ that they find it a special suffering to observe that they do not suffer.

8. People are incapable of reaching this sublime knowledge through any comparison or imagining of their own, because it transcends what is naturally attainable. Thus God effects in the soul what it is incapable of acquiring. God usually grants these divine touches, which cause certain remembrances of Him, at times when the soul is least expecting or thinking of them. Sometimes they are produced suddenly through some remembrance, which may only concern some slight detail. They are so sensible that they sometimes cause not only the soul but also the body to tremble. Yet at other times with a sudden feeling of spiritual delight and refreshment, and without any trembling, they occur very tranquilly in the spirit.

9. Or again they may occur on uttering or hearing a word from Sacred Scripture or from some other source. These touches do not always have the same efficacy, nor are they always felt so forcefully, because they are often very weak. Yet no matter how weak they may be, one of these divine touches is worth more to the soul than numberless other thoughts and ideas about God's creatures and works.

Since this knowledge is imparted to the soul suddenly, without exercise of free will, individuals do not have to be concerned about desiring it or not. They should simply remain humble and resigned about it, for God will do His work at the time and in the manner He wishes.

10. I do not affirm that people should be negative about this knowledge as they should be with the other apprehensions, because this knowledge is an aspect of the union toward which we are directing the soul and which is the reason for our doctrine about the denudation and detachment from all other apprehensions. God's demands for granting such a grace are humility, suffering for love of Him, and resignation as to all recompense. God does not bestow these favors on a possessive soul, since He gives them out of a very special love for the recipient. For the individual receiving them is one who loves with great detachment. The Son of God meant this when He stated: *Qui autem diligit me, diligetur a Patre meo, et ego diligam eum et manifestabo ei meipsum* (Those who love me will be loved by my Father, and I will love them and manifest Myself to them) [Jn 14:21]. This manifestation includes the knowledge and touches that God imparts to a person who has reached Him and truly loves Him. . . .

Chapter Twenty-Seven

The second kind of revelation: the disclosure of secrets and hidden mysteries. The ways in which this knowledge can be either a contribution or a hindrance toward union with God. How the devil can greatly deceive souls in this matter.

1. We stated that the second kind of revelation is the disclosure of secrets and hidden mysteries. It can be divided into two further categories:

The first concerns God Himself, which includes the revelation of the mystery of the three Persons in one God.

The second concerns God in His works; this comprises the remaining articles of our Catholic faith and the propositions of truths that can be explicitly formed about His works. . . .

4. Since there are no more articles to be revealed to the Church about the substance of our faith, people must not merely reject new revelations about the faith, but out of caution repudiate other kinds of knowledge mingled with them. In order to preserve the purity of faith,

a person should not believe already revealed truths because they are again revealed but because they were already sufficiently revealed to the Church. Closing one's mind to them, one should rest simply on the doctrine of the Church and its faith which, as St. Paul says, enters through hearing [Rom 10:17]. And if individuals want to escape delusion, they should not adapt their credence and understanding to those truths of faith revealed again no matter how true and conformed to the faith they may seem. To deceive and introduce lies, the devil first lures a person with truths and verisimilitudes that give assurance; and then he proceeds with his beguilement. These truths of his are like the bristle used in sewing leather: It is put through the holes first in order to pull along after it the soft thread; without the bristle the thread would never pass through. . . .

*   *   *

Chapter Twenty-Nine

The first kind of locution the recollected spirit sometimes forms. A discussion of its origin and of the profit or harm it may occasion.

1. Successive words always occur when the spirit is recollected and attentively absorbed in some consideration. Individuals will reason about their subject, proceeding thought by thought, forming precise words and judgments, deducing and discovering such unknown truths, with so much ease and clarity, that it will seem to them they are doing nothing and that another person is interiorly reasoning, answering, and teaching them. . . .

4. I knew someone who in his experience of these successive locutions formed, among some very true and solid ones about the Blessed Sacrament, others that were outright heresies. And I greatly fear what is happening in these times of ours: If any soul whatever after a bit of reflection has in its recollection one of these locutions, it will immediately baptize all as coming from God and with such a supposition say, "God told me," "God answered me." Yet this is not so, but, as we pointed out, these persons themselves are more often the origin of their locution. . . .

THE ASCENT OF MOUNT CARMEL

6. If you ask me why the intellect must be deprived of those truths since the Spirit of God illumines it through them, I answer: The Holy Spirit illumines the intellect that is recollected, and He illumines it according to the mode of its recollection; the intellect can find no better recollection than in faith, and thus the Holy Spirit will not illumine it in any other recollection more than in faith. The purer and more refined a soul is in faith, the more infused charity it possesses; and the more charity it has the more the Holy Spirit illumines it and communicates His gifts, because charity is the means by which they are communicated.[29]

In that illumination of truths the Holy Spirit indeed communicates some light to the soul, yet the light given in faith—in which there is no clear understanding—is qualitatively as different from the other as is the purest gold from the basest metal, and quantitatively as is the sea from a drop of water. In the first kind of illumination, wisdom concerning one, two, or three truths, and so on, is communicated; and in the second, all God's wisdom is communicated in general, that is, the Son of God, who is imparted to the soul in faith. . . .

* * *

---

29. John is not speaking of the gifts of the Holy Spirit in the strict theological sense by which they were considered as principles that dispose one to be moved passively by the Holy Spirit. John did not make use of this theory concerning the gifts. It is also worth noting that he establishes the same relation between faith and love in this "supernatural" sphere that exists naturally between knowledge and love.

Book Three

This book treats of the active night or purgation of the memory and the will. It presents doctrine about the attitude required in the apprehensions of these two faculties so that a soul may reach union with God in perfect hope and charity.

Chapter One

1. We have already given instructions for the intellect, the first faculty of the soul, so that in all its apprehensions it may be united with God through pure faith, the first theological virtue. The same has to be done for the other two faculties, memory and will. They must undergo a purification relative to their respective apprehensions in order to reach union with God in perfect hope and charity.

Our exposition in this third book will be brief. For it is unnecessary to enlarge so much in our treatise on these faculties, since in the instructions given for the intellect (the receptacle in its own way of all the other objects) we have covered a great portion of the matter. If spiritual persons direct their intellects in faith according to the doctrine given them, it is impossible for them not to instruct their other two faculties simultaneously in the other two virtues. For these faculties depend on one another in their operations. . . .

* * *

THE ASCENT OF MOUNT CARMEL

Chapter Three

Three kinds of harm resulting from not darkening the memory of its knowledge and discursive reflection. A discussion of the first kind.

1. Spiritual persons who still wish to make use of natural knowledge and discursive reflection in their journey to God, or for anything else, are subject to three kinds of harm and difficulty. Two are positive and one privative.

The first kind arises from the things of the world; the second from the devil; and the third, the privative, is the impediment and hindrance to the divine union that this knowledge causes.

2. The first, coming from the world, involves the subjection to many evils arising from this knowledge and reflection, such as: falsehoods, imperfections, appetites, judgments, loss of time, and numerous other evils engendering many impurities in the soul.

Manifestly, spiritual persons allowing themselves this knowledge and reflection will necessarily be the victims of many falsehoods. Often the true will appear false, and the certain doubtful, and vice versa, since we can hardly have complete understanding of truth. Those who darken their memory to all knowledge and reflection free themselves from all of this.

3. Imperfections meet them at every step if they turn their memories to the objects of hearing, sight, touch, smell, and taste. By so doing, some emotion will cling to them, whether it be sorrow, fear, hatred, vain hope, vain joy, or vainglory, and so on. All these are at least imperfections, and sometimes real venial sins. They subtly contaminate the soul with impurity, even though the knowledge and reflection concern God.

And it is also clear that appetites will be engendered since they naturally arise from this knowledge and reflection. And the mere desire for this knowledge and reflection is already an appetite.

Obviously these people will also meet with many occasions to judge others since by using their memories they cannot help but stumble on the good or evil deeds of others. And at times the evil seems good and the good evil. I am of the opinion that spiritual persons cannot free themselves entirely from all these evils if they do not blind and darken their memories as to all things.

4. You may say that people are easily capable of conquering all

THE ASCENT OF MOUNT CARMEL

these dangers when they come on them. I reply that it is simply impossible to achieve this completely if they pay attention to this knowledge, for intermingled with it are a thousand imperfections and trifles, some so subtle and slight that without one's realizing it they stick to one just as pitch does to those who touch it. These imperfections are better overcome all at once through complete denial of the memory.

You may also make the objection that the soul will suffer the deprivation of numerous holy thoughts and considerations about God, which are conducive to the reception of favors from God. I answer that purity of soul is more helpful toward this, for purity of soul indicates that no attachment or advertence to creatures or temporal things clings to the soul. I think these creatures will not fail to adhere to it a great deal because of the imperfections the faculties of themselves have in their operations. It is better to learn to silence and quiet the faculties so that God may speak. For in this state, as we pointed out, the natural operations must fade from sight. This is realized when the soul arrives at solitude in these faculties, and God speaks to its heart, as the prophet asserts [Os 2:14].

5. If you still insist, claiming that a person will obtain no benefits if the memory does not consider and reflect about God, and that many distractions and weaknesses will gradually find entrance, I answer that this is impossible. If the memory is recollected as to both heavenly and earthly things, there is no entry for evils, distractions, trifles, or vices—all of which enter through the wandering of the memory. Distractions would result if, on closing the door to considerations and discursive meditation, we opened it to thoughts about earthly matters. But in our case we close the memory to all ideas—from which distractions and evils arise—by rendering it silent and mute, and applying the hearing of the spirit to God in silence, saying with the prophet: *Speak Lord, for your servant is listening* [1 Sm 3:10].[1] The spouse in the Song of Songs proclaimed that this was to be the attitude of the bride: *My sister is a garden enclosed and a fountain sealed up* [Sg 4:12].

6. The soul should remain closed, then, without cares or afflictions, for He who entered the room of His disciples bodily, while the doors were closed (without their knowing how this was possible), and gave them peace, will enter the soul spiritually (without its knowing

---

1. In Chapter 27 of Book two, John discontinued for the most part the standard practice of citing biblical texts first in the Latin.

how or using any effort of its own), once it has closed the doors of its intellect, memory, and will to all apprehensions. And He will fill them with peace, descending on them, as the prophet says, like a river of peace [Is 66:12]. In this peace He will remove all the misgivings, suspicions, disturbances, and darknesses that made the soul fear it had gone astray. The soul should persevere in prayer and should hope in the midst of nakedness and emptiness, for its blessings will not be long in coming.

* * *

Chapter Five

The third kind of harm that follows from the natural, distinct knowledge of the memory.

1. The third kind of harm engendered by the natural apprehensions of the memory is privative. These apprehensions can be an impediment to moral good and deprive one of spiritual good.

An explanation of how these apprehensions are a hindrance to moral good demands a precise idea of moral good. Moral good consists in the control of the passions and the restriction of the inordinate appetites. The result for the soul is tranquillity, peace, repose, and moral virtue, which is the moral good.

The soul is incapable of truly acquiring the control of the passions and the restriction of the inordinate appetites without forgetting and withdrawing from the sources of these emotions. Disturbances never arise in a soul unless through the apprehensions of the memory. When all things are forgotten, nothing disturbs the peace or stirs the appetites. As the saying goes: What the eye does not see, the heart does not want.

2. We have experience of this all the time. We observe that as often as people begin to think about some matter, they are moved and aroused by it according to the kind of apprehension. If the apprehension is bothersome and annoying, they feel sadness or hatred, and so on; if agreeable, they will experience a desire and joy, and so on. Accordingly, when the apprehension is changed, agitation necessarily results. Thus they will sometimes be joyful, at other times sad; now they will feel hatred, now love. And they are unable to persevere in equanimity, the

effect of moral tranquillity, unless they endeavor to forget all things. Evidently, then, this knowledge is a serious impediment to the possession of the moral virtues.

3. That an encumbered memory is also a hindrance to the possession of spiritual good is clearly proved from our remarks. An unsettled soul, which has no foundation of moral good, is incapable as such of receiving spiritual good. For this spiritual good is only impressed on a restrained and peaceful soul.

Besides, if individuals bestow importance and attention on the apprehensions of the memory, they will find it impossible to remain free for the Incomprehensible, who is God, for they cannot advert to more than one thing. As we have always been insisting, the soul must go to God by not comprehending rather than by comprehending, and it must exchange the mutable and comprehensible for the Immutable and Incomprehensible.

Chapter Six

The benefits derived from forgetting the natural thoughts and knowledge of the memory.

1. From the kinds of harm occasioned by the apprehensions of the memory, we can also determine the opposite benefits that come from forgetting them; as the philosophers say: The doctrine for one thing serves also for its contrary.[2]

Contrary to the first kind of harm, spiritual persons enjoy tranquillity and peace of soul because of the absence of the disturbance and change that derive from the thoughts and ideas of the memory. And, as a consequence, these persons enjoy purity of conscience and soul, which is a greater benefit. As a result, they are excellently disposed for human and divine wisdom and virtues.

2. Contrary to the second, they are freed from many suggestions, temptations, and movements that the devil inserts in souls through their thoughts and ideas, thereby occasioning many impurities and sins; as David says: *They thought and spoke wickedness* [Ps 73:8]. When the

---

2. Aquinas makes use of this philosophical maxim in *Summa Theologica* 1–2, 54, 2.

THE ASCENT OF MOUNT CARMEL

thoughts are removed the devil has nothing naturally with which to wage his war on the spirit.

3. Contrary to the third, the soul is disposed by means of this recollection and forgetfulness of all things to be moved by the Holy Spirit and taught by Him. As the Wise Man declares: *He withdraws from thoughts that are without reason* [Wis 1:5].

Even though no other benefit would come to humans through this oblivion and void of the memory than freedom from afflictions and disturbances, it would be an immense advantage and blessing for them. For the afflictions and disturbances engendered in a soul through adversities are no help in remedying these adversities; rather, distress and worry ordinarily make things worse and even do harm to the soul itself. Thus David proclaimed: *Indeed every person is disturbed in vain* [Ps 39:7]. Clearly, it is always vain to be disturbed since being disturbed is never any help.

Thus if the whole world were to crumble and come to an end and all things were to go wrong, it would be useless to get disturbed, for this would do more harm than good. The endurance of all with tranquil and peaceful equanimity not only reaps many blessings but also helps the soul so that in these very adversities it may make a better judgment about them and employ the proper remedy.

4. Solomon, having clear knowledge of both this harm and this advantage, exclaimed: *I knew there was nothing better for a person than to rejoice and do good in life* [Eccl 3:12]. By this he indicates that in all events, however unfavorable, we ought to rejoice rather than be disturbed, and bear them all with equanimity so as not to lose a blessing greater than all prosperity: tranquillity of soul and peace in all things, in adversity as well as in prosperity. People would never lose their tranquillity if they were to forget ideas and lay aside their thoughts, and also, insofar as possible, withdraw from dealing with others and from hearing and seeing. Our nature is so unstable and fragile that even when well disciplined it will hardly fail to stumble on thoughts with the memory. And these thoughts become a disturbance to a soul that was residing in peace and tranquillity through the forgetfulness of all. As a result, Jeremiah proclaimed: *With the memory I shall remember, and my soul will faint in me with sorrow* [Lam 3:20].

* * *

THE ASCENT OF MOUNT CARMEL

Chapter Fifteen

A general rule of conduct for spiritual persons in their use of the memory.

1. To conclude this discussion on the memory, then, it will be worthwhile to delineate briefly a general method for the use of spiritual persons that they may be united with God according to this faculty. Even if the method is clearly understood from what we said, the reader will grasp it more easily in a summary.

The following must be kept in mind: Our aim is union with God in the memory through hope; the object of hope is something unpossessed; the less other objects are possessed, the more capacity and ability there is to hope for what one hopes for, and consequently the more hope; the greater the possessions, the less capacity and ability for hope, and consequently so much less of hope; accordingly, in the measure that individuals dispossess the memory of forms and objects, which are not God, they will fix it on God and preserve it empty, in the hope that God will fill it. That which people must do in order to live in perfect and pure hope in God is this: As often as distinct ideas, forms, and images occur to them, they should immediately, without resting in them, turn to God with loving affection, in emptiness of everything rememberable. If these things refer to their obligations, they should not think or look on them for a time any longer than is sufficient for the understanding and fulfillment of these obligations. And then they should consider these ideas without becoming attached or seeking gratification in them lest the effects of them remain in the soul. Thus spiritual persons are not required to cease recalling and thinking about what they must do and know. Since they are not attached to the possession of these thoughts, they will not be harmed. The verses of "The Mount," in Chapter 13 of the first book, are helpful for this practice.[3]

2. Yet it must be noted here that by our doctrine we are not in agreement, nor do we desire to be, with that of those pestiferous people who, persuaded by the pride and envy of Satan, have sought to remove from the eyes of the faithful the holy and necessary use of images of both God and the saints and of the renowned cult of these. Our doctrine

---

3. Cf. A. 1, 13, 10, note 16.

is far different from theirs.[4] We are not asserting, as they do, that there be no images or veneration of them. We are explaining the difference between these images and God, and how souls should use the painted image in such a way that they do not suffer an impediment in their movement toward the living image, and how they should pay no more attention to images than is required for advancing to what is spiritual.

The means is good and necessary for the attainment of the end, as are images for reminding us of God and the saints. But when people use and dwell on them more than they ought, their excessive use of them becomes as much an impediment as anything else. This is even truer in the case of supernatural visions and images with which I am more especially concerned here and which are the cause of many delusions and dangers.

There is no delusion or danger in the remembrance, veneration, and esteem of images, which the Catholic Church proposes to us in a natural manner, since in these images nothing else is esteemed than the person represented. The memory of these images will not fail to be profitable to people, because this remembrance is accompanied with love for whoever is represented. Images will always help individuals toward union with God, provided that no more attention is paid to them than is necessary, and that people allow themselves to soar—when God bestows the favor—from the painted image to the living God, in forgetfulness of all creatures and things pertaining to creatures.

Chapter Sixteen

The beginning of the treatise on the dark night of the will. A division of the emotions of the will.

1. We would achieve nothing by purging the intellect and memory in order to ground them in the virtues of faith and hope if we were to neglect the purification of the will through charity, the third virtue. Through charity, works done in faith are living works and have high value; without it they are worth nothing, as St. James affirms: *Without works of charity, faith is dead* [Jas 2:20].

---

4. Allusion to the iconoclasts of the eighth and ninth centuries and possibly to the *alumbrados* and Protestants of the sixteenth century.

THE ASCENT OF MOUNT CARMEL

For a treatise on the active night and denudation of this faculty, with the aim of instructing it and bringing it to perfection in this virtue of the love of God, I have found no more appropriate passage than the one in Chapter 6 of Deuteronomy, where Moses commands: *You shall love the Lord, your God, with all your heart, and with all your soul, and with all your strength* [Dt 6:5]. This passage contains all that spiritual persons must do and all that I must teach them here if they are to reach God by union of the will through charity. In it they receive the command to employ all the faculties, appetites, operations, and emotions of their soul in God so that they may avoid using their ability and strength for anything else, in accord with David's declaration: *Fortitudinem meam ad te custodiam* [Ps 58:10].[5]

2. The strength of the soul comprises the faculties, passions, and appetites. All this strength is ruled by the will. When the will directs these faculties, passions, and appetites toward God, turning them away from all that is not God, the soul preserves its strength for God, and comes to love Him with all its strength.

That individuals may bring this about, we will discuss here the purification of the will of all inordinate feelings. These inordinate feelings are the source of unruly appetites, affections, and operations, and the source as well of failure to preserve one's strength for God.

There are four of these feelings or passions: joy, hope, sorrow, and fear. These passions manifestly keep the strength and ability of the soul for God, and direct it toward Him, when they are so ruled that a person rejoices only in what is purely for God's honor and glory, hopes for nothing else, feels sorrow only about matters pertaining to this, and fears only God. The more people rejoice over something outside God, the less intense will be their joy in God; and the more their hope goes out toward something else, the less there is for God; and so on with the others.

3. To give a complete doctrine on this subject, we will as is our custom discuss individually these four passions as well as the appetites of the will.[6] The entire matter of reaching union with God consists in purging the will of its appetites and feelings, so that from a human and lowly will it may be changed into the divine will, made identical with the will of God.

---

5. I will keep my strength for you.
6. The theological virtues actually purify the whole human person, not just the spiritual

4. The less strongly the will is fixed on God, and the more dependent it is on creatures, the more these four passions combat the soul and reign in it. It then very easily finds joy in what deserves no rejoicing, and hope in what brings it no profit, and sorrow over what should perhaps cause rejoicing, and fear where there is no reason for fear.

5. When these feelings are unbridled, they are the source of all the vices and imperfections, and when they are in order and composed they give rise to all the virtues.

It should be known that, in the measure that one of the passions is regulated according to reason, the others are also. These four passions are so friendly that where one goes actually the others go virtually; if one is recollected actually, the other three in the same measure are recollected virtually. If the will rejoices over something, it must consequently in the same degree hope for it, with the virtual inclusion of sorrow and fear. And with the removal of satisfaction in this object, fear, sorrow, and hope will also be removed. . . .

6. Accordingly, you should keep in mind that wherever one of these passions goes, the entire soul with the will and the other faculties will go too, and all of these will live as prisoners of this passion. And the other three passions will dwell in the one passion to afflict the soul with their chains, and they will prevent it from soaring to the liberty and repose of sweet contemplation and union. As a result, Boethius claimed that if you desire a clear understanding of the truth, you must cast from yourself joys, hope, fear, and sorrow.[7] As long as these passions reign in the soul, they will not allow it to live in the tranquillity and peace that are necessary for the wisdom it can receive naturally and supernaturally.

Chapter Seventeen

The first emotion of the will. The nature of joy and a division of the objects of joy.

---

faculties. Love purifies the entire affective side of human nature: the will, the appetites, and the passions or emotions. Moreover, the will has a decisive role to play in the purification process because it is also the mover of the other spiritual faculties: intellect and memory.

7. *De Consolatione Philosophiae* 1, 7 (Migne PL 63, 656–658).

THE ASCENT OF MOUNT CARMEL

1. The first passion of the soul and emotion of the will is joy. Joy—to give a definition suited to our purpose—is nothing else than a satisfaction of the will with an object that is considered fitting and an esteem for it. For the will never rejoices unless in something that is valuable and satisfying to it.

We are speaking of active joy, which occurs when people understand distinctly and clearly the object of their joy and have the power either to rejoice or not. For there is another joy that is passive. In this kind of joy, the will finds itself rejoicing without any clear and distinct understanding of the object of its joy, although at times it does have this understanding. It has no power either to possess this joy or not to possess it. We will discuss this passive joy afterward. Our topic now is the joy derived from distinct and clear objects, insofar as it is active and voluntary.[8]

2. Joy can have as its source six kinds of objects or goods: temporal, natural, sensory, moral, supernatural, and spiritual. We must treat of these in their proper order, regulating the will according to reason lest it fail to concentrate the vigor of its joy on God because of the hindrance these goods may occasion.

We must in all of this presuppose a fundamental principle that will be like a staff, a continual support for our journey. It must be kept in mind because it is the light that will be our guide and master in this doctrine. By it we must, amid all these goods, direct joy to God. The principle is: The will should rejoice only in what is for the honor and glory of God, and the greatest honor we can give Him is to serve Him according to evangelical perfection; anything unincluded in such service is of no benefit or value to humans.[9]

* * *

---

8. The discussion of passive joy would belong more appropriately to *The Dark Night*. Actually, John never treats of passive joy.

9. John continues in the rest of the work applying this principle relative to the six kinds of goods that he mentions. His descriptions and applications of this principle brought him to Chapter 45, where he was still treating of joy, and this relative to provocative spiritual goods. He had still according to his promise to speak of directive and perfective spiritual goods and then of all that would pertain to hope, sorrow, and fear.

The Dark Night

Editor's Introduction

At the beginning of the *Ascent*, John set out with the express purpose of expounding on the theme of purificative contemplation, an experience referred to in his poem *The Dark Night*. But in putting together the manner in which he would develop his doctrine, he envisioned a much broader field in which the purgative contemplation would be just one aspect of the complete journey toward perfection. In fact *The Dark Night* deals with the night or purification insofar as it is passive. It represents what was promised as the subject matter of the fourth section of the *Ascent*. But John never finished the analyses he began in the *Ascent*, which led him into many divisions and subdivisions. The third book ends abruptly while he is dealing with the purification of the passion of joy. Rather than continue treating the many aspects of the purification that his divisions were leading him into and that were marginal to his main concern (to explain the passive purification since so little was written on it), John decided to begin a new work in which he could explain what he had always intended, the passive purification. Thus, though the work comes to us independently and its style differs from that of the *Ascent*, the theme is the same as that which was promised at the beginning of the *Ascent* and which was to form a part of that work. The *Night* then is a necessary complement to the *Ascent*.

If we take the symbol "night" as it appears in the poem, we find that night is not just a background or time of day but the very means by which the lover and beloved encounter each other. The poem contains the general meaning explicated in the commentary. The dark night is faith, the entire life of faith. At first faith is experienced simply as darkness and privation. Further on, it is presented as a valuable guide and a means to union. In the end faith itself is the person of the beloved in that it contains the object of the search, the subject of communion.

THE DARK NIGHT

The two basic situations are the painful passage and the ineffable joy of the encounter with God.

Since *The Dark Night* is linked with the *Ascent*, it lacks the usual kind of introduction. This was really provided in the prologue of the *Ascent*. In the brief prologue that does appear, John simply states his intention to comment on the stanzas of the poem. As things turn out, he comments only on the first two stanzas, explaining the first stanza twice. The third he hardly mentions and then discontinues the work. *The Dark Night* cannot be considered a commentary in the strict sense as is *The Spiritual Canticle*. The substance of the doctrine on the passive nights is contained in the explanation of the first verse alone. The content of the book deals with the experience of the night; the theological principles for understanding its causes and its purpose; the analysis of the human person before, during, and after the purification; and the fruits of love and illumination. John does not adapt an exhortatory method, nor does he give rules and counsels for obtaining the absolute poverty or *kenosis* implied in the radical purification. Rather, he insists on putting oneself at the disposal of God's work, that spiritual persons must allow themselves to be led by God so that the divine work of purification might be accomplished in them.

In the composition of the work, John uses only the stanzas and verses as marking points for his division of the material since he intended his words to be a real commentary on the poem and not a treatise as is the *Ascent*. His commentary on the first verse is so long, however, that the reader runs into difficulty and tends to get lost. Understandably, in the first edition (1618), Diego de Salablanca, the editor, introduced some further divisions. He divided the work into two books. The first of fourteen chapters contains all that pertains to the passive night of the senses. The second book, containing twenty-five chapters, includes all that refers to the passive night of the spirit. These divisions of the first editor have often been criticized because they give the work the appearance of a treatise rather than a commentary and because the chapters are not always well divided. Editors, though, with their eye on both reference and pedagogical needs, have wisely continued to use them.

In this work more than in any of his others, the double perspective of the author remains to the fore: the descriptive dimension of the spiritual process, presented in the poem, and the doctrinal dimension. The latter delves into the theological factors of this process. The first di-

THE DARK NIGHT

mension presents the author's experience; he offers it to others as a paradigm. But the two levels are not presented separately; they are fused, and this requires that we recall some presuppositions.

What is at stake in the spiritual journey to union with God is an ongoing work of purification of all that is repugnant to God's holiness. The purity implied is impossible without personal effort, but this effort, however intense, does not achieve the radical nakedness demanded by the union. The intervention of God through a purgation that comes about passively, that is not acquired through human effort, is necessary. The human work is simply a preparation for this particular divine action.

These two factors are not perfectly successive, but better considered as parallel and simultaneous. The predominance of one over the other permits a person to establish a certain relative succession. In the final stage of the purification the divine is clearly prevalent. The divine intervention may also come with greater or lesser intensity and efficacy. Thus there can be parts or periods of passive night. The high point of the dark night is that called the "passive night of the spirit." Chronologically it is situated within that period of the spiritual life that John calls the "spiritual betrothal."

The verses of the poem refer directly to this high point. Pedagogically the interpretation of them may be extended to periods or situations previous to this. John did precisely that in his commentary on the *Ascent* and in the first book of *The Dark Night*. Thus we have a twofold vision of the process: that of the poet, of the one who experienced, and that of the commentator, the teacher, the mystagogue.

What the person undergoing the dark night experiences is a painful lack or privation: darkness in the intellect, aridity in the exercise of love in the will, emptiness in the memory of all possessions, and affliction and torment as a consequence and general state. Such persons receive a vivid understanding of their own misery and think they will never escape from it. Their faculties seem powerless and bound; all outside help appears useless; they feel no hope for any breakthrough or remedy in the future. The effect of all this is the dread-filled experience of being abandoned by God. This becomes the worst part of the suffering since we are dealing with one who loves intensely.

All these painful experiences as well as the beneficial fruits of the transformation being wrought are attributable to contemplation. This contemplation is an inpouring of God, a divine loving knowledge, general, without images or concepts, obscure and hidden from the one who receives it, a knowledge that both purifies and illumines.[1] The one who receives it is in a kind of passive activity. But contemplation itself is not identifiable with dark night, for contemplation may be given in forms that do not produce these purifying effects. In addition, it is worth saying that if this night darkens, it does so only to give light; and if it humiliates it does so only to exalt; and if it impoverishes, it does so only to enrich.[2]

The point of arrival to which the night leads is "the new man," divinized in being and operation, living a life of faith, hope, and love, now fortified and without taint.

John's exposition of the night needs to be seen in relation to the rest of life. The night does not occur apart from the external situations of every day. In John's own experience we have the event of his imprisonment in Toledo with all its social and material deprivations. The horizon opens to many possible forms of realization according to the grace, state in life, and historical or personal circumstances of the individual. John leaves to each individual and each age the task of making the suitable applications. But if the sufferings and privations do not bring about a growing response of faith, hope, and love, the night would not be one that purifies and produces fruit.

The Dark Night may be divided as follows:

Book One
Chapters 1–7: Necessity of the passive night of the senses demonstrated by way of the seven capital vices
Chapters 8–10: The passive purgation of the senses: signs for recognizing it and appropriate response
Chapters 11–13: Benefits
Chapter 14: Duration and variations of trial

Book Two
Chapters 1–3: Intervening time and need for the passive night of the spirit
Chapters 4–10: The passive purgation of the spirit: nature, sufferings, duration, necessity

---

1. See N. 2, 5.
2. N. 2, 9, 1.

THE DARK NIGHT

Chapters 11–14: Benefits
Chapters 15–24: Commentary on the second stanza: secure, secret, ladder, disguised
Chapter 25: Begins commentary on the third stanza

For *The Dark Night* the two most trustworthy codices are the one know as *Hispalensis* (H), conserved in the National Library of Madrid, and that conserved in the general archives of the Discalced Carmelite Friars in Rome (R).

[Book One]

[A treatise on the passive night of the senses]

* * *

Stanza

One dark night
Fired with love's urgent longings
—Ah, the sheer grace!—
I went out unseen,
My house being now all stilled.

[Commentary]

1. In this first stanza, the soul is speaking of the way it followed in its departure from love of self and of all things through a method of true mortification, which causes it to die to itself and to all these things and to begin the sweet and delightful life of love with God. And it declares that this departure was a "dark night." As we will explain later, this dark night signifies here purgative contemplation, which passively causes in the soul this negation of self and of all things.[1]

2. The soul states that it was able to make this escape because of the vigor and warmth gained from loving its spouse in this obscure contemplation. It emphasized the intense happiness it possessed in journeying to God through this dark night. So great was the soul's success that none of the three enemies (the world, the flesh, and the devil, which are always in opposition to the journey along this road) could impede it, for that night of purifying contemplation lulled to sleep and

---

1. Purgative contemplation does not differ essentially from the contemplation of which he speaks in other places. Here he is speaking of contemplation insofar as it produces the effect of purifying the soul. By this reason it differs from contemplation insofar as it is illuminative or unitive.

THE DARK NIGHT

deadened all the inordinate movements of the passions and appetites in the house of sense.

The verse then states:

> One dark night.

Chapter One

[Begins to discuss the imperfections of beginners.]

1. Souls begin to enter this dark night when God, gradually drawing them out of the state of beginners (those who practice meditation on the spiritual road), begins to place them in the state of proficients (those who are already contemplatives) so that by passing through this state they might reach that of the perfect, which is the divine union of the soul with God.

We should first mention here some characteristics of beginners for the sake of a better explanation and understanding of the nature of this night and of God's motive for placing the soul in it. Although our treatment of these things will be as brief as possible, beginners will be helped by it to understand the feebleness of their state and take courage and desire that God place them in this night where the soul is strengthened in virtue and fortified for the inestimable delights of the love of God. And, although we shall be delayed for a moment, it will be for no longer than our discussion of this dark night requires.[2]

2. It should be known, then, that God nurtures and caresses the soul, after it has been resolutely converted to His service, like a loving mother who warms her child with the heat of her bosom, nurses it with good milk and tender food, and carries and caresses it in her arms. But as the child grows older, the mother withholds her caresses and hides her tender love; she rubs bitter aloes on her sweet breast and sets the child down from her arms, letting it walk on its own feet so that it may put aside the habits of childhood and grow accustomed to greater and more important things. The grace of God acts just as a loving mother by reengendering in the soul new enthusiasm and fervor in the service

---

2. This whole treatment of the imperfections of beginners brings about a delay in John's proposed plan, which was to treat of the purgative night, proper to proficients.

of God. With no effort on the soul's part, this grace causes it to taste sweet and delectable milk and to experience intense satisfaction in the performance of spiritual exercises, because God is handing the breast of His tender love to the soul, just as if it were a delicate child.

3. The soul finds its joy, therefore, in spending lengthy periods at prayer, perhaps even entire nights; its penances are pleasures; its fasts, happiness; and the sacraments and spiritual conversations are its consolations. Although spiritual persons do practice these exercises with great profit and persistence and are very careful about them, they conduct themselves, spiritually speaking, in a very weak and imperfect manner. Since their motivation in their spiritual works and exercises is the consolation and satisfaction they experience in them, and since they have not been conditioned by the arduous struggle of practicing virtue, they possess many faults and imperfections in the discharge of their spiritual activities. For, assuredly, peoples' actions are in direct conformity to the habit of perfection they have acquired, and since these persons have not had time to acquire those firm habits, their work must of necessity be feeble, like that of weak children.

For a clearer understanding of this and of how imperfect beginners truly are, insofar as they practice virtue readily because of the satisfaction attached to it, we will describe, using the seven capital vices as our basis, some of the numerous imperfections beginners commit. Thus we will see how very similar are their deeds to those of children. Then the benefits of the dark night will become evident since it cleanses and purifies the soul of all these imperfections.

Chapter Two

Some of the imperfections of pride possessed by beginners.

1. These beginners feel so fervent and diligent in their spiritual exercises and undertakings that a certain kind of secret pride is generated in them, which begets a complacency with themselves and their accomplishments, despite the fact that holy works do of their very nature cause humility. Then they develop a desire somewhat vain—at times very vain—to speak of spiritual things in others' presence, and sometimes even to instruct rather than be instructed; in their hearts they condemn others who do not seem to have the kind of devotion they would

THE DARK NIGHT

like them to have, and sometimes they give expression to this criticism, like the pharisee who despised the publican while he boasted and praised God for the good deeds he himself accomplished [Lk 18:11–12].

2. The devil, desiring the growth of pride and presumption in these beginners, often increases their fervor and readiness to perform such works, and other ones, too. For he is quite aware of the fact that all these works and virtues are not only worthless for them, but even become vices. Some of these persons become so evil-minded that they do not want anyone except themselves to appear holy; and so by both word and deed, they condemn and detract others whenever the occasion arises, seeing the little mote in their neighbor's eye, and failing to consider the beam in their own eye [Mt 7:23]; they strain at the other's gnat and swallow their own camel [Mt 23:24].

3. And when at times their spiritual directors, their confessors or superiors, disapprove their spirit and method of procedure, they feel that these directors do not understand, or perhaps that this failure to approve derives from a lack of holiness, since they want these directors to regard their conduct with esteem and praise. So they quickly search for some other spiritual adviser more to their liking, someone who will congratulate them and be impressed by their deeds, and they flee, as they would death, those who attempt to place them on the safe road by forbidding these things—and sometimes they even become hostile toward such spiritual directors. Frequently, in their presumption, they make many resolutions but accomplish very little. Sometimes they want others to recognize their spirit and devotion, and as a result occasionally contrive to make some manifestations of it, such as movements, sighs, and other little ceremonies; sometimes, with the assistance of the devil, they experience raptures, more often in public than in private, and they are quite pleased, and often eager, for others to take notice of these.

4. Many want to be the favorites of their confessors, and thus they are consumed by a thousand envies and disquietudes. Embarrassment forbids them from relating their sins clearly, lest their reputation diminish in their confessor's eyes. They confess their sins in the most favorable light so as to appear better than they actually are, and thus they approach the confessional to excuse themselves rather than accuse themselves. Sometimes they confess the evil things they do to a different confessor so that their own confessor might think they commit no sins at all. Therefore, in their desire to appear holy, they enjoy relating their good behavior to their confessor, and in such careful terms that

these good deeds appear greater than they actually are. It would be more humble of them, as we will point out later on, to make light of the good they do and to wish that no one, neither their confessor nor anybody else, should consider it of any importance at all.

5. Sometimes they minimize their faults, and at other times they become discouraged by them since they felt they were already saints, and they become impatient and angry with themselves, which is yet another fault.

They are often extremely anxious that God remove their faults and imperfections, but their motive is personal peace rather than God. They fail to realize that were God to remove their faults they might very well become more proud and presumptuous.

They dislike praising anyone else, but they love to receive praise, and sometimes they even seek it. In this they resemble the foolish virgins who had to seek oil from others when their own lamps were extinguished [Mt 25:8].

6. The number of these imperfections in some people is serious and causes them a good deal of harm. Some have fewer, some have more, and yet others have little more than the first movements toward them. But there are scarcely any beginners who at the time of their initial fervor do not fall victim to some of these imperfections.

Souls, however, who are advancing in perfection act in an entirely different manner and with a different quality of spirit during this period.[3] They receive great benefit from their humility by which they not only place little importance on their deeds, but also take very little self-satisfaction from them. They think everyone else is far better than themselves, and usually possess a holy envy of them and would like to emulate their service of God. Since they are truly humble, their growing fervor and the increased number of their good deeds and the gratification they receive from them only cause them to become more aware of their debt to God and the inadequacy of their service to Him, and thus the more they do, the less satisfaction they derive from it. Their charity and love makes them want to do so much for God that what they actually do accomplish seems as nothing. This loving solicitude goads them, preoccupies them, and absorbs them to such an ex-

---

3. Here by way of comparison he begins to speak of the virtue of proficients and the perfect.

tent that they never notice what others do or do not accomplish, but if they should, they then think, as I say, that everyone is better than they. They think they themselves are insignificant, and want others to think this also and to belittle and slight their deeds. Moreover, even though others do praise and value their works, these souls are unable to believe them; such praises seem strange to them.

7. These souls humbly and tranquilly long to be taught by anyone who might be a help to them. This desire is the exact opposite of that other desire we mentioned above, of those who want to be themselves the teachers in everything. When these others notice that someone is trying to give them some instruction, they themselves take the words from their very mouths as though they already know everything.

Yet these humble souls, far from desiring to be anyone's teacher, are ready to take a road different from the one they are following, if told to do so. For they do not believe they could ever be right themselves. They rejoice when others receive praise, and their only sorrow is that they do not serve God as these others do.

Because they consider their deeds insignificant, they do not want to make them known. They are even ashamed to speak of them to their spiritual directors because they think these deeds are not worth mentioning.

They are more eager to speak of their faults and sins, and reveal these to others, than of their virtues. They have an inclination to seek direction from one who will have less esteem for their spirit and deeds. Such is the characteristic of a pure and simple and true spirit, one that is very pleasing to God. Since the wise Spirit of God dwells within these humble souls, He moves them to keep these treasures hidden, and to manifest only their faults. God gives this grace to the humble, together with the other virtues, just as He denies it to the proud.

8. These souls would give their life's blood to anyone who serves God, and they will do whatever they can to help others serve Him. When they see themselves fall into imperfections, they suffer this with humility, with docility of spirit, and with loving fear of God and hope in Him.

Yet I believe very few souls are so perfect in the beginning. We would be happy enough if they managed not to fall into these imperfections of pride. As we will point out later, then, God places these souls in the dark night so as to purify them of these imperfections and make them advance.

THE DARK NIGHT

Chapter Three

Some imperfections of spiritual avarice commonly found in beginners.

1. Many beginners also at times possess great spiritual avarice. They will hardly ever seem content with the spirit God gives them. They become unhappy and peevish owing to a lack of the consolation they desire to have in spiritual things.

Many never have enough of hearing counsels, or of learning spiritual maxims, or of keeping them and reading books about them. They spend more time doing this than striving after mortification and the perfection of the interior poverty to which they are obliged. Furthermore, they weigh themselves down with overdecorated images and rosaries. They will now put these down, now take up others; at one moment they are exchanging, and at the next reexchanging. Now they want this kind, now they want another. And they will prefer one cross to another because of its elaborateness. Others you will see decked out in *agnusdeis* and relics and lists of saints' names, like children in trinkets.[4]

What I condemn in this is possessiveness of heart and attachment to the number, workmanship, and overdecoration of these objects. For this attachment is contrary to poverty of spirit which is intent only on the substance of the devotion, benefits by no more than what procures this sufficiently, and tires of all other multiplicity and elaborate ornamentation. Since true devotion comes from the heart and looks only to the truth and substance represented by spiritual objects, and since everything else is imperfect attachment and possessiveness, any appetite for these things must be uprooted if some degree of perfection is to be reached.

2. I knew a person who for more than ten years profited by a cross roughly made out of a blessed palm and held together by a pin twisted around it. She carried it about and never would part with it until I took it from her—and she was not a person of poor judgment or little intelligence. I saw someone else who prayed with beads made out of bones from the spine of a fish. Certainly, the devotion was not for this reason

---

[4]. An agnusdei was a little wax disk with the image of a lamb on it and blessed by the pope. This blessing by the pope took place with special ceremonies every seven years. Agnusdeis were worn as protection against storms, fire, lightning, and pestilence.

less precious in the sight of God.[5] In neither of these two instances, obviously, did these persons base their devotion on the workmanship and value of a spiritual object.

They, therefore, who are well guided from the outset do not become attached to visible instruments or burden themselves with them. They do not care to know any more than what is necessary to accomplish good works, because their eyes are fixed only on God, on being His friend and pleasing Him; this is what they long for. They very generously give all they have. Their pleasure is to know how to live for love of God or neighbor without these spiritual or temporal things. As I said, their eyes are fastened on the substance of interior perfection, on pleasing God and not themselves.

3. Yet until a soul is placed by God in the passive purgation of that dark night, which we will soon explain, it cannot purify itself completely of these imperfections or from the others. But people should insofar as possible strive to do their part in purifying and perfecting themselves and thereby merit God's divine cure. In this cure God will heal them of what through their own efforts they were unable to remedy. No matter how much individuals do through their own efforts, they cannot actively purify themselves enough to be disposed in the least degree for the divine union of the perfection of love. God must take over and purge them in that fire that is dark for them, as we will explain.

Chapter Four

The imperfections of lust, the third capital vice, usually found in beginners.

1. A number of these beginners have many more imperfections in each vice than those I am mentioning. But to avoid prolixity, I am omitting them and touching on some of the principal ones which are as it were the origin of the others.

As for the vice of lust—aside from what it means for spiritual persons to fall into this vice, since my intent is to treat of the imperfections

---

5. The identity of these persons is not known. Some think this one with the roughly made cross could have been St. Teresa.

that have to be purged by means of the dark night—spiritual persons have numerous imperfections, many of which can be called spiritual lust, not because the lust is spiritual but because it proceeds from spiritual things. It happens frequently that in one's spiritual exercises themselves, without one's being able to avoid it, impure movements will be experienced in the sensory part of the soul, and even sometimes when the spirit is deep in prayer or when receiving the sacraments of Penance or of the Eucharist. These impure feelings arise from any of three causes outside one's control.

2. First, they often proceed from the pleasure human nature finds in spiritual exercises. Since both the spiritual and the sensory part of the soul receive gratification from that refreshment, each part experiences delight according to its own nature and properties. The spirit, the superior part of the soul, experiences renewal and satisfaction in God; and the sense, the lower part, feels sensory gratification and delight because it is ignorant of how to get anything else, and hence takes whatever is nearest, which is the impure sensory satisfaction. It will happen that while a soul is with God in deep spiritual prayer, it will on the other hand passively experience sensual rebellions, movements, and acts in the senses, not without its own great displeasure. This frequently happens at the time of Communion. Since the soul receives joy and gladness in this act of love—for the Lord grants the grace and gives Himself for this reason—the sensory part also takes its share, as we said, according to its mode. Since, after all, these two parts form one *suppositum*, each one usually shares according to its mode in what the other receives. As the Philosopher says: Whatever is received is received according to the mode of the receiver.[6] Because in the initial stages of the spiritual life, and even more advanced ones, the sensory part of the soul is imperfect, God's spirit is frequently received in this sensory part with this same imperfection. Once the sensory part is reformed through the purgation of the dark night, it no longer has these infirmities. For then the spiritual part of the soul rather than the sensory part receives God's spirit, and the soul thus receives everything according to the mode of the spirit.

3. The second origin of these rebellions is the devil. To bring dis-

---

6. This saying of the Philosopher has not been found as such in Aristotle. It was used by Aquinas. See, for example, *Summa Theologica* 1, 79, 6.

THE DARK NIGHT

quietude and disturbance on a soul when it is praying, or trying to pray, he endeavors to excite impure feelings in the sensory part. And if people pay any attention to these, the devil does them great harm. Through fear, some souls grow slack in their prayer—which is what the devil wants—in order to struggle against these movements, and others give it up entirely, for they think these feelings come while they are engaged in prayer rather than at any other time. And this is true because the devil excites these feelings while souls are at prayer, instead of when they are engaged in other works, so that they might abandon prayer. And that is not all; for to make them cowardly and afraid, he brings vividly to their minds foul and impure thoughts. And sometimes the thoughts will concern spiritual things and persons who have been a help to them. Those who attribute any importance to such thoughts, therefore, do not even dare look at anything or think about anything lest they thereupon stumble into them.

These impure thoughts so affect people who are afflicted with melancholia that one should have great pity for them; indeed, these people suffer a sad life. In some who are troubled with this bad humor the trial reaches such a point that they clearly feel that the devil has access to them without their having the freedom to prevent it. Yet some of these melancholiacs are able through intense effort and struggle to forestall this power of the devil.

If these impure thoughts and feelings arise from melancholia, individuals are not ordinarily freed from them until they are cured of that humor, unless the dark night flows in on the soul and deprives it successively of all things.

4. The third origin from which these impure feelings usually proceed and wage war on the soul is fear of them. The fear that springs up at the sudden remembrance of these thoughts, caused by what one sees, is dealing with, or thinking of, produces impure feelings without one's being at fault.

5. Some people are so delicate that when gratification is received spiritually or in prayer, they immediately experience a lust that so inebriates them and caresses their senses that they become as it were engulfed in the delight and satisfaction of that vice; and this experience will continue passively with the other. Sometimes these individuals become aware that certain impure and rebellious acts have taken place.

The reason for such occurrences is that since these natures are, as I say, delicate and tender, their humors and blood are stirred up by any

THE DARK NIGHT

change. For these persons will also experience these feelings when they are inflamed with anger or agitated by some other disturbance or affliction.

6. Sometimes, too, in their spiritual conversations or works, they manifest a certain sprightliness and gallantry on considering who is present, and they carry on with a kind of vain satisfaction. Such behavior is also a by-product of spiritual lust (in the way we here understand it), which generally accompanies complacency of the will.

7. Some will spiritually acquire a liking for other individuals, which often arises from lust rather than from the spirit. This lustful origin will be recognized if, on recalling that affection, there is not an increase in the remembrance and love of God, but remorse of conscience. The affection is purely spiritual if the love of God grows when it grows, or if the love of God is remembered as often as the affection is remembered, or if the affection gives the soul a desire for God—if by growing in one the soul grows also in the other. For this is a trait of God's spirit: The good increases with the good since there is likeness and conformity between them.

But when the love is born of this sensual vice it has the contrary effects. As the one love grows greater, the other lessens, and the remembrance of it lessens too. If the inordinate love increases, then, as will be seen, the soul will grow cold in the love of God, and, owing to the recollection of that other love, forget Him—not without the feeling of some remorse of conscience. On the other hand, as the love of God increases, the soul will grow cold in the inordinate affection and come to forget it. For not only do these loves fail to benefit one another, but, since they are contrary loves, the predominating one, while becoming stronger itself, will stifle and extinguish the other, as the philosophers say.[7] Hence our Savior proclaimed in the gospel: *That which is born of the flesh is flesh, and that which is born of the spirit is spirit* [Jn 3:16], that is: Love derived from sensuality terminates in sensuality, and the love that is of the spirit terminates in the spirit of God, and brings it increase. And this, then, is the difference between these two loves, which enables us to discern the one from the other.

8. The dark night, when it enters the soul, puts all these loves in reasonable order. It strengthens and purifies the love of God, and takes

---

7. Cf. A. 1, 4, 2, note 10.

THE DARK NIGHT

away and destroys the other. But in the beginning it will cause the soul to lose sight of both of them, as will be explained.

Chapter Five

The imperfections of the capital vice of anger into which beginners fall.

1. Because of the strong desire of many beginners for spiritual gratification, they usually have many imperfections of anger. For when the delight and satisfaction procured in their spiritual exercises passes, these beginners are naturally left without any spiritual savor. And because of this distastefulness, they become peevish in the works they do and easily angered by the least thing, and occasionally they are so unbearable that nobody can put up with them. This frequently occurs after they have experienced in prayer some recollection pleasant to the senses. After the delight and satisfaction is gone, the sensory part of the soul is naturally left vapid and zestless, just as a child when withdrawn from the sweet breast. These souls are not at fault if they do not allow this dejection to influence them for it is an imperfection that must be purged through the dryness and distress of the dark night.

2. Among these spiritual persons there are also those who fall into another kind of spiritual anger. Through a certain indiscreet zeal they become angry over the sins of others, reprove these others, and sometimes even feel the impulse to do so angrily, which in fact they occasionally do, setting themselves up as lords of virtue. All such conduct is contrary to spiritual meekness.

3. Others, in becoming aware of their own imperfections, grow angry with themselves in an unhumble impatience. So impatient are they about these imperfections that they would want to become saints in a day.

Many of these beginners will make numerous plans and great resolutions, but since they are not humble and have no distrust of themselves, the more resolves they make the more they break, and the greater becomes their anger. They do not have the patience to wait until God gives them what they need when He so desires. Their attitude is contrary to spiritual meekness and can only be remedied by the purgation of the dark night. Some, however, are so patient about their desire for advancement that God would prefer to see them a little less so.

THE DARK NIGHT

Chapter Six

The imperfections of spiritual gluttony.

1. A great deal can be said on spiritual gluttony, the fourth vice. There are hardly any persons among these beginners, no matter how excellent their conduct, who will not fall into some of the many imperfections of this vice. These imperfections arise because of the delight beginners find in their spiritual exercises.

Many, lured by the delight and satisfaction procured in their religious practices, strive more for spiritual savor than for spiritual purity and discretion; yet it is this purity and discretion that God looks for and finds acceptable throughout a soul's entire spiritual journey. Besides the imperfection of seeking after these delights, the sweetness these persons experience makes them go to extremes and pass beyond the mean in which virtue resides and is acquired.

Some, attracted by the delight they feel in their spiritual exercises, will kill themselves with penances, and others will weaken themselves by fasts and, without the counsel or command of another, overtax their weakness; indeed they try to hide these penances from the one to whom they owe obedience in such matters. Some will even dare perform these penances contrary to obedience.

2. Such individuals are unreasonable and most imperfect. They subordinate submissiveness and obedience (which is a penance of reason and discretion, and consequently a sacrifice more pleasing and acceptable to God) to corporal penance. But corporal penance without obedience is no more than a penance of beasts. And like beasts, they are motivated in these penances by an appetite for the pleasure they find in them. Since all extremes are vicious and since by such behavior these persons are doing their own will, they grow in vice rather than in virtue. For through this conduct they at least become spiritually gluttonous and proud, since they do not tread the path of obedience.

The devil, increasing the delights and appetites of these beginners and thereby stirring up this gluttony in them, so impels many of them that when they are unable to avoid obedience they either add to, change, or modify what was commanded them. Any obedience in this matter is distasteful to them. Some will reach such a point that the mere obligation of obedience to perform their spiritual exercises makes them lose all desire and devotion. Their only yearning and satisfaction is to

THE DARK NIGHT

do what they feel inclined to do, whereas it would be better in all likelihood for them not to do this at all.

3. Some are very insistent that their spiritual director allow them to do what they themselves want to do, and finally almost force the permission from him. And if they do not get what they want, they become sad and go about like testy children. They are under the impression that they do not serve God when they are not allowed to do what they want. Since they take gratification and their own will as their support and their god, they become sad, weak, and discouraged when their director takes these from them and desires that they do God's will. They think that gratifying and satisfying themselves is serving and satisfying God.

4. Others, too, because of this sweetness have so little knowledge of their own lowliness and misery and such lack of the loving fear and respect they owe to God's grandeur that they do not hesitate to insist boldly that their confessors allow them the frequent reception of Communion. And worse than this, they often dare to receive Communion without the permission and advice of the minister and dispenser of Christ. They are guided here solely by their own opinion, and they endeavor to hide the truth from him. As a result, with their hearts set on frequent Communion, they make their confessions carelessly, more eager just to receive Communion than to receive it with a pure and perfect heart. It would be sounder and holier of them to have the contrary inclination and to ask their confessor not to let them receive Communion so frequently. Humble resignation, though, is better than either of these two attitudes. But the bold things referred to first will bring great evil and chastisement on one.

5. In receiving Communion they spend all their time trying to get some feeling and satisfaction rather than humbly praising and reverencing God dwelling within them. And they go about this in such a way that, if they do not procure any sensible feeling and satisfaction, they think they have accomplished nothing. As a result they judge very poorly of God and fail to understand that the sensory benefits are the least among those that this Most Blessed Sacrament bestows, for the invisible grace it gives is a greater blessing. God often withdraws sensory delight and pleasure so that souls might set the eyes of faith on this invisible grace. Not only in receiving Communion, but in other spiritual exercises as well, beginners desire to feel God and taste Him as if he were comprehensible and accessible. This desire is a serious imper-

fection and, because it involves impurity of faith, opposed to God's way.

6. They have the same defect in their prayer, for they think the whole matter of prayer consists in looking for sensory satisfaction and devotion. They strive to procure this by their own efforts and tire and weary their heads and their faculties. When they do not get this sensible comfort, they become very disconsolate and think they have done nothing. Because of their aim they lose true devotion and spirit, which lie in distrust of self and in humble and patient perseverance so as to please God. Once they do not find delight in prayer, or any other spiritual exercise, they feel extreme reluctance and repugnance in returning to it, and sometimes even give it up. For after all, as was mentioned, they are like children who are prompted to act not by reason but by pleasure.

All their time is spent looking for satisfaction and spiritual consolation; they can never read enough spiritual books, and one minute they are meditating on one subject and the next on another, always in search for some gratification in the things of God. God very rightly and discreetly and lovingly denies this satisfaction to these beginners. If He did not, they would fall into innumerable evils because of their spiritual gluttony and craving for sweetness. Wherefore it is important for these beginners to enter the dark night and be purged of this childishness.

7. Those who are inclined toward these delights have also another serious imperfection; that is, they are weak and remiss in treading the rough way of the cross. A soul given up to pleasure naturally feels aversion toward the bitterness of self-denial.

8. These people incur many other imperfections because of this spiritual gluttony, of which the Lord in time will cure them through temptations, aridities, and other trials, which are all a part of the dark night. So as not to be too lengthy, I do not want to discuss these imperfections any more, but only point out that spiritual sobriety and temperance beget another very different quality, one of mortification, fear, and submissiveness in all things. Individuals thereby become aware that the perfection and value of their works do not depend on their number or the satisfaction found in them but on knowing how to practice self-denial in them. These beginners ought to do their part in striving after this self-denial until God in fact brings them into the dark night and purifies them. In order to get to our discussion of this dark night, I am passing over these imperfections hurriedly.

THE DARK NIGHT

Chapter Seven

The imperfections of spiritual envy and sloth.

1. As for the other two vices, spiritual envy and sloth, these beginners also have many imperfections. In regard to envy, many of them will feel sad about the spiritual good of others and experience sensible grief in noting that their neighbor is ahead of them on the road to perfection, and they will not want to hear others praised. Learning of the virtues of others makes them sad. They cannot bear to hear others being praised without contradicting and undoing these compliments as much as possible. Their annoyance grows because they themselves do not receive these plaudits and because they long for preference in everything. All of this is contrary to charity, which, as St. Paul says, rejoices in goodness [1 Cor 13:6]. If any envy accompanies charity, it is a holy envy by which they are saddened at not having the virtues of others, rejoice that others have them, are happy that all others are ahead of them in the service of God since they are so wanting in His service.

2. Also, regarding spiritual sloth, these beginners usually become weary in the more spiritual exercises and flee from them since these exercises are contrary to sensory satisfaction. Since they are so used to finding delight in spiritual practices, they become bored when they do not find it. If they do not receive in prayer the satisfaction they crave—for after all it is fit that God withdraw this so as to try them—they do not want to return to it, or at times they either give up prayer or go to it begrudgingly. Because of their sloth, they subordinate the way of perfection (which requires the denial of one's own will and satisfaction for God's sake) to the pleasure and delight of their own will. As a result they strive to satisfy their own will rather than God's.

3. Many of these beginners want God to desire what they want, and they become sad if they have to desire God's will. They feel an aversion toward adapting their will to God's. Hence they frequently believe that what is not their will, or that which brings them no satisfaction, is not God's will, and, on the other hand, that if they are satisfied, God is too. They measure God by themselves and not themselves by God, which is in opposition to His teaching in the gospel, that those who lose their life for His sake will gain it and that those who desire to gain it will lose it [Mt 16:25].

4. Beginners also become bored when told to do something unpleasant. Because they look for spiritual gratifications and delights,

they are extremely lax in the fortitude and labor perfection demands. Like those who are reared in luxury, they run sadly from everything rough, and they are scandalized by the cross, in which spiritual delights are found. And in the more spiritual exercises their boredom is greater. Since they expect to go about in spiritual matters according to the whims and satisfactions of their own will, entering by the narrow way of life, about which Christ speaks, is saddening and repugnant to them [Mt 7:14].

5. It is enough to have referred to the many imperfections of those who live in this beginner's state to see the need there is that God put them in the state of proficients. He does this by introducing them into the dark night, of which we will now speak. There, through pure dryness and interior darkness, He weans them from the breasts of these gratifications and delights, takes away all these trivialities and childish ways, and makes them acquire the virtues by very different means. No matter how earnestly beginners in all their actions and passions practice the mortification of self, they will never be able to do so entirely—far from it—until God accomplishes it in them passively by means of the purgation of this night. May God be pleased to give me His divine light that I may say something worthwhile about this subject, for in a night so dark and a matter so difficult to treat and expound His enlightenment is very necessary.

The verse, then, is:

One dark night.

Chapter Eight

[The beginning of the exposition of this dark night.]

1. This night, which as we say is contemplation, causes two kinds of darkness or purgation in spiritual persons according to the two parts of the soul, the sensory and the spiritual. Hence the one night of purgation will be sensory, by which the senses are purged and accommodated to the spirit; and the other night or purgation will be spiritual, by which the spirit is purged and denuded as well as accommodated and prepared for union with God through love.

The sensory night is common and happens to many. These are the beginners of whom we will treat first. The spiritual night is the lot of very few, of those who have been tried and are proficient, and of whom we will speak afterward.

2. The first purgation or night is bitter and terrible to the senses. But nothing can be compared to the second, for it is horrible and frightful to the spirit. Because the sensory night is first in order, we will speak of it now briefly; since it is a more common occurrence one finds more written on it. Then we will pass on to discuss more at length the spiritual night, for hardly anything has been said of it, in sermons or in writing; and even the experience of it is rare.[8]

3. Since the conduct of these beginners in the way of God is lowly and not too distant from love of pleasure and of self, as we explained, God desires to withdraw them from this base manner of loving and lead them on to a higher degree of divine love. And He desires to liberate them from the lowly exercise of the senses and of discursive meditation, by which they go in search of Him so inadequately and with so many difficulties, and lead them into the exercise of spirit, in which they become capable of a communion with God that is more abundant and freer of imperfections. God does this after beginners have exercised themselves for a time in the way of virtue and have persevered in meditation and prayer. For it is through the delight and satisfaction they experience in prayer that they have become detached from worldly things and have gained some spiritual strength in God. This strength has helped them somewhat to restrain their appetites for creatures, and through it they will be able to suffer a little oppression and dryness without turning back. Consequently, it is at the time they are going about their spiritual exercises with delight and satisfaction, when in their opinion the sun of divine favor is shining most brightly on them, that God darkens all this light and closes the door and spring of the sweet spiritual water they were tasting as often and as long as they desired. For since they were weak and tender, no door was closed to them, as St. John says in the Book of Revelation [Rv 3:8]. God now leaves them in such darkness that they do not know which way to turn in their

---

8. In speaking again of the forms or levels of night, he follows the same basic division he made in A. 1, 1, 2: the night of the senses and that of the spirit. The first, which is common, is the lot of beginners as they pass into the stage of proficients; the second, which is rare, is the lot of proficients as they pass into the stage of the perfect. But as the commentary progresses it becomes clear that, in accord with the *Ascent*, because of the interdependence of sense and spirit, the one night or purification is not present without the other. In order of time, the effect is experienced predominantly first in the senses and then in the spirit.

discursive imaginings. They cannot advance a step in meditation, as they used to, now that the interior sense faculties are engulfed in this night. He leaves them in such dryness that they not only fail to receive satisfaction and pleasure from their spiritual exercises and works, as they formerly did, but also find these exercises distasteful and bitter. As I said, when God sees that they have grown a little, He weans them from the sweet breast so that they might be strengthened, lays aside their swaddling bands, and puts them down from His arms that they may grow accustomed to walking by themselves. This change is a surprise to them because everything seems to be functioning in reverse.

4. This usually happens to recollected beginners sooner than to others since they are freer from occasions of backsliding and more quickly reform their appetites for worldly things. A reform of the appetites is the requirement for entering the happy night of the senses. Not much time ordinarily passes after the initial stages of their spiritual life before beginners start to enter this night of sense. And the majority of them do enter it because it is common to see them suffer these aridities.

5. We could adduce numerous passages from Sacred Scripture, for since this sensory purgation is so customary, we find a great many references to it throughout, especially in the psalms and the prophets. But I do not want to spend time citing them, because the prevalence of the experience of this night should be enough for those who are unable to find the scriptural references to it.

Chapter Nine

Signs for discerning whether a spiritual person is treading the path of this sensory night and purgation.

1. Because the origin of these aridities may not be the sensory night and purgation, but sin and imperfection, or weakness and lukewarmness, or some bad humor or bodily indisposition, I will give some signs here for discerning whether the dryness is the result of this purgation or of one of these other defects. I find there are three principal signs for knowing this.[9]

---

9. Regarding these three signs: Two are negative (aridity and inability to meditate), and one is positive. The positive sign (solicitude and painful care) is the sign that best reveals the

THE DARK NIGHT

2. The first is that since these souls do not get satisfaction or consolation from the things of God, they do not get any out of creatures either. Since God puts a soul in this dark night in order to dry up and purge its sensory appetite, He does not allow it to find sweetness or delight in anything. Through this sign it can in all likelihood be inferred that this dryness and distaste is not the outcome of newly committed sins and imperfections. If this were so, some inclination or propensity to look for satisfaction in something other than the things of God would be felt in the sensory part. For when the appetite is allowed indulgence in some imperfection, the soul immediately feels an inclination toward it, little or great in proportion to the degree of its satisfaction and attachment. Yet, because the want of satisfaction in earthly or heavenly things could be the product of some indisposition or melancholic humor, which frequently prevents one from being satisfied with anything, the second sign or condition is necessary.

3. The second sign for the discernment of this purgation is that the memory ordinarily turns to God solicitously and with painful care, and the soul thinks it is not serving God but turning back, because it is aware of this distaste for the things of God. Hence it is obvious that this aversion and dryness is not the fruit of laxity and tepidity, for lukewarm people do not care much for the things of God nor are they inwardly solicitous about them.

There is, consequently, a notable difference between dryness and lukewarmness. The lukewarm are very lax and remiss in their will and spirit, and have no solicitude about serving God. Those suffering from the purgative dryness are ordinarily solicitous, concerned, and pained about not serving God. Even though the dryness may be furthered by melancholia or some other humor—as it often is—it does not thereby fail to produce its purgative effect in the appetite, for the soul will be deprived of every satisfaction and concerned only about God. If this humor is the entire cause, everything ends in displeasure and does harm to one's nature, and there are none of these desires to serve God that accompany the purgative dryness. Even though in this purgative dryness the sensory part of the soul is very cast down, slack, and feeble in its actions because of the little satisfaction it finds, the spirit is ready and strong.

4. The reason for this dryness is that God transfers His goods and

---

presence and activity of the theological virtues or divine life. The similar signs given in A. 2, 13 represent a later phase than this initial one of the *Night*. The difference lies in the positive sign, which in the *Ascent* is a loving peaceful awareness.

THE DARK NIGHT

strength from sense to spirit. Since the sensory part of the soul is incapable of the goods of spirit, it remains deprived, dry, and empty. Thus, while the spirit is tasting, the flesh tastes nothing at all and becomes weak in its work.[10] But the spirit through this nourishment grows stronger and more alert, and becomes more solicitous than before about not failing God. If in the beginning the soul does not experience this spiritual savor and delight, but dryness and distaste, the reason is due to the novelty involved in this exchange. Since its palate is accustomed to these other sensory tastes, the soul still sets its eyes on them. And since, also, its spiritual palate is neither purged nor accommodated for so subtle a taste, it is unable to experience the spiritual savor and good until gradually prepared by means of this dark and obscure night. The soul rather experiences dryness and distaste because of a lack of the gratification it formerly enjoyed so readily.

5. Those whom God begins to lead into these desert solitudes are like the children of Israel. When God began giving them the heavenly food, which contained in itself all savors and, as is there mentioned, changed to whatever taste each one hungered after [Wis 16:2–21], they nonetheless felt a craving for the tastes of the fleshmeats and onions they had eaten in Egypt, for their palate was accustomed and attracted to them more than to the delicate sweetness of the angelic manna. And in the midst of that heavenly food, they wept and sighed for fleshmeat [Nm 11:4–6]. The baseness of our appetite is such that it makes us long for our own miserable goods and feel aversion for the incommunicable heavenly good.

6. Yet, as I say, when these aridities are the outcome of the purgative way of the sensory appetite, the spirit feels the strength and energy to work, which is obtained from the substance of that interior food, even though in the beginning, for the reason just mentioned, it may not experience the savor. This food is the beginning of a contemplation that is dark and dry to the senses. Ordinarily this contemplation, which is secret and hidden from the very one who receives it, imparts to the soul, together with the dryness and emptiness it produces in the senses, an inclination to remain alone and in quietude. And the soul will be unable to dwell on any particular thought, nor will it have the desire to do so.

---

10. Cf. A. 2, 17, 5.

THE DARK NIGHT

If those in whom this occurs know how to remain quiet, without care or solicitude about any interior or exterior work, they will soon in that unconcern and idleness delicately experience the interior nourishment. This refection is so delicate that usually if the soul desires or tries to experience it, it cannot. For, as I say, this contemplation is active while the soul is in idleness and unconcern. It is like air that escapes when one tries to grasp it in one's hand.

7. In this sense we can interpret what the spouse said to the bride in the Song of Songs: *Turn your eyes from me, because they make me fly away* [Sg 6:4]. God conducts the soul along so different a path, and so puts it in this state that a desire to work with the faculties would hinder rather than help His work; whereas in the beginning of the spiritual life everything was quite the contrary.

The reason is that now in this state of contemplation, when the soul has left discursive meditation and entered the state of proficients, it is God who works in it. He therefore binds the interior faculties and leaves no support in the intellect, nor satisfaction in the will, nor remembrance in the memory. At this time a person's own efforts are of no avail, but an obstacle to the interior peace and work God is producing in the spirit through that dryness of sense. Since this peace is something spiritual and delicate, its fruit is quiet, delicate, solitary, satisfying, and peaceful, and far removed from all the other gratifications of beginners, which are very palpable and sensory. For this is the peace that David says God speaks in the soul in order to make it spiritual [Ps 85:9]. The third sign follows from this one.

8. The third sign for the discernment of this purgation of the senses is the powerlessness, in spite of one's efforts, to meditate and make use of the imagination, the interior sense, as was one's previous custom. At this time God does not communicate Himself through the senses as He did before, by means of the discursive analysis and synthesis of ideas, but begins to communicate Himself through pure spirit by an act of simple contemplation, in which there is no discursive succession of thought. The exterior and interior senses of the lower part of the soul cannot attain to this contemplation. As a result the imaginative power and phantasy can no longer rest in any consideration or find support in it.

9. From the third sign it can be deduced that this dissatisfaction of the faculties is not the fruit of any bad humor. For if it were, people would be able with a little care to return to their former exercises and find support for their faculties when that humor passed away, for it is

by its nature changeable. In the purgation of the appetite this return is not possible, because on entering it the powerlessness to meditate always continues. It is true, though, that at times in the beginning the purgation of some souls is not continuous in such a way that they are always deprived of sensory satisfaction and the ability to meditate. Perhaps, because of their weakness, they cannot be weaned all at once. Nevertheless, if they are to advance, they will ever enter further into the purgation and leave further behind their work of the senses. Those who do not walk the road of contemplation act very differently. This night of the aridity of the senses is not so continuous in them, for sometimes they experience the aridities and at other times not, and sometimes they can meditate and at other times they cannot. God places them in this night solely to exercise and humble them, and reform their appetite lest in their spiritual life they foster a harmful attraction toward sweetness. But He does not do so in order to lead them to the life of the spirit, which is contemplation. For God does not bring to contemplation all those who purposely exercise themselves in the way of the spirit, nor even half. Why? He best knows. As a result He never completely weans their senses from the breasts of considerations and discursive meditations, except for some short periods and at certain seasons, as we said.

Chapter Ten

The conduct required of souls in this dark night.

1. At the time of the aridities of this sensory night, God makes the exchange we mentioned by withdrawing the soul from the life of the senses and placing it in that of spirit—that is, He brings it from meditation to contemplation—where the soul no longer has the power to work or meditate with its faculties on the things of God. Spiritual persons suffer considerable affliction in this night, owing not so much to the aridities they undergo as to their fear of having gone astray. Since they do not find any support or satisfaction in good things, they believe there will be no more spiritual blessings for them and that God has abandoned them. They then grow weary and strive, as was their custom, to concentrate their faculties with some satisfaction on a subject of meditation, and they think that if they do not do this and do not feel

that they are at work, they are doing nothing. This effort of theirs is accompanied by an interior reluctance and repugnance on the part of the soul, for it would be pleased to dwell in that quietude and idleness without working with the faculties.

They consequently impair God's work and do not profit by their own. In searching for spirit, they lose the spirit which was the source of their tranquillity and peace. They are like someone who turns from what has already been done in order to do it again, or like one who leaves a city only to reenter it, or they are like a hunter who abandons the prey in order to go hunting again. It is useless, then, for the soul to try to meditate because it will no longer profit by this exercise.

2. If there is no one to understand these persons, they either turn back and abandon the road or lose courage, or at least they hinder their own progress because of their excessive diligence in treading the path of discursive meditation. They fatigue and overwork themselves, thinking that they are failing because of their negligences or sins. Meditation is now useless for them because God is conducting them along another road, which is contemplation and which is very different from the first. For the one road belongs to discursive meditation and the other is beyond the range of the imagination and discursive reflection.

3. Those who are in this situation should feel comforted; they ought to persevere patiently and not be afflicted. Let them trust in God who does not fail those who seek Him with a simple and righteous heart; nor will He fail to impart what is needful for the way until getting them to the clear and pure light of love. God will give them this light by means of that other night, the night of spirit, if they merit that He place them in it.

4. The attitude necessary in the night of sense is to pay no attention to discursive meditation since this is not the time for it. They should allow the soul to remain in rest and quietude even though it may seem very obvious to them that they are doing nothing and wasting time, and even though they think this disinclination to think about anything is due to their laxity. Through patience and perseverance in prayer, they will be doing a great deal without activity on their part. All that is required of them here is freedom of soul, that they liberate themselves from the impediment and fatigue of ideas and thoughts and care not about thinking and meditating. They must be content simply with a loving and peaceful attentiveness to God, and live without the concern, without the effort, and without the desire to taste or feel Him. All these

desires disquiet the soul and distract it from the peaceful quiet and sweet idleness of the contemplation that is being communicated to it.[11]

5. And even though more scruples come to the fore concerning the loss of time and the advantages of doing something else, since it cannot do anything nor think of anything in prayer, the soul should endure them peacefully, as though going to prayer means remaining in ease and freedom of spirit. If individuals were to desire to do something themselves with their faculties, they would hinder and lose the goods that God engraves on their souls through that peace and idleness. If a model for the painting or retouching of a portrait should move because of a desire to do something, the artist would be unable to finish, and the work would be spoiled. Similarly, any operation, affection, or advertency a soul might desire when it wants to abide in interior peace and idleness would cause distraction and disquietude, and make it feel sensory dryness and emptiness. The more a person seeks some support in knowledge and affection the more the soul will feel the lack of these, for this support cannot be supplied through these sensory means.

6. Accordingly, people should not mind if the operations of their faculties are being lost to them; they should desire rather that this be done quickly so that they themselves may be no obstacle to the operations of the infused contemplation that God is bestowing, that they may receive it with more peaceful plenitude and make room in their spirits for the enkindling and burning of the love that this dark and secret contemplation bears and communicates to the soul. For contemplation is nothing else than a secret and peaceful and loving inflow of God, which, if not hampered, fires the soul in the spirit of love, as is brought out in the following verse:

Fired with love's urgent longings.

Chapter Eleven
[Explains three verses of the stanza.]

1. The fire of love is not commonly felt at the outset, either because it does not have a chance to take hold, owing to the impurity of the sen-

---

11. The night insofar as it is produced by contemplation is identical with the general loving knowledge as presented in A. 2, 13–16.

sory part, or because the soul for want of understanding has not made within itself a peaceful place for it; although at times with or without these conditions a person will begin to feel a certain longing for God. In the measure that the fire increases, the soul becomes aware of being attracted by the love of God and enkindled in it, without knowing how or where this attraction and love originates. At times this flame and enkindling increases to such an extent that the soul desires God with urgent longings of love, as David, while in this night, said of himself: *Because my heart was inflamed* (in contemplative love), *my reins were likewise changed* [Ps 73:21]. That is, my appetites of sensible affection were changed from the sensory life to the spiritual life, which implies dryness and cessation of all those appetites we are speaking of. *And*, he says, *I was brought to nothing and annihilated, and I knew not* [Ps 73:22]. For, as we pointed out, the soul, with no knowledge of its destination, sees itself annihilated in all heavenly and earthly things in which it formerly found satisfaction. And it only sees that it is enamored, but knows not how.

Because the enkindling of love in the spirit sometimes increases exceedingly, the longings for God become so intense that it will seem to individuals that their bones are drying up in this thirst, their nature withering away, and their ardor and strength diminishing through the liveliness of the thirst of love. They will feel that this is a living thirst. David also had such experience when he proclaimed: *My soul thirsts for the living God* [Ps 42:3], as though to say, this thirst my soul experiences is a living thirst. Since this thirst is alive, we can assert that it is a thirst that kills. Yet it should be noted that its vehemence is not continual, but only experienced from time to time; although usually some thirst is felt.

2. Yet it must be kept in mind that, as I explained before, people generally do not perceive this love in the beginning, but they experience rather the dryness and void we are speaking of. Then, instead of this love that is afterward enkindled, they will, in the midst of the dryness and emptiness of their faculties, harbor a habitual care and solicitude for God accompanied by grief or fear about not serving Him. A spirit in distress and solicitude for His love is a sacrifice most pleasing to God.

Secret contemplation produces this solicitude and concern in the soul until, after having somewhat purged the sensory part of its natural propensities by means of this aridity, it begins to enkindle in the spirit this divine love. Meanwhile, however, as in one who is undergoing a cure, all is suffering in this dark and dry purgation of the appetite, and

THE DARK NIGHT

the soul being relieved of numerous imperfections acquires many virtues, thereby becoming capable of this love, as will be shown in the explanation of the following verse:

—Ah, the sheer grace!—

3. God introduces people into this night to purge their senses and accommodate, subject, and unite the lower part of their souls to the spiritual part by darkening it and causing a cessation of discursive meditation, just as afterward in order to purify the spirit and unite it to Himself, He brings it into the spiritual night. As a result, they gain so many benefits—though at the time this may not be apparent—that they consider their departure from the fetters and straits of the senses a sheer grace. The verse therefore proclaims: "Ah, the sheer grace!"

We ought to point out the benefits procured in this night,[12] for it is because of them that the soul says it was a sheer grace to have passed through this night. All these benefits are included in the next verse:

I went out unseen.

4. This going out bears reference to the subjection the soul had to its senses, in seeking God through operations so feeble, limited, and exposed to error as are those of this lower part. At every step the soul stumbled into numerous imperfections and much ignorance as was noted above in relation to the seven capital vices. This night frees the soul from all these vices by quenching all its earthly and heavenly satisfactions, darkening its discursive meditations, and producing in it other innumerable goods through the acquisition of the virtues, as we will now explain. For it will please and comfort one who treads this path to know that a way seemingly so rough and adverse and contrary to spiritual gratification engenders so many blessings.

These blessings are attained when the soul departs from all created things, in its affection and operation, by means of this night and marches on toward eternal things. This is a great happiness and grace: first, because of the signal benefit of quenching one's appetite and affection for all things; second, because there are very few who will endure the night and persevere in entering through this small gate and in treading this narrow road that leads to life, as our Savior says [Mt 7:14]. . . .

---

12. Here he begins a new theme: the benefits or fruits of the purgation. The basic benefit

THE DARK NIGHT

Chapter Twelve

The benefits this night causes in the soul.

1. This glad night and purgation causes many benefits, even though the soul thinks it is being deprived of them. So numerous are these benefits that, just as Abraham made a great feast on the day of his son Isaac's weaning [Gn 21:8], there is rejoicing in heaven: that God now has taken from this soul its swaddling clothes; that He has put it down from His arms and is making it walk alone; that He is weaning it from the delicate and sweet food of infants and making it eat bread with crust; and that the soul is beginning to taste the food of the strong (the infused contemplation of which we have spoken), which in these sensory aridities and darknesses is given to the spirit that is dry and empty of the satisfactions of sense.

2. The first and chief benefit that this dry and dark night of contemplation causes is the knowledge of self and of one's own misery. Besides the fact that all the favors God imparts to the soul are ordinarily enwrapped in this knowledge, the aridities and voids of the faculties in relation to the abundance previously experienced, and the difficulty encountered in the practice of virtue, make the soul recognize its own lowliness and misery, which was not apparent in the time of its prosperity.

There is a good figure of this in Exodus where God, desiring to humble the children of Israel and make them know themselves, ordered them to remove their festive garments and adornments which they were ordinarily wearing in the desert: *From now on leave aside your festive ornaments and put on common working garments that you may be aware of the treatment you deserve* [Ex 33:5]. This was like saying: Since the clothing you wear, being of festivity and mirth, is an occasion for your not feeling as lowly as you in fact are, put it aside so that seeing the foulness of your dress you may know yourself and your deserts.

As a result the soul recognizes the truth about its misery, of which it was formerly ignorant. When it was walking in festivity, gratification, consolation, and support in God, it was more content, believing that it was serving God in some way. Though this idea of serving God may not be explicitly formed in one's mind, at least some notion of it

---

is the knowledge of self and of God (ch. 12). The other benefits (ch. 13) are the virtues opposite the imperfections of beginners of which he spoke.

THE DARK NIGHT

is deeply embedded within owing to the satisfaction derived from one's spiritual exercises. Now that the soul is clothed in these other garments of labor, dryness, and desolation, and that its former lights have been darkened, it possesses more authentic lights in this most excellent and necessary virtue of self-knowledge. It considers itself to be nothing and finds no satisfaction in self because it is aware that of itself it neither does nor can do anything.

God esteems this lack of self-satisfaction and the dejection individuals have about not serving Him more than all former deeds and gratifications, however notable these may have been, since they were the occasion of many imperfections and a great deal of ignorance. Not only the benefits we mentioned result from this garment of dryness but also those of which we will now speak, and many more, for they flow from self-knowledge as from their fount.

3. First, individuals commune with God more respectfully and courteously, the way one should always converse with the Most High. In the prosperity of their satisfaction and consolation as beginners, they did not act thus, for that satisfying delight made them somewhat more daring with God than was proper, and more discourteous and inconsiderate. This is what happened to Moses: When he heard God speaking to him, he was blinded by that gratification and desire and without any further thought would have dared to approach God if he had not been ordered to stop and take off his shoes [Ex 3:4–5]. This instance denotes the respect and discretion, the nakedness of appetite, with which one ought to commune with God. Consequently when Moses was obedient to this command, he was so discreet and cautious that Scripture says he not only dared not approach but did not even dare look [Ex 3:6; Acts 7:32]. Having left aside the shoes of his appetites and gratifications, he became fully aware of his misery in the sight of God; for this was the manner in which it was fitting for him to hear God's word.

Similarly, Job was not prepared for converse with God by means of those delights and glories of which he tells he was accustomed to experience in his God. But the preparation for this converse embodied the following: nakedness on a dunghill; abandonment and even persecution by his friends; the fullness of anguish and bitterness; and the sight of the earth round about him covered with worms [Jb 2:8, 30:17–18]. Yet then the most high God, He who raises the poor from the dunghill [Ps 113:7], was pleased to descend and speak face to face with Job and reveal the deep mysteries of His wisdom, which He never did before in the time of Job's prosperity [Jb 38–41].

THE DARK NIGHT

4. Since this is the proper moment, we ought to point out another benefit resulting from this night and dryness of the sensory appetite. So that the prophecy—*Your light will illumine the darkness* [Is 58:10]—may be verified, God will give illumination by bestowing on the soul not only knowledge of its own misery and lowliness but also knowledge of His grandeur and majesty. When the sensory appetites, gratifications, and supports are quenched, the intellect is left limpid and free to understand the truth. For even though these concern spiritual things they blind and impede the spirit. Similarly the anguish and dryness of the senses illumine and quicken the intellect, as Isaiah affirms: *Vexation makes one understand* [Is 28:19]. But God also, by means of this dark and dry night of contemplation, supernaturally instructs in His divine wisdom the soul that is empty and unhindered (which is the requirement for His divine inflow), which He did not do through the former satisfactions and pleasures.

5. Isaiah explains this clearly: *To whom shall God teach His knowledge? And to whom shall He explain His message? To them that are weaned,* he says, *from the milk, and to them who are drawn away from the breasts* [Is 28:9]. This passage indicates that the preparation for this divine influx is not the former milk of spiritual sweetness or aid from the breast of the discursive meditations of the sensory faculties that the soul enjoyed, but the privation of the one and a withdrawal from the other.

In order to hear God, people should stand firm and be detached in their sense life and affections, as the prophet himself declares: *I will stand on my watch* (with detached appetite) *and will fix my foot* (I will not meditate with the sensory faculties) *in order to contemplate* (understand) *what God says to me* [Hb 2:1].

We conclude that self-knowledge flows first from this dry night, and that from this knowledge as from its source proceeds the other knowledge of God. Hence St. Augustine said to God: *Let me know myself, Lord, and I will know You.*[13] For as the philosophers say, one extreme is clearly known by the other.[14]

6. For a more complete proof of the efficacy of this sensory night in further occasioning through its dryness and destitution the light here received from God, we will quote that passage from David in which the great power of this night in relation to the lofty knowledge of God is

---
13. *Soliloquia* 2, 1, 1 (Migne PL 32, 885).
14. Cf. A. 1, 4, 2, note 10; N. 1, 4, 7, note 7.

clearly shown. He proclaims: *In a desert land, without water, dry, and without a way, I appeared before You to be able to see Your power and Your glory* [Ps 63:2–3]. David's teaching here is admirable: that the means to the knowledge of the glory of God were not the many spiritual delights and gratifications he had received, but the sensory aridities and detachments referred to by the dry and desert land. And it is also wonderful that, as he says, the way to the experience and vision of the power of God did not consist in ideas and meditations about God, of which he had made extensive use, but embodied his inability both to grasp God with ideas and to walk by means of discursive, imaginative meditation. This inability is referred to by the land without a way.

Hence the dark night with its aridities and voids is the means to the knowledge of God and self, although the knowledge given in this night is not as plenteous and abundant as that of the other night of spirit, for the knowledge of this night is as it were the foundation of the other.[15]

7. In the dryness and emptiness of this night of the appetite, a person also procures spiritual humility, that virtue opposed to the first capital vice, spiritual pride. Through this humility acquired by means of self-knowledge, individuals are purged of all those imperfections of the vice of pride into which they fell in the time of their prosperity. Aware of their own dryness and wretchedness, the thought of their being more advanced than others does not even occur in its first movements, as it did before; on the contrary, they realize that others are better.

8. From this humility stems love of neighbor, for they will esteem them and not judge them as they did before when they were aware that they enjoyed an intense fervor while others did not.

These persons will know only their own misery and keep it so much in sight that they will have no opportunity to watch anyone else's conduct. David while in this night gives an admirable manifestation of such a state of soul: *I became dumb and was humbled, and I kept silent in good things, and my sorrow was renewed* [Ps 38:3]. He says this because it seemed to him that his blessings had so come to an end that not only was he unable to find words for them, but he also became silent concerning his neighbor, in the sorrow he experienced from the knowledge of his own misery.

---

15. The first editor, who divided this commentary into chapters, should have ended Chapter 12 here. John now takes up the subject of the particular benefits and continues dealing with them in Chapter 13.

9. These individuals also become submissive and obedient in their spiritual journey. Since they are so aware of their own wretchedness, they not only listen to the teaching of others but even desire to be directed and told what to do by anyone at all.

The affective presumption they sometimes had in their prosperity leaves them. And, finally, as they proceed on their journey, all the other imperfections of this first vice, spiritual pride, are swept away.

Chapter Thirteen
Other benefits of this night of senses.

1. In this arid and obscure night the soul undergoes a thorough reform in its imperfections of avarice, in which it coveted various spiritual objects and was never content with any of its spiritual exercises because of the gratification derived from them and the covetousness of its appetite. Since it does not obtain the delight it formerly did in its spiritual practices, but rather finds them distasteful and laborious, it uses them so moderately that now perhaps it might fail through defect rather than excess. Nevertheless, God usually imparts to those whom He brings into this night the humility and the readiness, even though they feel displeasure, to do what is commanded of them for His sake alone, and they become detached from many things because of this lack of gratification.

2. It is also evident regarding spiritual lust that through the sensory dryness and distaste experienced in its spiritual exercises, the soul is freed of those impurities we noted. For we said that they ordinarily proceed from the delight of the spirit redounding in the senses.

3. The imperfections of the fourth vice, spiritual gluttony, from which a person is freed in this dark night are listed above, although not all of them since they are innumerable. Thus I will not refer to them here, since I am anxious to conclude this dark night in order to pass on to the important doctrine we have concerning the other night.

To understand the countless benefits gained from this night in regard to the vice of spiritual gluttony, let it suffice to say that the soul is liberated from all the imperfections we mentioned and from many other greater evils and foul abominations, not listed, into which many have fallen, as we know from experience, because they did not reform their desire for this spiritual sweetness.

THE DARK NIGHT

God so curbs concupiscence and bridles the appetite through this arid and dark night that the soul cannot feast on any sensory delight from earthly or heavenly things, and He continues this purgation in such a way that the concupiscence and the appetites are brought into subjection, reformed, and mortified. The passions, as a result, lose their strength and become sterile from not receiving any satisfaction, just as the courses of the udder dry up when milk is not drawn through them daily.

Once the soul's appetites have withered, and it lives in spiritual sobriety, admirable benefits besides those mentioned result. For when the appetites and concupiscences are quenched, the soul dwells in spiritual peace and tranquillity. Where neither the appetites nor concupiscence reign, there is no disturbance but only God's peace and consolation.

4. A second benefit following on this one is that the soul bears a habitual remembrance of God, accompanied by a fear and dread of turning back on the spiritual road. This is a notable benefit and by no means one of the least in this dryness and purgation of the appetite, because the soul is purified of the imperfections which of themselves make it dull and dark, and cling to it by means of appetites and affections.

5. Another very great benefit for the soul in this night is that it exercises all the virtues together. In the patience and forbearance practiced in these voids and aridities, and through perseverance in its spiritual exercises without consolation or satisfaction, the soul practices the love of God, since it is no longer motivated by the attractive and savory gratification it finds in its work but only by God. It also practices the virtue of fortitude because it draws strength from weakness in the difficulties and aversions experienced in its work, and thus becomes strong. Finally, in these aridities the soul practices corporally and spiritually all the virtues, theological as well as cardinal and moral.

6. David affirms that a person obtains in this night these four benefits: the delight of peace; a habitual remembrance of God, and solicitude concerning Him; cleanness and purity of soul; and the practice of virtue. For David himself had this experience on enduring the night: *My soul refused consolations, I remembered God and found consolation, and exercised myself, and my soul swooned away* [Ps 77:3–4]; and then he adds: *I meditated at night in my heart, and I exercised myself, and swept and purified my spirit* (of all its imperfections) [Ps 77:7].

7. In relation to the imperfections of the other three vices (anger,

envy, and sloth), the soul is also purged in this dryness of appetite, and it acquires the virtues to which these vices are opposed. Softened and humbled by aridities and hardships and by other temptations and trials in which God exercises the soul in the course of this night,[16] individuals become meek toward God and themselves and also toward their neighbor. As a result, they will no longer become impatiently angry with themselves and their faults or with their neighbor's faults. Neither are they displeased or disrespectfully querulous with God for not making them perfect quickly.

8. As for envy, they will also be charitable toward others. For if they do have envy, it will not be vicious as before, when they were distressed that others were preferred to them and more advanced. Now, aware of how miserable they are, they are willing to concede that others are more advanced. The envy they have—if they do have any—is a holy envy that desires to imitate others, which indicates solid virtue.

9. The sloth and tedium they feel in spiritual things are not vicious as before. Previously this sloth was the outcome of the spiritual gratification they either enjoyed or tried to obtain when it was not experienced. But the tedium experienced now does not flow from any weakness relative to sensory gratification, for in this purgation of the appetite God takes from the soul all its satisfaction.

10. Besides these benefits, innumerable others flow from this dry contemplation. In the midst of these aridities and straits, God frequently communicates to the soul, when it least expects, spiritual sweetness, a very pure love, and a spiritual knowledge that is sometimes most delicate.[17] Each of these communications is more valuable than all that the soul previously sought. Yet in the beginning one will not think so, because the spiritual inflow is very delicate and the senses do not perceive it.

11. Finally, insofar as individuals are purged of their sensory affections and appetites, they obtain liberty of spirit in which they acquire the twelve fruits of the Holy Spirit.

They are also wondrously liberated from the hands of their ene-

---

16. There are other means (hardships, temptations, and trials) by which this passive purification is effected in addition to what is brought about through the contemplative purgation. The general principles are open to many possibilities in individual experience.

17. In the passage through the passive night of the senses there are alternating periods of dry and obscure contemplation and of the serene and loving contemplation he speaks of in the A. 2, 13–15.

mies, the world, the flesh, and the devil. For when the sensory delight and gratification coming from things are quenched, neither the devil, nor the world, nor sensuality has arms or power against the spirit.

12. These aridities, then, make people walk with purity in the love of God. No longer are they moved to act by the delight and satisfaction they find in a work, as they perhaps were when they derived this from their deeds, but by the desire to please God. They are neither presumptuous nor self-satisfied, as was their custom in the time of their prosperity, but fearful and disquieted about themselves and lacking in any self-satisfaction. This is the holy fear that preserves and gives increase to the virtues.

This dryness also quenches the natural concupiscences and vigor, as we also said. Were it not for the satisfaction God Himself sometimes infuses, it would be a wonder if the soul through its own diligence could get any sensible gratification or consolation out of its spiritual works and exercises.

13. In this arid night solicitude for God and yearnings about serving Him increase. Since the sensory breasts (through which the appetites pursued by these souls were sustained and nurtured) gradually dry up, only the anxiety about serving God remains, in dryness and nakedness. These yearnings are very pleasing to God, since as David proclaims: *The afflicted spirit is a sacrifice to God* [Ps 51:19].

14. Since the soul knows that from this dry purgation, through which it passed, it procured so many and such precious benefits, as are those referred to here, the verse of this stanza is no exaggeration: "Ah, the sheer grace!—I went out unseen." That is, I went out from subjection to my sensory appetites and affections unseen, so that the three enemies were unable to stop me. These enemies entrap the soul—as with snares—in its appetites and gratifications and keep it from going forth to the freedom of the love of God. But without these satisfactions and appetites the enemies cannot fight against the soul.

15. Having calmed the four passions (joy, sorrow, hope, and fear) through constant mortification, and having lulled to sleep the natural sensory appetites, and having achieved harmony in the interior senses by discontinuing discursive operations (all of which pertains to the household or dwelling of the lower part of the soul, here referred to as its house), the soul says:

My house being now all stilled.

THE DARK NIGHT

When this house of the senses was stilled, that is, mortified, its passions quenched, and its appetites calmed and put to sleep through this happy night of the purgation of the senses, the soul went out in order to begin its journey along the road of the spirit, which is that of proficients and which by another terminology is referred to as the illuminative way or the way of infused contemplation, in which God Himself pastures and refreshes the soul without any of its own discursive meditation or active help.

* * *

[Book Two]

[The more intimate purgation, which is the night of the spirit.]

* * *

Chapter Three

An explanation of what is to follow.

1. These souls, then, are now proficients. Their senses have been fed with sweet communications so that, allured by the gratification flowing from the spirit, they could be accommodated and united to the spirit. Each part of the soul can now in its own way receive nourishment from the same spiritual food and from the same dish of only one *suppositum* and subject. These two parts thus united and conformed are jointly prepared to suffer the rough and arduous purgation of the spirit which awaits them. In this purgation, these two portions of the soul will undergo complete purification, for one part is never adequately purged without the other. The real purgation of the senses begins with the spirit. Hence the night of the senses we explained should be called a certain reformation and bridling of the appetite rather than a purgation. The reason is that all the imperfections and disorders of the sensory part are rooted in the spirit and from it receive their strength. All good and evil habits reside in the spirit and until these habits are purged, the senses cannot be completely purified of their rebellions and vices.

2. In this night that follows, both parts are jointly purified. This was the purpose of the reformation of the first night and the calm that resulted from it: that the sensory part united in a certain way with the spirit might undergo the purgation and suffering with greater fortitude. Such is the fortitude necessary for so strong and arduous a purgation that if the lower part in its weakness is not reformed first, and afterward

strengthened in God through the experience of sweet and delightful communion with Him, it has neither the fortitude nor the preparedness to endure it.

3. These proficients are still very lowly and natural in their communion with God and in their activity directed toward Him because the gold of the spirit is not purified and illumined. They still think of God and speak of Him as little children, and their knowledge and experience of Him is like that of little children, as St. Paul asserts [1 Cor 13:11]. The reason is that they have not reached perfection, which is union of the soul with God. Through this union, as full-grown persons, they do mighty works in their spirit, since their faculties and works are more divine than human, as we will point out. Wishing to strip them in fact of this old man and clothe them with the new, which is created according to God in the newness of sense, as the Apostle says [Col 3:9–10; Eph 4:22–24], God divests the faculties, affections, and senses, both spiritual and sensory, interior and exterior. He leaves the intellect in darkness, the will in aridity, the memory in emptiness, and the affections in supreme affliction, bitterness, and anguish, by depriving the soul of the feeling and satisfaction it previously obtained from spiritual blessings. For this privation is one of the conditions required that the spiritual form, which is the union of love, may be introduced into the spirit and united with it. The Lord works all of this in the soul by means of a pure and dark contemplation, as is indicated in the first stanza. Although we explained this stanza in reference to the first night of the senses, the soul understands it mainly in relation to this second night of the spirit, since this night is the principal purification of the soul. With this in mind we will quote it and explain it again.[18]

Chapter Four

[The first stanza and its commentary.]

One dark night,
Fired with love's urgent longings
—Ah, the sheer grace!—

---

18. The poem beginning with the first stanza speaks chiefly of this passive night of the spirit.

THE DARK NIGHT

> I went out unseen,
> My house being now all stilled.

Commentary

1. Understanding this stanza now to refer to contemplative purgation or nakedness and poverty of spirit (which are all about the same), we can thus explain it, as though the soul says:

Poor, abandoned, and unsupported by any of the apprehensions of my soul (in the darkness of my intellect, the distress of my will, and in the affliction and anguish of my memory), left to darkness in pure faith, which is a dark night for these natural faculties, and with only my will touched by the sorrows, afflictions, and longings of love of God, I went out from myself. That is, I departed from my low manner of understanding, and my feeble way of loving, and my poor and limited method of finding satisfaction in God. I did this unhindered by either the flesh or the devil.

2. This was great happiness and a sheer grace for me, because through the annihilation and calming of my faculties, passions, appetites, and affections, by which my experience and satisfaction in God was base, I went out from my human operation and way of acting to God's operation and way of acting. That is, my intellect departed from itself, changing from human and natural to divine. For, united with God through this purgation, it no longer understands by means of its natural vigor and light but by means of the divine wisdom to which it was united.

And my will departed from itself and became divine. United with the divine love, it no longer loves in a lowly manner, with its natural strength, but with the strength and purity of the Holy Spirit; and thus the will does not operate humanly in relation to God.

And finally, all the strength and affections of the soul, by means of this night and purgation of the old man, are renewed with divine qualities and delights.

Chapter Five

Begins to explain how this dark contemplation is not only night for the soul but also affliction and torment.

1. This dark night is an inflow of God into the soul that purges it of its

THE DARK NIGHT

habitual ignorances and imperfections, natural and spiritual, and which contemplatives call infused contemplation or mystical theology.[19] Through this contemplation, God teaches the soul secretly and instructs it in the perfection of love without its doing anything or understanding how this happens.

Insofar as infused contemplation is loving wisdom of God, it produces two principal effects in the soul: It prepares the soul for the union with God through love by both purging and illumining it. Hence the same loving wisdom that purges and illumines the blessed spirits purges and illumines the soul here on earth.

2. Yet a doubt arises: Why, if it is a divine light (for it illumines souls and purges them of their ignorances), does one call it a dark night? In answer to this, there are two reasons why this divine wisdom is not only night and darkness for the soul, but also affliction and torment. First, because of the height of the divine wisdom, which exceeds the capacity of the soul. Second, because of the soul's baseness and impurity; and on this account the wisdom is painful, afflictive, and also dark for the soul.

3. To prove the first reason, we must presuppose a certain principle of the Philosopher: that the clearer and more obvious divine things are in themselves, the darker and more hidden they are to the soul naturally. The brighter the light the more the owl is blinded; and the more one looks at the brilliant sun, the more the sun darkens the faculty of sight, deprives it and overwhelms it in its weakness.[20]

Hence when the divine light of contemplation strikes souls not yet entirely illumined, it causes spiritual darkness, for it not only surpasses them but also deprives and darkens their act of understanding. This is why St. Dionysius and other mystical theologians call this infused contemplation a ray of darkness; that is, for the soul not yet illumined and purged.[21] For this great supernatural light overwhelms the intellect and deprives it of its natural vigor.

David also said that clouds and darkness are near God and surround Him [Ps 18:12], not because this is true in itself but because it appears thus to our weak intellects, which in being unable to attain so

---

19. In identifying the dark night with infused contemplation or mystical theology, John is mainly considering the cause or root of the night, not its effects. Cf. A. 2, 8, 6, note 10.
20. Aristotle, *Metaphysica* 2, 1. Cf. A. 2, 8, 6, note 11.
21. Dionysius the Pseudo-Areopagite, *De Mystica theologia* 1, 1 (Migne PG 3, 999).

THE DARK NIGHT

bright a light are blinded and darkened. Hence, he immediately added: *Clouds passed before the great splendor of His presence* [Ps 18:12], that is, between God and our intellect. As a result, when God communicates this bright ray of His secret wisdom to the soul not yet transformed, He causes thick darkness in its intellect.

4. It is also evident that this dark contemplation is painful to the soul in these beginnings. Since this divine infused contemplation has many extremely good properties, and the still unpurged soul that receives it has many extreme miseries, and because two contraries cannot coexist in one subject, the soul must necessarily undergo affliction and suffering. Because of the purgation of its imperfections caused by this contemplation, the soul becomes a battlefield in which these two contraries combat one another. We will prove this by induction in the following way.

5. In regard to the first cause of one's affliction: Because the light and wisdom of this contemplation is very bright and pure, and the soul in which it shines is dark and impure, a person will be deeply afflicted on receiving it. When eyes are sickly, impure, and weak, they suffer pain if a bright light shines on them.

The soul, because of its impurity, suffers immensely at the time this divine light truly assails it. When this pure light strikes in order to expel all impurity, persons feel so unclean and wretched that it seems God is against them and they are against God.

Because it seems that God has rejected them, these souls suffer such pain and grief that when God tried Job in this way it proved one of the worst of Job's trials, as he says: *Why have you set me against you, and I am heavy and burdensome to myself?* [Jb 7:20]. Clearly beholding its impurity by means of this pure light, although in darkness, the soul understands distinctly that it is worthy neither of God nor of any creature. And what most grieves it is that it thinks it will never be worthy, and that there are no more blessings for it. This divine and dark light causes deep immersion of the mind in the knowledge and feeling of one's own miseries and evils; it brings all these miseries into relief so that the soul sees clearly that of itself it will never possess anything else. We can interpret that passage from David in this sense: *You have corrected people for their iniquity and have undone and consumed their souls, as a spider is eviscerated in its work* [Ps 39:12].

6. Souls suffer affliction in the second manner because of their natural, moral, and spiritual weakness. Since this divine contemplation assails them somewhat forcibly in order to subdue and strengthen their

soul, they suffer so much in their weakness that they almost die, particularly at times when the light is more powerful. Both the sense and the spirit, as though under an immense and dark load, undergo such agony and pain that the soul would consider death a relief. The prophet Job, having experienced this, declared: *I do not want Him to commune with me with much strength that He might not overwhelm me with the weight of His greatness* [Jb 23:6].

7. Under the stress of this oppression and weight, individuals feel so far from all favor that they think, and so it is, that even that which previously upheld them has ended along with everything else, and that there is no one who will take pity on them. It is in this sense that Job also cried out: *Have pity on me, at least you my friends, for the hand of the Lord has touched me* [Jb 19:21].

How amazing and pitiful it is that the soul be so utterly weak and impure that the hand of God, though light and gentle, should feel so heavy and contrary. For the hand of God does not press down or weigh on the soul, but only touches it; and this mercifully, for God's aim is to grant it favors and not chastise it.

* * *

Chapter Eight

[Other afflictions that trouble the soul.] . . .

4. This, precisely, then, is what the divine ray of contemplation does. In striking the soul with its divine light, it surpasses the natural light and thereby darkens and deprives individuals of all the natural affections and apprehensions they perceive by means of their natural light. It leaves their spiritual and natural faculties not only in darkness but in emptiness too. Leaving the soul thus empty and dark, the ray purges and illumines it with divine spiritual light, while the soul thinks it has no light and that it is in darkness, as illustrated in the case of the ray of sunlight that is invisible even in the middle of a room if the room is pure and void of any object on which the light may reflect.[22] Yet when this spiritual light finds an object on which to shine, that is, when something is to be understood spiritually concerning perfection or imper-

---

22. Cf. A. 2, 14, 9.

THE DARK NIGHT

fection, no matter how slight, or about a judgment on the truth or falsity of some matter, individuals will understand more clearly than they did before they were in this darkness. And easily recognizing the imperfection that presents itself, they grow conscious of the spiritual light they possess; for the ray of light is dark and invisible until a hand or some other thing passes through it, and then both the object and the ray are recognized. . . .

Chapter Nine

[Although this night darkens the spirit, it does so to give light.]

1. It remains to be said, then, that even though this happy night darkens the spirit, it does so only to impart light concerning all things. And even though it humbles persons and reveals their miseries, it does so only to exalt them. And even though it impoverishes and empties them of all possessions and natural affection, it does so only that they may reach out divinely to the enjoyment of all earthly and heavenly things, with a general freedom of spirit in them all.

That elements be commingled with all natural compounds, they must be unaffected by any particular color, odor, or taste, and thus they can concur with all tastes, odors, and colors. Similarly, the spirit must be simple, pure, and naked as to all natural affections, actual and habitual, in order to be able to freely communicate in fullness of spirit with the divine wisdom, in which, on account of the soul's purity, the delights of all things are tasted in a certain eminent degree. Without this purgation the soul would be wholly unable to experience the satisfaction of all this abundance of spiritual delight. Only one attachment or one particular object to which the spirit is actually or habitually bound is enough to hinder the experience or reception of the delicate and intimate delight of the spirit of love, which contains eminently in itself all delights. . . .

6. Individuals suffer these afflictive purgations of spirit that they may be reborn in the life of the spirit by means of this divine inflow, and through these sufferings the spirit of salvation is brought forth in fulfillment of the words of Isaiah: *In your presence, O Lord, we have conceived and been in the pains of labor and have brought forth the spirit of salvation* [Is 26:17–18].

Moreover, the soul should leave aside all its former peace because it is prepared by means of this contemplative night to attain inner peace, which is of such a quality and so delightful that, as the Church says, it surpasses all understanding.[23] That former peace was not truly peace, because it was clothed with many imperfections, although to the soul walking in delight it seemed to be peace. It seemed to be a twofold peace, sensory and spiritual, since the soul beheld within itself a spiritual abundance. This sensory and spiritual peace, since it is still imperfect, must first be purged; the soul's peace must be disturbed and taken away. In the passage we quoted to demonstrate the distress of this night, Jeremiah felt disturbed and wept over his loss of peace: *My soul is withdrawn and removed from peace* [Lam 3:17]. . . .

Chapter Ten

[Explains this purgation thoroughly by means of a comparison.]

1. For the sake of further clarity in this matter, we ought to note that this purgative and loving knowledge, or divine light we are speaking of, has the same effect on a soul that fire has on a log of wood. The soul is purged and prepared for union with the divine light just as the wood is prepared for transformation into the fire. Fire, when applied to wood, first dehumidifies it, dispelling all moisture and making it give off any water it contains. Then it gradually turns the wood black, makes it dark and ugly, and even causes it to emit a bad odor. By drying out the wood, the fire brings to light and expels all those ugly and dark accidents that are contrary to fire. Finally, by heating and enkindling it from without, the fire transforms the wood into itself and makes it as beautiful as the fire itself. Once transformed, the wood no longer has any activity or passivity of its own, except for its weight and its quantity, which is denser than the fire. For it possesses the properties and performs the actions of fire: it is dry and it dries; it is hot and it gives off heat; it is brilliant and it illumines; and it is also much lighter than before. It is the fire that produces all these properties in the wood.

2. Similarly, we should philosophize about this divine, loving fire

---

23. Instead of referring to Phil 4:7, he refers to the Church, probably having in mind the text as used in the Divine Office.

of contemplation. Before transforming the soul, it purges it of all contrary qualities. It produces blackness and darkness and brings to the fore the soul's ugliness; thus the soul seems worse than before and unsightly and abominable. This divine purge stirs up all the foul and vicious humors of which the soul was never before aware. Never did it realize there was so much evil in itself, for these humors were so deeply rooted. And now that they may be expelled and annihilated they are brought to light and seen clearly through the illumination of this dark light of divine contemplation. Although the soul is no worse than before, neither in itself nor in its relationship with God, it feels undoubtedly so bad as to be not only unworthy that God should see it but deserving of His abhorrence; in fact, it feels that God now does abhor it.

This comparison illustrates many of the things we have been saying.

3. First, we can understand that the very loving light and wisdom into which the soul will be transformed is that which in the beginning purges and prepares it, just as the fire which transforms the wood by incorporating it into itself is that which was first preparing it for this transformation.

4. Second, we discern that the experience of these sufferings does not derive from this wisdom—for as the Wise Man says: *All good things come to the soul together with her* [Wis 7:11]—but from the soul's own weakness and imperfection. Without this purgation it cannot receive the divine light, sweetness, and delight of wisdom, just as the log of wood until prepared cannot be transformed by the fire that is applied to it. And this is why the soul suffers so intensely. Sirach confirms our assertion by telling what he suffered in order to be united with wisdom and enjoy it: *My soul wrestled for her, and my entrails were disturbed in acquiring her; therefore shall I possess a good possession* [Sir 51:19–21].

5. Third, we can infer the manner in which souls suffer in purgatory. The fire, when applied, would be powerless over them if they did not have imperfections from which to suffer. These imperfections are the fuel that catches fire, and once they are gone there is nothing left to burn. So it is here on earth; when the imperfections are gone, the soul's suffering terminates, and joy remains.

6. Fourth, we deduce that as the soul is purged and purified by this fire of love, it is further enkindled in love, just as the wood becomes hotter as the fire prepares it. Individuals, however, do not always feel this enkindling of love. But sometimes the contemplation shines less

THE DARK NIGHT

forcibly so that they may have the opportunity of observing and rejoicing in the work being achieved, for then these good effects are revealed. It is as though one were to stop work and take the iron out of the forge to observe what is being accomplished. Thus the soul is able to perceive the good of which it was unaware while the work was proceeding. So, too, when the flame stops acting on the wood, there is a chance to see how much the wood has been enkindled by it.

7. Fifth, we can also gather from this comparison why, as we previously mentioned, the soul after this alleviation suffers again, more intensely and inwardly than before. After that manifestation and after a more exterior purification of imperfections, the fire of love returns to act more interiorly on the consumable matter of which the soul must be purified. The suffering of the soul becomes more intimate, subtle, and spiritual in proportion to the inwardness, subtlety, spiritual character, and deep-rootedness of the imperfections that are removed. This more interior purgation resembles the action of fire on wood: As the fire penetrates, its action becomes stronger and more vehement, preparing the innermost part in order to gain possession of it.

8. Sixth, we discover the reason the soul thinks that all blessings are past and that it is full of evil. For at this time it is conscious of nothing but its own bitterness; just as in the example of the wood, for neither the air nor anything else reaches it; only the consuming fire. Yet, when other manifestations like the previous are made, the soul's joy will be more interior because of the more intimate purification.

9. Seventh, we deduce that when the purification is soon to return, even though the soul's joy is ample during these intervals (so much so that it sometimes seems, as we pointed out, that the bitterness will never recur), there is a feeling, if the soul adverts (and sometimes it cannot help adverting), that some root remains. And this advertence does not allow complete joy, for it seems that the purification is threatening to assail it again. And when the soul does have this feeling, the purification soon returns. Finally, that more inward part still to be purged and illumined cannot be completely concealed by the portion already purified, just as there is a very perceptible difference between that inmost part of the wood still to be illumined and that which is already purged. When this purification returns to attack more interiorly, it is no wonder that once again the soul thinks all its good has come to an end and that its blessings are over. Placed in these more interior sufferings, it is blinded as to all exterior good.

10. With this example in mind as well as the explanation of verse

THE DARK NIGHT

1 of the first stanza concerning this dark night and its terrible traits, it will be a good thing to leave these sad experiences and begin now to discuss the fruit of the soul's tears and the happy traits about which it begins to sing in the second verse:

> Fired with love's ugent longings.

Chapter Eleven

[The beginning of an explanation of verse 2 of the first stanza. Tells how the fruit of these dark straits is a vehement passion of divine love.]

1. In this second verse the soul refers to the fire of love that, like material fire acting on wood, penetrates it in this night of painful contemplation. Although this enkindling of love we are now discussing is in some way similar to that which occurs in the sensory part of the soul, it is as different from it in another way as is the soul from the body, or the spiritual part from the sensory part. For the enkindling of love occurs in the spirit and through it the soul in the midst of these dark conflicts feels vividly and keenly that it is being wounded by a strong divine love, and it has a certain feeling and foretaste of God. Yet it understands nothing in particular, for as we said the intellect is in darkness.

2. The spirit herein experiences an impassioned and intense love because this spiritual inflaming engenders the passion of love. Since this love is infused, it is more passive than active and thus generates in the soul a strong passion of love. This love is now beginning to possess something of union with God and thereby shares to a certain extent in its properties. These properties are actions of God more than of the soul, and they reside in it passively, although the soul does give its consent. But only the love of God, which is being united to the soul, imparts the heat, strength, temper, and passion of love, or fire, as the soul terms it here. The more the soul is equipped to receive the wound and union the more this love finds that all the soul's appetites are brought into subjection, alienated, incapacitated, and unable to be satisfied by any heavenly or earthly thing.

3. This happens very particularly in this dark purgation, as we said, since God so weans and recollects the appetites that they cannot

THE DARK NIGHT

find satisfaction in any of their objects. God proceeds thus so that by withdrawing the appetites from other objects and recollecting them in Himself, He may strengthen the soul and give it the capacity for this strong union of love, which He begins to accord by means of this purgation. In this union the soul will love God intensely with all its strength and all its sensory and spiritual appetites. Such love is impossible if these appetites are scattered by their satisfaction in other things. In order to receive the strength of this union of love, David proclaimed to God: *I will keep my strength for You* [Ps 59:10], that is, all the ability, appetites, and strength of my faculties, by not desiring to make use of them or find satisfaction in anything outside of You.[24] . . .

* * *

---

[24]. John continues commenting on the verses of this stanza in relation to the passive purification of the spirit. His commentary on the second stanza (chs. 15–24) refers to the same period and does not represent any new stage along the spiritual journey. When he comes to the third stanza (ch. 25), he gives a general explanation of it but then interrupts his work. Although the work is left materially unfinished, he had achieved what he set out to do: explain the dark night or passive purification. As he draws to the close of his explanation of the passive purification, he begins to speak of the beloved, of Christ as the bridegroom, of the soul as the bride. His perspective now approaches that of *The Spiritual Canticle*.

The Spiritual Canticle

Editor's Introduction

In the confinement of his dark and cramped prison cell in Toledo, John of the Cross discovered a means of inner expansion in the images of the Song of Songs: mountains, valleys, rivers, fountains, flowers, caverns; all that we associate with being outside, free in the open country. His mind filled with these images of Solomon's Song, which he knew by heart, John began composing his own song based on Solomon's. The result was the first thirty-one stanzas of *The Spiritual Canticle*. What John found in the biblical symbolism was a remarkable resource for the expression of his own mystical experience, because "the Holy Spirit, unable to express the fullness of His meaning in ordinary words, utters mysteries in strange figures and likenesses."[1] In the genesis of *The Spiritual Canticle*, there came first John's own mystical experience and then the "love flowing from the abundant mystical understanding"[2] that stirred the poet to sing of his love in verse.

The poem is dramatic in form with a dialogue between two persons who search for and are lovingly moved by each other. The bride speaks five times and at length; the bridegroom, three times, and only briefly. In one stanza, creatures themselves speak. The author of the poem is looking back over the panorama of his spiritual life and interpreting its realities in terms of love, but in a lyrical language that adds enrichment to the whole. The progression is painted from the bride's vantage point. There are the urgent longings of the lover who is searching for her beloved, a beloved who seems to be far away and passive. He apparently stirs up love only so as to hide and make himself loved more. The effort to come close is on the part of the lover, who turns to

---

1. C. prol. 1.
2. Ibid.

all creatures along her path and begs them to tell her why the beloved is fleeing and not answering. But after she meets him again, she becomes aware that her initial longings for union were the work of her beloved and begins to interpret her search in a new light. When the bridegroom finally speaks, he shows with what interest he has been following the search. He has been desiring her intensely and efficaciously and rejoices in the bride's triumph even more than she.

After John had escaped from prison he added more stanzas to the original thirty-one. Stanzas 32–34 were composed during the period in which he was rector in Baeza (1577–1578). The five final stanzas, 35–39, represent the initial months of his stay in Granada (1582). In the second redaction of the poem, he added stanza 11, bringing the number to forty, but the time of its composing remains unknown.

In the first part of the poem, the stanzas speak of the longings of love. The soul is wounded with love for the beloved and moans for him who is absent. She then encounters him and finds in him every joy. But after her union with the beloved, the lover's perspective varies: She looks backward sometimes, sometimes forward, or at other times to the present. The final stanzas speak of the intimate life of the lovers together. The poem is in fact a poem about the exchange of love between the soul (the bride) and Christ (the bridegroom), as John later was to point out.

But those with whom John shared his mystical verses were so taken by what his genius was suggesting that they kept begging him for explanations; in many respects the verses had an extremely mysterious sound to them. John felt reluctance about responding to the requests of the nuns, for "who can describe the understanding He gives to loving souls in whom He dwells?"[3] Would it not be best for the poet to pour out the abundance of his spirit, its secrets and mysteries, only in the strange figures and similes of his poetry? John compromised, in the end, by agreeing to try to shed some general light on their meaning, but no more than that.

Knowing the deep caverns into which his own experience had penetrated, the mystical poet discredited his work as a commentator. But from the viewpoint of the reader, we could easily fail, relying on our ordinary experience, to reach the deep and rich meanings contained in the verses. That being true, John desired, nonetheless, that we always

---

3. Ibid.

return from his commentary to the poem and the symbols by which he expresses himself there.

As for his being brief, John points out some reasons for this in addition to the ineffability of mystical understanding. One is that there are many things written about the spiritual life, especially for beginners. Another is that those for whom he is writing, particularly Madre Ana de Jesús, to whom he gave the commentary, have gone beyond the stage of beginners into the depths of divine love. With readers like these before him, he will enlarge only at times and when dealing with some of the more elevated effects of prayer.

In the end, John would want readers to interpret the poem for themselves and at their own level. He explains the verses in their broadest sense so that we can adapt them to our own mode, and urges us not to bind ourselves to his explanation.[4] In fact, John himself interprets the stanzas variously and on different levels. At the outset, his commentary on the first stanza offers a three-level interpretation—for beginners, for proficients, and for the perfect.

But the commentary also led John to the awareness of the need for a different arrangement of the stanzas if he wanted to bring out more consistently the difference between the stage of spiritual betrothal and that of spiritual marriage. Greater correspondence to the real time sequence was needed. This involved him in a rearrangement of the stanzas in the middle section of the poem. Thus John has left us two major redactions of his commentary on *The Spiritual Canticle*. Editors refer to the first as CA, and to the second, rearranged version, as CB.

In addition to this major change of CB, John also adds an introduction to most of the stanzas. Doing so enabled him to link them together so that he could put forth a gradual and doctrinally justifiable journey of love. He also in these introductions takes the opportunity to place the *Canticle* within the framework of his overall synthesis as presented in his other works.

In CB, moreover, the five last stanzas, which in CA were interpreted in the light of something proper to this life, open onto a new horizon with aspirations toward the life of glory.

John also added another stanza to this second redaction of the *Canticle* and commented on it. This new stanza (no. 11) was inserted in a suitable place, bringing the final total of stanzas to forty.

---

4. C. prol. 2.

THE SPIRITUAL CANTICLE

In the 1920s doubts about the authenticity of the second redaction were raised. The arguments put forth against CB led to some polemics as well as to a good number of extremely detailed and careful critical studies. The result of these studies has been a strong case in favor of the authenticity of the second redaction. The arguments for its reliableness begin with the abundant historical documentation that endorses it. In addition, the style, language, and doctrine are patently John's and provide a weighty defense. As things have turned out, in fact, no adequate reasons for opposing the authenticity of the second redaction have come forth. Editors continue with certainty to include this second redaction among John's works. Since it gives a clearer and more complete presentation of the general theme of the *Canticle*, the selections for this volume come from it. Among other things, this final draft gives more attention to beginners, places emphasis in its middle section on the anxious love that has a role in the purification, and turns our gaze in the end to the vision of glory, of which the soul in the state of perfection has a foretaste.[5]

In the *Canticle*, the way of perfection is a journey shaped and colored by divine love. The stages as well as the summit of the spiritual path have to do with this love as it gradually increases, pervades, and transforms the soul. The advance along such a path progressively disengages a person from every appetite contrary to this love, and all the other elements of the spiritual life function in terms of the exercise of love. In sum, the *Canticle* deals with the love that is exercised and exchanged "between the soul and Christ its bridegroom."[6]

Love nourishes a longing for the object, that is, for the other. To know Christ, to surrender oneself to Him, to possess and be possessed by Him, these are the ideals suggested by the symbol "spiritual marriage." The spiritual marriage is the furthest reach for which the bride quests, and she continues untiringly until she obtains it. The theme of love, in the end, will embody three stages: the impatient and anxious longings of love, the union of love, and the glory of love.

The first period is equivalent to what John presented in other works as a "dark night." Purification entails feelings of privation, emptiness, and absence. But the order here is inverted. The bride first re-

---

5. For a good presentation in English of the critical questions surrounding the *Canticle* see Colin P. Thompson, *The Poet and the Mystic: A Study of the Cantico Espiritual of San Juan de la Cruz* (Oxford: Oxford University Press, 1977).

6. See the theme announced just before the prologue.

ceives; then she empties or goes out of herself. The stress is placed on the anxious searching. Her longings turn in the direction of full knowledge, full possession. Messengers are not enough; she desires the person.

Union with Christ, the bridegroom, lies at the core of the *Canticle*. So absorbed is the bride in the beloved that she loses sight of herself. The whole journey is powerfully Christ-centered. Moreover, the bridegroom does not remain just passively waiting while the bride is searching for Him. "Great was the desire of the bridegroom to free and ransom his bride completely."[7] He is "like the good shepherd rejoicing and holding on his shoulders the lost sheep for which He had searched along many winding paths."[8] The startling thing is that now the bride becomes aware that it was she who was lost and hidden. Indeed, when the bridegroom does give the longing soul some glimpses of himself, she cannot bear them. She is still weak; even the slight glimpse of him is too much to bear. The whole sensitive part of her nature needs further purification and strengthening. This weakness is a characteristic of the state of spiritual betrothal. Here the bride enjoys a relative tranquillity in the spiritual part of her being, but she still suffers from afflictions in her sensitive part. She needs to undergo further purifying periods of his absence, which will help her bring all her energies into subjection to him. The senses must be fully adapted to the life of the spirit. The bride, then, feels, at intervals, joy and presence, pain and absence, light, darkness.

In the spiritual marriage the bride is finally freed from "the hands of sensuality and the devil,"[9] and transformed into her God. All the temptations, disturbances, pains, solicitude, and cares are now forgotten in the abundance and fullness of God, in which she receives an intimate spiritual embrace; through it she lives the life of God. The gifts (virtues) of each to the other are concrete examples of the total surrender made and received. They are manifestations of love. But not only that, the persons themselves are the gift. The exercise of the virtues is now seen not merely as a good habit ascetically acquired; it is an offering, a service to the beloved. "Let us rejoice in the communication of the sweetness of love, not only in that sweetness we already possess in our habitual union, but in that which overflows into the effective and actual practice of love, either interiorly with the will in the affective act, or

---

7. C. 22, 1.
8. Ibid.
9. C. 22, 1.

exteriorly in works directed to the service of the beloved."[10] The soul fully transformed in God turns now to the beloved not to beg and seek but to praise, extol, and thank. It would ring hollow, though, to think that this transformation of love is equivalent to a lack of all suffering. If suffering is lacking, it is the suffering of impatient love, of those anxieties and afflictions that were a preparation for the full union of spiritual marriage. But the thicket of trials and tribulations is still beneficial even in the spiritual marriage in that it provides the opportunity to express more love and enter thereby further into the thicket of the delectable wisdom of God.

The final stanzas deal with the soul's aspirations, within the state of union, for the vision of glory. Perhaps John elevated these stanzas, which at first referred only to union on this earth, because of a development that he had undergone himself. In the passing of time, he would have experienced the insufficiency of all earthly perfection, however sublime. So these stanzas open up new territories, pointing out how the bride and the bridegroom give each other love, a love identified with the Holy Spirit. God gives Himself to the soul so that, in John's surprising words, the soul may in turn through its love give God to God through God Himself.[11] The bride's aim had always been to love God as much as He loves her, and she now has the signs and traces of such love through the Holy Spirit. On earth, however, this love will never have all the excellence and power of the love that will be possessed in the strong union of glory, and so, in the end, she still desires to be dissolved and to be with Christ, to see Him face to face.

The stanzas of *The Spiritual Canticle* may be divided briefly as follows:

1–12: The anxious longings and the searching by every means
13–21: Encounters of loving union and the urgent desires for complete freedom from inner and outer impediments
22–35: The full union, the mutual and total surrender and gift of self
36–40: The aspirations to glory

The copy generally followed for CB is the codex of *Jaen* conserved by the Discalced Carmelite nuns in Jaen.

---

10. C. 36, 4.
11. C. 38, 3–4; 39, 3–4; F. 3, 78.

Spiritual Canticle

This commentary on the stanzas that deal with the exchange of love between the soul and Christ, its bridegroom, explains certain matters about prayer and its effects. It was written at the request of Madre Ana de Jesús, prioress of the Discalced Carmelite nuns of St. Joseph's in Granada, 1584.[1]

Prologue

1. These stanzas, Reverend Mother, were obviously composed with a certain burning love of God. The wisdom and charity of God is so vast, as the Book of Wisdom states, that it reaches from end to end [Wis 8:1], and those informed and moved by it bear in some way this very abundance and impulsiveness in their words. As a result I do not plan to expound these stanzas in all the breadth and fullness that the fruitful spirit of love conveys to them. It would be foolish to think that expressions of love arising from mystical understanding, like these stanzas, are fully explainable. The Spirit of the Lord, who abides in us and aids our weakness, as St. Paul says [Rom 8:26], pleads for us with unspeakable groanings in order to manifest what we can neither fully understand nor comprehend.

Who can describe the understanding He gives to loving souls in whom He dwells? And who can express the experience He imparts to them? Who, finally, can explain the desires he gives them? Certainly, no one can! Not even they who receive these communications. As a result these persons let something of their experiences overflow in fig-

---

1. Ana de Jesús (Lobera) (1545–1621) was born in Medina del Campo and entered the Teresian Carmel of St. Joseph's in Avila in 1571. She made her profession in Salamanca and was prioress in Beas, Granada, and Madrid. In 1604 she left Spain for France and Belgium where she founded Carmels. She died in Brussels. The cause for her beatification is in process.

ures and similes, and from the abundance of their spirit pour out secrets and mysteries rather than rational explanations.

If these similitudes are not read with the simplicity of the spirit of knowledge and love they contain, they will seem to be absurdities rather than reasonable utterances, as will those comparisons of the divine Canticle of Solomon and other books of Sacred Scripture where the Holy Spirit, unable to express the fullness of His meaning in ordinary words, utters mysteries in strange figures and likenesses. The saintly doctors, no matter how much they have said or will say, can never furnish an exhaustive explanation of these figures and comparisons, since the abundant meanings of the Holy Spirit cannot be caught in words. Thus the explanation of these expressions usually contains less than what they themselves embody.

2. Since these stanzas, then, were composed in a love flowing from abundant mystical understanding, I cannot explain them adequately, nor is it my intention to do so. I only wish to shed some general light on them, since Your Reverence has desired this of me. I believe such an explanation will be more suitable. It is better to explain the utterances of love in their broadest sense so that individuals may derive profit from them according to the mode and capacity of their own spirit, rather than narrow them down to a meaning unadaptable to every palate. As a result, though we give some explanation of these stanzas, there is no reason to be bound to this explanation. For mystical wisdom, which comes through love and is the subject of these stanzas, need not be understood distinctly in order to cause love and affection in the soul, for it is given according to the mode of faith, through which we love God without understanding Him.

3. I will then be very brief, although I do intend to give a lengthier explanation when necessary and where the occasion arises for a discussion of some matters concerning prayer and its effects. Since these stanzas refer to many of the effects of prayer, I ought to treat of at least some of these effects.

Yet, passing over the more common effects, I will deal briefly with the more extraordinary ones, which take place in those who with God's help have passed beyond the state of beginners. I do this for two reasons: first, because there are many writings for beginners; second, because I am addressing Your Reverence, at your request. And our Lord has favored you and led you beyond the state of beginners into the depths of His divine love.

I hope that, although some scholastic theology is used here in reference to the soul's interior converse with God, it will not prove vain to speak in such a manner to the pure of spirit. Even though Your Reverence lacks training in scholastic theology by which the divine truths are understood, you are not wanting in mystical theology, which is known through love and by which one not only knows but at the same time experiences.

4. And that my explanations—which I desire to submit to anyone with better judgment than mine and entirely to Holy Mother the Church—may be worthy of belief, I do not intend to affirm anything of myself or trust in any of my own experiences or in those of other spiritual persons whom I have known or heard of. Although I plan to make use of these experiences, I want to explain and confirm at least the more difficult matters through passages from Sacred Scripture. In using these passages, I will quote the words in Latin,[2] and then interpret them in regard to the matter being discussed.

I will now record the stanzas in full and then in due order quote each one separately before its explanation; similarly, I will quote each verse before commenting on it.

End of the Prologue

Stanzas between the Soul and the Bridegroom

Bride

1. Where have you hidden,
Beloved, and left me moaning?
You fled like the stag
After wounding me;
I went out calling you, and you were gone.

2. Shepherds, you that go
Up through the sheepfolds to the hill,
If by chance you see
Him I love most,
Tell him that I sicken, suffer, and die.

---

2. In the unaltered passages from CA the biblical texts are cited first in Latin, but those texts representing the second draft, or CB, are not first cited in Latin because, as noted in the *Ascent,* John after a time discontinued this practice. See Book Three, note 1.

THE SPIRITUAL CANTICLE

3. Seeking my love
I will head for the mountains and for watersides,
I will not gather flowers,
Nor fear wild beasts;
I will go beyond strong men and frontiers.

4. O woods and thickets
Planted by the hand of my beloved!
O green meadow,
Coated, bright with flowers.
Tell me, has he passed by you?

5. Pouring out a thousand graces,
He passed these groves in haste;
And having looked at them,
With his image alone,
Clothed them in beauty.

6. Ah, who has the power to heal me?
Now wholly surrender yourself!
Do not send me
Any more messengers,
They cannot tell me what I must hear.

7. All who are free
Tell me a thousand graceful things of you;
All wound me more
And leave me dying
Of, ah, I-don't-know-what behind their stammering.

8. How do you endure
O life, not living where you live?
And being brought near death
By the arrows you receive
From that which you conceive of your beloved.

9. Why, since you wounded
This heart, don't you heal it?
And why, since you stole it from me,

THE SPIRITUAL CANTICLE

Do you leave it so,
And fail to carry off what you have stolen?

10. Extinguish these miseries,
Since no one else can stamp them out;
And may the vision of your beauty be my death;
For the sickness of love
Is not cured
Except by your very presence and image.

12. O spring like crystal!
If only, on your silvered-over face,
You would suddenly form
The eyes I have desired,
Which I bear sketched deep within my heart.

13. Withdraw them, beloved,
I am taking flight!

Bridegroom

Return, dove,
The wounded stag
Is in sight on the hill,
Cooled by the breeze of your flight.

Bride

14. My beloved, the mountains
And lonely wooded valleys,
Strange islands,
And resounding rivers,
The whistling of love-stirring breezes,

15. The tranquil night
At the time of the rising dawn,
Silent music,
Sounding solitude,
The supper that refreshes, and deepens love.

16. Catch us the foxes,
For our vineyard is now in flower,

THE SPIRITUAL CANTICLE

While we fashion a cone of roses
Intricate as the pine's;
And let no one appear on the hill.

17. Be still, deadening north wind;
South wind come, you that waken love,
Breathe through my garden,
Let its fragrance flow,
And the beloved will feed amid the flowers.

18. You girls of Judea,
While among flowers and roses
The amber spreads its perfume,
Stay away, there on the outskirts:
Do not so much as seek to touch our thresholds.

19. Hide yourself, my love;
Turn your face toward the mountains,
And do not speak;
But look at those companions
Going with her through strange islands.

Bridegroom

20. Swift-winged birds,
Lions, stags, and leaping roes,
Mountains, lowlands, and river banks,
Waters, winds, and ardors,
Watching fears of night:

21. By the pleasant lyres
And the siren's song, I conjure you
To cease your anger
And not touch the wall,
That the bride may sleep in deeper peace.

22. The bride has entered
The sweet garden of her desire,
And she rests in delight,
Laying her neck
On the gentle arms of her beloved.

THE SPIRITUAL CANTICLE

23. Beneath the apple tree:
There I took you for my own,
There I offered you my hand,
And restored you,
Where your mother was corrupted.

Bride

24. Our bed is in flower,
Bound round with linking dens of lions,
Hung with purple,
Built up in peace,
And crowned with a thousand shields of gold.

25. Following your footprints
Maidens run along the way;
The touch of a spark,
The spiced wine,
Cause flowings in them from the sacred balsam.

26. In the inner wine cellar
I drank of my beloved, and when I went abroad
Through all this valley
I no longer knew anything,
And lost the herd that I was following.

27. There he gave me his breast;
There he taught me a sweet and living knowledge;
And I gave myself to him,
Keeping nothing back;
There I promised to be his bride.

28. Now I occupy my soul
And all my energy in his service;
I no longer tend the herd,
Nor have I any other work
Now that my every act is love.

30. With flowers and emeralds
Chosen on cool mornings
We shall weave garlands

THE SPIRITUAL CANTICLE

Flowering in your love,
And bound with one hair of mine.

31. You considered
That one hair fluttering at my neck;
You gazed at it upon my neck;
And it captivated you;
And one of my eyes wounded you.

32. When you looked at me
Your eyes imprinted your grace in me;
For this you loved me ardently;
And thus my eyes deserved
To adore what they beheld in you.

33. Do not despise me;
For if, before, you found me dark,
Now truly you can look at me
Since you have looked
And left in me grace and beauty.

Bridegroom

34. The small white dove
Has returned to the ark with an olive branch;
And now the turtledove
Has found its longed-for mate
By the green river banks.

35. She lived in solitude,
And now in solitude has built her nest;
And in solitude he guides her,
He alone, who also bears
In solitude the wound of love.

Bride

36. Let us rejoice, beloved,
And let us go forth to behold ourselves in your beauty,
To the mountain and to the hill,
To where the pure water flows,
And further, deep into the thicket.

37. And then we will go on
To the high caverns in the rock
Which are so well concealed;
There we shall enter
And taste the fresh juice of the pomegranates.

38. There you will show me
What my soul has been seeking,
And then you will give me,
You, my life, will give me there
What you gave me on that other day:

39. The breathing of the air,
The song of the sweet nightingale
The grove and its living beauty
In the serene night,
With a flame that is consuming and painless.

40. No one looked at her,
Nor did Aminidab appear;
The siege was still;
And the cavalry,
At the sight of the waters, descended.

* * *

Stanza 10

Introduction

1. The soul, then, in this condition of love is like those who are sick, who are extremely tired and, having lost their taste and appetite, find all food nauseating and everything a disturbance and annoyance. In everything they think about or see they have only one desire, the desire for health, and all that does not lead to health is a bother and a burden to them.

Since the soul has reached this sickness of love of God, she has three traits. The first is that in all things that are offered to her, or with which she deals, she has ever before her that longing for her health, which is her beloved. Even though she cannot help being occupied with them, she always has her heart fixed on him. The second trait, arising from this first, is the loss of taste for all things. The third, then, results, which is that all these things molest her and that all dealings with others are burdensome and annoying.

2. The reason for these traits, deduced from what has been said, is that, since the palate of the soul's will has tasted this food of love of God, her will is inclined immediately to seek and enjoy her beloved in everything that happens and in all her occupations, without looking for any satisfaction or concern of her own. Mary Magdalene acted similarly when with ardent love she was searching for Him in the garden: Thinking that He was the gardener, without any further reasoning or considerations, she pleaded with Him: *If you have taken Him from me, tell me, and I will take Him away* [Jn 20:15]. Having a similar yearning to find Him in all things, and not immediately finding Him as she desires—but rather quite the contrary—not only does the soul fail to find satisfaction in these things, but they also become a torment to her, and sometimes a very great one. Such souls suffer much in dealing with people and with business matters, for these contacts hinder rather than help them to their goal.

3. The bride clearly indicates in the Canticle these three traits she had when searching for her bridegroom: *I looked for him and did not find him. But they who go about the city found me and wounded me, and the guards of the walls took my mantle from me* [Sg 5:6–7]. Those who go about the city refer to the affairs of the world. When they find the soul who is searching for God, they inflict on her many wounds of sorrow, pain, and displeasure, for not only does she fail to find her desire in them, but she is also impeded by them. Those who guard the wall of contemplation, to prevent the soul from entering, are the devils and the negotiations of the world, and they take away the mantle of the peace and quietude of loving contemplation.[3]

The soul that loves God derives a thousand displeasures and annoyances from all of these. Conscious that as long as she is in this life without the vision of God, she cannot free herself from them to either a small or a great degree, she continues her prayers to the beloved and recites the following stanza:

---

3. This introduction bears resemblance to what he says in A. 1, 13 and N. 1, 1 about the signs of contemplation.

THE SPIRITUAL CANTICLE

> Extinguish these miseries,
> Since no one else can stamp them out;
> And may my eyes behold you,
> Because you are their light,
> And I would open them to you alone.

Commentary

4. She continues in this stanza to ask the beloved to put an end to her longings and pains since he alone can do this, and no one else; and to accomplish this so that the eyes of her soul may be able to see him since he alone is the light they behold, and she wants to employ them in him alone:

5.   Extinguish these miseries

A characteristic of the desires of love is that all deeds and words unconformed with what the will loves, weary, tire, annoy, and displease the soul as she beholds that her desire goes unfulfilled. She refers to this weariness that she suffers in order to see God as "these miseries." And nothing but possession of the beloved can extinguish them. She says he extinguishes them by his presence and refreshes her as cool water soothes a person exhausted from the heat. She uses the word "extinguish" to indicate that she is suffering from the fire of love.

6.   Since no one else can stamp them out

To further urge and persuade her beloved to grant her petition, she declares that, since he alone suffices to satisfy her need, he must be the one to extinguish these miseries. It is noteworthy that God is very ready to comfort and satisfy the soul in her needs and afflictions when she neither has nor desires consolation and satisfaction outside of Him. The soul possessing nothing that might withhold her from God cannot remain long without a visit from the beloved.

7.   And may my eyes behold you,

That is: May I see You face to face with the eyes of my soul,

8.   Because you are their light

Regardless of the fact that God is the supernatural light of the soul's eyes, and that without this light she is enveloped in darkness, she affectionately calls Him here the light of her eyes, just as any lover might call the one she loves the light of her eyes in order to show her affection.

These two verses are like saying: Since my eyes have no other light (neither through nature nor through love) than you, may my eyes behold you because you are their light in every way. David noted the absence of this light when he lamented: *The light of my eyes itself is not with me* [38:11]. Tobit did the same: *What joy can be mine since I am seated in darkness and do not see the light of heaven?* [Tb 5:10]. Through these words he gave expression to his desire for the clear vision of God because the light of heaven is the Son of God, as St. John says: *The heavenly city has no need of the sun or of the moon to shine in it, because the brightness of God illumines it, and the Lamb is the lamp thereof* [Rv 21:23].

9. And I would open them to you alone.

With this line the soul desires to oblige the bridegroom to reveal this light of her eyes, not only because she lives in darkness in that her eyes have no other light, but also because she wants to keep her eyes for him alone. As the soul longing to focus the eyes of her will on the light of something outside of God is justly deprived of the divine light—insofar as the spiritual powers she has for receiving God's light are occupied with this other light—so also does the soul that closes its eyes to all things in order to open them to God alone merit congruously the illumination of the divine light.

Stanza 11

Introduction

1. It should be known that the loving bridegroom of souls cannot long watch them suffering alone—as this soul is suffering—because as he says through Zechariah, their afflictions touch him in the apple of his eye [Zec 2:12]; especially when these afflictions are the outcome of love for him, as are those of this soul. He also declares through Isaiah: *Before they call, I will hear; while they are yet with the word in their mouth, I will hear them* [Is 65:24]. The Wise Man says of him, that if the soul seeks him as money, she will find him [Prv 2:4–5].

Apparently God granted a certain spiritual feeling of His presence to this loving soul whose prayers are so enkindled and who seeks Him more covetously than one would seek money, since she has left herself and all things for him. In this spiritual sense of his presence, he revealed some deep glimpses of his divinity and beauty by which he greatly increased her fervor and desire to see him. As a man throws water into the forge to stir up and intensify the fire, so the Lord usually grants to some souls that walk in these fiery longings of love certain signs of His excellence to make them more fervent and further prepare them for the favors He wishes to grant them later.

Since the soul saw and experienced through that obscure presence the Supreme Good and Beauty hidden there, she recites the following stanza, dying with the desire to see Him:

> Reveal your presence,
> And may the vision of your beauty be my death;
> For the sickness of love
> Is not cured
> Except by your very presence and image.

Commentary

2. The soul desiring to be possessed by this immense God, for love of whom she feels that her heart is robbed and wounded, unable to endure her sickness any longer, deliberately asks Him in this stanza to show her His beauty, His divine essence, and to kill her with this revelation, and thereby free her from the flesh since she cannot see and enjoy Him as she wants. She makes this request by displaying before Him the sickness and yearning of her heart, in which she perseveres suffering for love of Him, unable to find a cure in anything less than this glorious vision of His divine essence. The verse follows:

3.   Reveal your presence,

In explanation of this verse it should be known that God's presence can be of three kinds:

The first is His presence by essence. In this way He is present not only in the holiest souls, but also in sinners and in all other creatures. For with this presence He gives them life and being. Should this essential presence be lacking to them, they would all be annihilated. Thus this presence is never wanting to the soul.

The second is His presence by grace, in which He abides in the soul, pleased and satisfied with it. Not all have this presence of God; those who fall into mortal sin lose it. The soul cannot know naturally if it has this presence.

The third is His presence by spiritual affection, for God usually grants His spiritual presence to devout souls in many ways, by which He refreshes, delights, and gladdens them.

Yet, these many kinds of spiritual presence, just as the others, are all hidden, for in them God does not reveal Himself as He is, since the conditions of this life will not allow such a manifestation. Thus the above verse, "reveal your presence," could be understood of any of these three ways in which God is present.

4. Since it is certain that at least in the first way God is ever present in the soul, she does not ask Him to be present in her, but that He so reveal His hidden presence, whether natural, spiritual, or affective, that she may be able to see Him in His divine being and beauty. As He gives the soul natural being through His essential presence, and perfects her through His presence by grace, she begs Him to glorify her also with His manifest glory.

Yet insofar as this soul is full of fervor and tender love of God, we should understand that this presence she asks the beloved to reveal refers chiefly to a certain affective presence which the beloved accords her. This presence is so sublime that the soul feels an immense hidden being is there from which God communicates to her some semi-clear glimpses of His divine beauty.[4] And these bear such an effect on the soul that she ardently longs and faints with desire for what she feels hidden there in that presence, which is similar to what David felt when he exclaimed: *My soul longs and faints for the courts of the Lord* [Ps 84:3].

At this time the soul faints with longing to be engulfed in that Supreme Good she feels present and hidden, for although it is hidden she has a notable experience of the good and delight present there. Accordingly, she is drawn and carried toward this good more forcibly than any material object is pulled toward its center by gravity. With this longing and heartfelt desire, unable to contain herself any longer, the soul begs: Reveal your presence.

5. Moses had this very experience on Mount Sinai. While standing in God's presence, he was able to get such sublime and profound glimpses of the height and beauty of the hidden divinity that, unable to endure it, he asked God twice to reveal His glory: *You say that you know me by name and that I have found favor before you. If therefore I have found favor in your presence, show me your face that I may know you and find*

---

4. The experiences of absence and presence, so much a part of the theme of this work, refer principally to the third kind of presence, "affective," of which John speaks in his analysis of the presence of God in the soul. But this is also a hidden presence.

before your eyes the grace that I desire fulfilled [Ex 33:12-13]—that is, to reach the perfect love of the glory of God. Yet the Lord answered: *You shall not be able to see my face, for no one shall see me and live* [Ex 33:20]. This is like saying: You ask a difficult thing of me, Moses, for such is the beauty of my face and the delight derived from the sight of my being that your soul will be unable to withstand it in a life as weak as this.

The soul knows that she cannot see Him in His beauty in this kind of life. She knows this either through God's answer to Moses or through her experience of what is hidden here in the presence of God. For even though He appears but vaguely, she faints. Hence she anticipates the reply that can be made to her as it was to Moses and says:

6. And may the vision of your beauty be my death; This is like saying: Since the delight arising from the sight of your being and beauty is unendurable, and since I must die in seeing you, may the vision of your beauty be my death.

7. It is known that there are two visions that will kill a person because of the inability of human nature to suffer their force and vigor: One is that of the basilisk, from which it is said one dies immediately; the other is the vision of God. Yet the causes are very different, for the sight of one kills with a terrible poison, and that of God by an immense health and glorious good.

The soul does nothing very outstanding by wanting to die at the sight of the beauty of God in order to enjoy Him forever. Were she to have but a foreglimpse of the height and beauty of God, she would not only desire death in order to see Him now forever, as she here desires, but she would very gladly undergo a thousand singularly bitter deaths to see Him only for a moment; and having seen Him, she would ask to suffer just as many more that she might see Him for another moment.

8. To shed further light on this verse, it should be known that when the soul asks that the vision of His beauty be her death she speaks conditionally, under the supposition that she cannot see Him without dying. Were she able to see Him without dying, she would not ask Him to slay her, for to desire death is a natural imperfection. Yet with the supposition that this corruptible life of humans is incompatible with the other incorruptible life of God, she says: "May the vision of your beauty be my death."

9. St. Paul teaches this doctrine to the Corinthians, saying: *We do not wish to be unclothed, but we desire to be clothed over, that that which is mortal may be absorbed in life* [2 Cor 5:4]. This is like saying: We do not desire to be despoiled of the flesh but to be clothed over with glory. Yet

observing that one cannot live simultaneously in glory and in the mortal flesh, he says to the Philippians that he desires to be loosed and to be with Christ [Phil 1:23]. . . .

10. . . . Death cannot be bitter to the soul that loves, for in it she finds all the sweetness and delight of love. The thought of death cannot sadden her, for she finds that gladness accompanies this thought. Neither can the thought of death be burdensome and painful to her, for death will put an end to all her sorrows and afflictions and be the beginning of all her bliss. She thinks of death as her friend and bridegroom, and at the thought of it she rejoices as she would over the thought of her betrothal and marriage, and she longs for that day and that hour of her death more than earthly kings long for kingdoms and principalities.

The Wise Man proclaims of this kind of death: *O death! Your sentence is welcome to the one who feels need* [Sir 41:2]. If it is welcome to those who feel need for earthly things, even though it does not provide for these needs but rather despoils these persons of the possessions they have, how much better will its sentence be for the soul in need of love, as is this one who is crying out for more love. For death will not despoil her of the love she possesses, but rather be the cause of love's completeness, which she desires, and the satisfaction of all her needs.

The soul is right in daring to say, may the vision of your beauty be my death, since she knows that at the instant she sees this beauty she will be carried away by it, and absorbed in this very beauty, and transformed in this same beauty, and made beautiful like this beauty itself, and enriched and provided for like this very beauty.

David declares, consequently, that the death of the saints is precious in the sight of the Lord [Ps 116:15]. This would not be true if they did not participate in His very grandeurs, for in the sight of God nothing is precious but what He in Himself is. Accordingly, the soul does not fear death when she loves; rather, she desires it. Yet sinners are always fearful of death. They foresee that death will take everything away and bring them all evils. As David says, *The death of sinners is very evil* [Ps 34:22]. And hence, as the Wise Man says, the remembrance of it is bitter [Sir 41:1]. Since sinners love the life of this world intensely and have little love for that of the other, they have an immense fear of death.

The soul that loves God lives more in the next life than in this, for the soul lives where it loves more than where it gives life, and thus has but little esteem for this temporal life. She says then: "May the vision of your beauty be my death."

11. For the sickness of love
   Is not cured
   Except by your very presence and image.

The reason love-sickness has no other remedy than the presence and the image of the beloved is that, since this sickness differs from others, its medicine also differs. In other sicknesses, following sound philosophy, contraries are cured by contraries, but love is incurable except by what is in accord with love.[5]

The reason for this is that love of God is the soul's health, and the soul does not have full health until love is complete. Sickness is nothing but a want of health, and when the soul has not even a single degree of love, she is dead. But when she possesses some degrees of love of God no matter how few, she is then alive, yet very weak and infirm because of her little love. In the measure that love increases she will be healthier, and when love is perfect she will have full health.

12. It should be known that love never reaches perfection until the lovers are so alike that one is transfigured in the other. And then the love is in full health. The soul experiences within herself a certain sketch of love, which is the sickness she mentions, and she desires the completion of the sketch of this image, the image of her bridegroom, the Word, the Son of God, who as St. Paul says, *is the splendor of His glory and the image of His substance* [Heb 1:3], for this is the image referred to in this verse and into which the soul desires to be transfigured through love. As a result she says: For the sickness of love is not cured except by your very presence and image.

13. She does well to call imperfect love "sickness." For just as a sick person is too weak for work, so is the soul, feeble in love, too weak to practice heroic virtue.

14. It is also noteworthy that those who feel in themselves the sickness of love, a lack of love, show that they have some love because they are aware of what they lack through what they have. Those who do not feel this sickness show that they either have no love or are perfect in love.

---

5. Cf. A. 3, 6, 1, note 2.

THE SPIRITUAL CANTICLE

Stanza 12

Introduction

1. At this period the soul feels that she is rushing toward God as impetuously as a falling stone when nearing its center. She also feels that she is like wax in which an impress is being made, but not yet completed. She knows too that she is like a sketch or the first draft of a drawing and calls out to the one who did this sketch to finish the painting and image. And her faith is so enlightened that it gives her a glimpse of some clear divine reflections of the height of her God. As a result she does not know what to do other than turn to this very faith, which contains and hides the image and the beauty of her beloved, and from which she also receives these sketches and tokens of love, and speak to it in the following stanza:

> O spring like crystal!
> If only, on your silvered-over face,
> You would suddenly form
> The eyes I have desired,
> Which I bear sketched deep within my heart. . . .

Commentary

2. Since the soul longs so ardently for union with the bridegroom and is aware that she finds no remedy in any creature, she turns to speak to faith, as to that which most vividly sheds light concerning her beloved, and takes it as a means toward this union. Indeed, there is no other means by which one reaches true union and spiritual espousal with God, as Osee indicates: *I will espouse you to me in faith* [Os 2:20]. With this burning desire she exclaims the following, which is the meaning of the stanza: O faith of Christ, my Spouse, would that you might show me clearly now the truths of my beloved, which you have infused in my soul and which are covered with obscurity and darkness (for faith, as the theologians say, is an obscure habit), in such a way that, what you communicate to me in inexplicit and obscure knowledge, you would show suddenly, clearly, and perfectly, changing it into a manifestation of glory! Would that you might do this by drawing back from these truths (for faith is the veil of the truths of God)! The verse then runs:

THE SPIRITUAL CANTICLE

3.   O spring like crystal!

She says faith is like crystal for two reasons: first, because it concerns Christ, her spouse; second, because it has the characteristics of crystal. It is pure in its truths, and strong and clear, cleansed of errors and natural forms.

And she calls it a spring because from it the waters of all spiritual goods flow into the soul. Christ, our Lord, speaking with the Samaritan woman, called faith a spring, declaring that in those who believed in Him He would make a fountain whose waters would leap up unto life everlasting [Jn 4:14]. This water was the Spirit, which believers were to receive through faith [Jn 7:39].

4.   If only, on your silvered-over face,

She calls the propositions and articles of faith a silvered-over face. To understand this verse as well as the others, it should be known that faith is compared to silver in the propositions it teaches us, and that the truths and substance it contains are compared to gold. For in the next life we shall see and enjoy openly this very substance that, clothed and covered with the silver of faith, we now believe. . . .

Faith, consequently, gives us God, but covered with the silver of faith. Yet it does not for this reason fail to give Him to us truly. Were we to be given a gold vase plated with silver, we would not fail to receive a gold vase merely because of the silver plating. God promised the bride of the Song of Songs who wanted this possession of Him that, insofar as possible in this life, He would make her gold earrings plated with silver [Sg 1:10]. He thereby promised to give Himself to her, but hidden in faith.

The soul, then, exclaims to faith: Oh, if only on your silvered-over face (the articles we mentioned) by which you cover the gold of the divine rays (the eyes I have desired), and she adds:

You would suddenly form
The eyes I have desired,

The eyes refer to the divine truths and rays. Faith, as we mentioned, proposes these truths to us in its covered and inexplicit articles. The soul, in other words, says: Oh, if only the truths hidden in your articles, which you teach me in an inexplicit and dark manner, you would give me now completely, clearly, and explicitly, freed of their covering, as my desire begs!

She calls these truths eyes because of the remarkable presence of the beloved she experiences. It seems that he is now always looking at her. Thus she says:

6.   Which I bear sketched deep within my heart.

She says these truths are sketched deep within her, that is, in her soul, in her intellect and will.

For these truths are infused by faith into her intellect. And since the knowledge of them is imperfect, she says they are sketched. Just as a sketch is not a perfect painting, so the knowledge of faith is not perfect knowledge. Hence, the truths infused in the soul through faith are as though sketched, and when they will be clearly visible they will be like a perfect and finished painting in the soul. As the Apostle says: *Cum autem venerit quod perfectum est evacuabitur quod ex parte est* [1 Cor. 13–10]; this means that when what is perfect, the clear vision, comes, that which is in part, the knowledge of faith, will end. . . .

9. The soul's state at this time is such that, regardless of the fact that it is indescribable, I do not want to neglect saying something about it even though briefly. It seems to the soul that its bodily and spiritual substance is drying up with thirst for this living spring of God. Its thirst is like David's when he said: *As the hart longs for the fount of waters, so does my soul long for you, my God. My soul has thirsted for God the living fount; when shall I see and appear before the face of God?* [Ps 42:2–3]. This thirst so exhausts the soul that she would think nothing of breaking through the midst of the camp of the Philistines, as did David's strong men, to fill their containers with water from the cistern of Bethlehem, which was Christ [1 Cor 11:18]. She would consider all the difficulties of this world, and the fury of demons, and infernal afflictions nothing if by passing through them she could plunge into the unfathomable spring of love. In this respect it is said in the Song of Songs: *Love is as strong as death and its jealousy as hard as hell* [Sg 8:6].

It is incredible how ardent the longing and pain is that the soul experiences when she sees that she is near the enjoyment of that good, and that yet it is not given to her. The more the object of her desire comes into sight and the closer it draws, while yet being denied her, so much more pain and torment does it cause. In this spiritual sense Job says: *Before I eat, I sigh; and the roaring and bellowing of my soul is like overflowing waters* [Jb 3:24], with craving for food. By the food is meant God, and the craving for food, or for the knowledge of God, is commensurate with the suffering for Him.

THE SPIRITUAL CANTICLE

Stanza 13

Introduction

1. This is the reason the soul's suffering for God at this time is so intense: She is drawing nearer to Him, and so she has greater experience within herself of the void of God, of very heavy darkness, and of spiritual fire, which dries up and purges her, so that thus purified she may be united with Him. Inasmuch as God does not communicate some supernatural ray of light from Himself, He is intolerable darkness to her when He is spiritually near her, for the supernatural light darkens with its excess the natural light. David indicated all this when he said: *Clouds and darkness are round about Him; fire goes before Him* [Ps 97:2–3]. In another psalm he asserts: *He made darkness His covert and hiding place, and His tent round about Him is dark water in the clouds of the air; because of His great splendor there are in His presence clouds, hail and coals of fire* [Ps 18:12–13], that is, for the soul drawing near Him. As the soul comes closer to Him, and until God introduces her into His divine splendors through transformation of love, she experiences within herself all that David described. In the meantime, like Job, she exclaims over and over: *Who will grant me to know Him and find Him and come unto His throne?* [Jb 23:3].

God through His immense mercy grants the soul favors and consolations in the measure of her darknesses and voids, for *sicut tenebrae ejus ita et lumen ejus* [Ps 139:12], and in exalting and glorifying her He humbles and wearies her. In a like way He sends the soul suffering these fatigues some of His divine rays with such strong love and glory that He stirs her completely and causes her to go out of her senses.[6] Thus in great fear and trembling, she spoke to her beloved the first part of the following stanza, and her beloved then spoke the remaining verses.

> Withdraw them, beloved,
> I am taking flight!

---

6. This stanza marks the beginning of a new stage in which there are frequent visits from the beloved. John calls this period the spiritual betrothal. The reason for the suffering experienced in the divine communications is, as was also explained in the *Night*, that the soul is not entirely purified.

THE SPIRITUAL CANTICLE

Bridegroom

Return, dove,
The wounded stag
Is in sight on the hill,
Cooled by the breeze of your flight.

Commentary

2. The beloved usually visits his bride chastely, delicately, and with strong love amid the intense loving desires and ardors she has shown in the previous stanzas. God's favors and visits are generally in accord with the intensity of the yearnings and ardors of love that precede them.

Since, as the soul just finished saying in the previous stanza, she desired these divine eyes with such yearnings, the beloved revealed to her some rays of his grandeur and divinity. He communicated these so sublimely and forcibly that he carried her out of herself in rapture and ecstasy. At the beginning this is accompanied by great pain and fear in the sensory part. Unable in her weakness to endure such excess, she proclaims in this stanza: "Withdraw them, beloved," that is, these your divine eyes, "for they cause me to take flight and go out of myself to supreme contemplation, which is beyond what the sensory part can endure." This flight from the body is what she desired; this is why she begged him to withdraw his eyes, to cease communicating them to her in the body, in which she is unable to suffer and enjoy them as she would, and communicate them to her in her flight outside the body.

The bridegroom then impedes this desire and flight, saying: "Return, dove, for the communication you receive from me is not yet of the state of glory to which you now aspire. Return to me, for I am he whom you, wounded with love, seek. For I too, like the stag, wounded by your love, begin to reveal myself to you in your high contemplation, and I am refreshed and renewed in the love which arises from your contemplation."

The soul, then, says to the bridegroom:

3.   Withdraw them, beloved!

As we mentioned, the soul in accordance with her intense desire for these divine eyes, for the divinity, received interiorly from the beloved such divine communication and knowledge that she had to say: "Withdraw them, beloved."

The misery of human nature is such that when the communication and knowledge of the beloved, which gives more life to the soul and for which she longs so ardently, is about to be imparted, she cannot receive it save almost at the cost of her life. When she receives the eyes she has been searching for so anxiously and in so many ways, she cries: "Withdraw them, beloved!"

4. The torment experienced in these rapturous visits is such that there is no other which so disjoins the bones and endangers the sensory part. Were God not to provide, she would die. And indeed, it seems so to the soul in which this happens, that she is being loosed from the flesh and is abandoning the body.

The reason for this is that such favors cannot be received wholly in the body, for the spirit is elevated to commune with the divine Spirit who comes to the soul. Thus the soul must in some fashion abandon the body. As a result the body must suffer and, consequently, the soul in the body, because of their unity in one *suppositum*.[7] The torment she experiences at the time of this visit and the terror arising from her awareness of being treated in this supernatural way make her cry: "Withdraw them, beloved!"

5. Yet, it should not be thought that because she says withdraw them, she desires him to do so. Those words spring from natural fear, as we said. No matter what the cost, she would not want to lose these visits and favors of the beloved. Although the sensory part suffers, the spirit takes flight to supernatural recollection and enjoyment of the beloved's Spirit, which is what she desired and sought. Yet she would not want to receive the Spirit in the body, for there she cannot receive Him fully, but only in a small degree and with considerable suffering. But she would want to receive Him in the flight of the spirit, outside the body, where she can freely rejoice with Him. Accordingly, she says, "Withdraw them, beloved," that is, cease communicating them to me in the body.

6.   I am taking flight!

This is like saying: I am taking flight from the body in order that you may communicate them to me outside of it, since they cause me to fly out of the body.

For a better understanding of the nature of this flight, it should be noted that, as we said, in this visit of the divine Spirit, the spirit of the

---

7. Here again he stresses the unity of the human person, or of the *suppositum*, the technical scholastic term.

THE SPIRITUAL CANTICLE

soul is carried away violently to communicate with Him, and it abandons the body and ceases to have its feelings and actions in it, for they are in God. Thus St. Paul said that in his rapture he did not know if his soul was receiving the communication in the body or out of the body [2 Cor 12:2].

However, it should not be thought because of this that the soul forsakes the body, which is its sensory life, but rather that the soul's actions are not in the body. This is why in these raptures and flights the body has no feeling, and even though severely painful things are done to it, it does not feel them. This rapture is not like other natural transports and swoons in which one returns to self when pain is inflicted.

These feelings are experienced in such visits by those who have not yet reached the state of perfection, but are advancing along in the state of proficients.[8] Those who have reached perfection receive all communications in peace and gentle love. These raptures then cease, for they are communications preparatory to the reception of the total communication.

7. This would be an apt place to treat of the different kinds of raptures, ecstasies, and other elevations and flights of the soul that are customarily experienced by spiritual persons. But since, as I promised in the prologue, my intention is only to give a brief explanation of these stanzas, such a discussion will have to be left for someone who knows how to treat the matter better than I. Then too, the blessed Teresa of Jesus, our Mother, left writings about these spiritual matters, which are admirably done and which I hope will soon be printed and brought to light.[9]

What the soul then says about flight here should be understood in reference to rapture and ecstasy of the spirit in God.

And the beloved then says:

8.   Return, dove.

The soul went out of the body very willingly in that spiritual flight and

---

8. The high experiences explained here still belong to the state of proficients or illuminative way and alternate with the trials of the passive purification.

9. This reference would include especially *The Life* 20; and *The Interior Castle* VI, 4–5. In a Council session of the order, with John present as a councillor, in 1586, it was decreed that Teresa's books be published. The influence of Teresa on John's writing is more extensive than usually realized. He who once displeased some by calling her "his daughter" now calls her "our Mother" and speaks with admiration of her works.

thought that now her life was at an end and that she would be able to see her bridegroom openly and enjoy him forever. But the bridegroom intercepted her flight saying, "Return, dove." This is like saying: In your sublime and swift contemplation and in your burning love and in the simplicity of your advance—for the dove has three properties—return from this lofty flight in which you aim after true possession of me; the time has not yet come for such high knowledge, adapt yourself to this lower knowledge that I am communicating to you in this rapture of yours. And it is as follows:

9. The wounded stag.

The bridegroom in this verse compares himself to a stag. It is characteristic of the stag to climb to high places and when wounded to race in search of refreshment and cool waters. If he hears the cry of his mate and senses that she is wounded, he immediately runs to her to comfort and coddle her.

The bridegroom now acts similarly. Beholding that the bride is wounded with love for him, he also, because of her moan, is wounded with love for her. Among lovers, the wound of one is a wound for both, and the two have but one feeling. Thus, in other words, he says: Return to me, my bride, because if you go about wounded with love for me, I too, like the stag, will come to you wounded by your wound.

10. Also by appearing in a high place I am like the stag. Hence he says, the stag

is in sight on the hill,

That is, in the height of your contemplation in this flight. For contemplation is a high place where God in this life begins to communicate and show Himself to the soul, but not completely. Hence He does not say that He is fully in sight, but that He is in sight. However sublime may be the knowledge God gives the soul in this life, it is but like a glimpse of Him from a great distance.

The third characteristic of the stag, contained in the next verse, follows:

11. Cooled by the breeze of your flight.

By the "flight," he means the contemplation received in that ecstasy, and by the breeze, the spirit of love that this flight of contemplation causes in the soul. He very appropriately terms this love that is caused by the flight a breeze, because the Holy Spirit, who is Love, is also compared to a breeze in Scripture, for the Holy Spirit is the breath of the Father and the Son. And just as the Holy Spirit is like a breeze from the flight (that is, He proceeds through spiration from the contemplation and wisdom of the Father and the Son), so the bridegroom calls this love of the soul a breeze because it proceeds from the contemplation and knowledge that she has of God at this time.

It is noteworthy that the bridegroom does not say he comes at the flight, but at the breeze of the flight, because, properly speaking, God does not communicate Himself to the soul through its flight (the knowledge it has of Him), but through the love it has from this knowledge. For just as love is the union of the Father and the Son, so it is the union of the soul with God. Hence it is that even though a soul may have the highest knowledge and contemplation of God and know all mysteries, yet if it does not love, this knowledge will be of no avail to its union with God, as St. Paul teaches [1 Cor 13:2]. St. Paul also says: *Charitatem habete quod est vinculum perfectionis* (Have this charity which is the bond of perfection) [Col 3:14]. This charity, then, causes the bridegroom to run to the spring of his bride's love, as the wounded and thirsty stag races for refreshment to the cool waters. Consequently he uses the word "cooled."

12. As a breeze cools and refreshes a person worn out by the heat, so this breeze of love refreshes and renews the one burning with the fire of love. The fire of love bears this property: The breeze by which it is cooled and refreshed makes it increase. For in the lover, love is a flame that burns with a desire to burn more, like the flame of natural fire. He refers to the fulfillment of this desire to burn more in his ardent love for his bride as "being cooled." In other words, he says: In the ardor of your flight you burn more, because one love enkindles another.

It is worthy of note that God does not place His grace and love in the soul except according to its desire and love. Those truly loving God must strive not to fail in this love, for they will thereby induce God, if we may so express it, to further love them and find delight in their soul.

And to obtain this charity, the soul must practice what St. Paul taught: *Charity is patient, is kind, is not envious, does no evil, does not become proud, is not ambitious, seeks not its own, does not become disturbed, thinks no evil, rejoices not in iniquity but rejoices in the truth, suffers all things* (that are to be suffered), *believes all things* (that must be believed), *hopes all things, and endures all things* (that are in accord with charity) [1 Cor 13:4–7].

THE SPIRITUAL CANTICLE

Stanzas 14 and 15

Introduction

1. Since this little dove was flying in the breeze of love above the flood waters of her loving fatigues and yearnings, which she has shown until now, and could find nowhere to alight, the compassionate father Noah, stretching out his merciful hand, caught her on her last flight and placed her in the ark of his charity [Gn 8:9]. This occurred when in the stanza we just explained the bridegroom said, "Return dove."

Finding in this recollection all that she desired and more than is expressible, the soul begins to sing the praises of her beloved in the following stanzas. They apply to his grandeurs, which she experiences and enjoys in this union.

> My beloved, the mountains,
> And lonely wooded valleys,
> Strange islands
> And resounding rivers,
> The whistling of love-stirring breezes,
>
> The tranquil night
> At the time of the rising dawn,
> Silent music,
> Sounding solitude,
> The supper that refreshes, and deepens love.

2. Before commenting on these stanzas, we should call to mind for the sake of a clearer understanding of them, and those that follow, that this spiritual flight denotes a high state and union of love, in which, after much spiritual exercise, the soul is placed by God. This state is called spiritual espousal with the Word, the Son of God. And at the beginning, when this flight is experienced the first time, God communicates to the soul great things about Himself, beautifies her with grandeur and majesty, adorns her with gifts and virtues, and clothes her with the knowledge and honor of God, as the betrothed is clothed on the day of her betrothal.

Not only do her vehement longings and complaints of love cease, but, in being graced with the blessings mentioned, a state of peace and delight and gentleness of love begins in her. This state is indicated in

THE SPIRITUAL CANTICLE

these stanzas, in which she does no more than tell in song her beloved's grandeurs, which she knows and enjoys in him through this union of espousal. In the remaining stanzas she no longer speaks of sufferings and longings as she did before, but of communion and exchange of sweet and peaceful love with her beloved, because now in this state all those sufferings have ceased.

It should be noted that these two stanzas describe the most that God communicates to the soul at this time. Yet it must not be thought that He communicates to all those who reach this state everything declared in these two stanzas, or that He does so in the same manner and measure of knowledge and feeling. To some souls He gives more and to others less, to some in one way and to others in another, although all alike may be in this same state of spiritual espousal. But the greatest possible communication is recorded here because it includes everything else. The commentary follows.[10]

Commentary on the two stanzas

3. In Noah's ark, as Sacred Scripture says, there were many rooms for different kinds of animals, and all the food that could be eaten [Gn 6:14, 19–21]. It should be noted that, similarly, the soul in her flight to the divine ark, the bosom of God, not only sees there the many dwelling places that His Majesty through St. John declared were in His Father's house [Jn 14:2], but sees and knows there all the foods (all the grandeurs the soul can enjoy) included in these two stanzas and signified by these common terms. These grandeurs in substance are as follows.

4. The soul sees and tastes abundance and inestimable riches in this divine union. She finds all the rest and recreation she desires, and understands secrets and strange knowledge of God, which is another one of the foods that taste best to her. She experiences in God an awesome power and strength which sweeps away every other power and strength. She tastes there a splendid spiritual sweetness and gratification, discovers true quiet and divine light, and tastes sublimely the wisdom of God reflected in the harmony of His creatures and works. She has the feeling of being filled with blessings and of being empty of evils and far removed from them. And above all she understands and enjoys inestimable refreshment of love which confirms her in love. These in substance are the affirmations of the two stanzas.

---

10. John wishes to leave room for a wide variety of possibilities within the same spiritual state.

5. The bride says in these stanzas that the beloved is all these things in himself and that he is so also for her, because in such superabundant communications from God, the soul experiences and knows the truth of St. Francis's prayer: *My God and all things.*[11] Since God is all things to the soul and the good that is in all things, the communication of this superabundance is explained through its likeness to the goodness of the things mentioned in these stanzas, which we shall explain in our commentary on each of the verses. It should be known that what is explained here is present in God eminently and infinitely, or, better, each of these sublime attributes is God, and all of them together are God.

Inasmuch as the soul in this case is united with God, she feels that all things are God, as St. John experienced when he said: *Quod factum est, in ipso vita erat* (That which was made, had life in Him) [Jn 1:4]. It should not be thought that what the soul is said to feel here is comparable to seeing things by means of the light, or creatures by means of God; rather in this possession the soul feels that God is all things for her. Neither must it be thought that, because the soul has so sublime an experience of God, we are asserting that she has essential and clear vision of Him. This experience is nothing but a strong and overflowing communication and glimpse of what God is in Himself, in which the soul feels the goodness of the things mentioned in these verses, which we will now comment on. . . .

12. The soul refers to two things in this verse: the breezes and the whistling. By "love-stirring breezes" is understood the attributes and graces of the beloved which by means of this union assail the soul and lovingly touch it in its substance.

This most sublime and delightful knowledge of God and His attributes that overflows into the intellect from the touch these attributes of God produce in the substance of the soul, she calls the whistling of these breezes. This is the most exalted delight of all the soul here enjoys.

13. To understand this better it should be noted that just as two things are felt in the breeze (the touch and the whistling or sound), so in this communication of the bridegroom two things are experienced: knowledge and a feeling of delight. As the feeling of the breeze delights

---

11. Bartholomew of Pisa in his book *Liber Conformitatum* speaks of how St. Francis spent the whole night in prayer repeating the words: "My God and all things."

the sense of touch, and its whistling delights the sense of hearing, so the feeling of the beloved's attributes are experienced and enjoyed by the soul's power of touch, which is in its substance, and the knowledge of these attributes is experienced in its hearing, which is its intellect.

It should also be known that the love-stirring breeze is said to come when it wounds in a pleasant way by satisfying the appetite of the one desiring such refreshment, because the sense of touch is then filled with enjoyment and refreshment; and the hearing, through the delectable touch, experiences great pleasure and gratification in the sound and whistling of the breeze. The delight of hearing is much greater than that of feeling because the sound in the sense of hearing is more spiritual; or, better, it more closely approaches the spiritual than does feeling. Consequently, the delight of hearing is more spiritual than that of feeling.

14. Since this touch of God gives intense satisfaction and enjoyment to the substance of the soul, and gently fulfills her desire for this union, she calls this union, or these touches, love-stirring breezes. As we have said, the beloved's attributes are lovingly and sweetly communicated in this breeze, and from it the intellect receives the knowledge or whistling.

She calls the knowledge a whistling, because just as the whistling of the breeze pierces deeply into the hearing organ, so this most subtle and delicate knowledge penetrates with wonderful savoriness into the innermost part of the substance of the soul, and the delight is greater than all other.[12]

The reason for the delight is that the substance understood, stripped of its accidents and phantasms, is bestowed. For this knowledge is given to that intellect that philosophers call the passive or possible intellect, and the intellect receives it passively without any efforts of its own. This knowing is the soul's main delight because it is pertinent to the intellect, and, as theologians say, fruition, the vision of God, is proper to the intellect.[13]

---

12. In distinguishing the knowledge received from the communication and the knowledge penetrating to the substance of the soul, John is distinguishing between conceptual knowledge and experiential knowledge of the divine realities.

13. His thought may come from *De Beatitudine*, an apocryphal work that had been attributed to Aquinas. See volume 28 of the works of St. Thomas (ed. Vives, Paris 1875). This work had a good deal of influence on John. See C.M.A. Diez, "La reentrega de amor asi en la tierra como en el cielo. Influjo de un opusculo pseudotomista en San Juan de la Cruz," *Ephemerides Carmeliticae* 13 (1962): 299–352.

THE SPIRITUAL CANTICLE

Since this whistling refers to the substantial knowledge mentioned, some theologians think our Father Elijah saw God in that whistling of the gentle breeze heard on the mount at the mouth of his cave [1 Kgs 19:11–13]. Scripture calls it the whistling of the gentle breeze because knowledge was begotten in his intellect from the delicate spiritual communication. This knowledge is called the whistling of love-stirring breezes because it flows over into the intellect from the loving communication of the beloved's attributes. As a result the soul calls the knowledge the whistling of love-stirring breezes.

15. This divine whistling, which enters through the soul's hearing, is, as I have said, not only the substance understood but also an unveiling of truths about the divinity and a revelation of God's secrets. When Scripture refers to a communication of God that enters by hearing, this communication ordinarily amounts to a manifestation of these naked truths to the intellect, or a revelation of the secrets of God. These are pure spiritual revelations or visions, which are given only to the spirit without the service and help of the senses. Thus what is called the communication of God through hearing is very certain and lofty. Accordingly, St. Paul, in order to declare the height of his revelation, did not say: *Vidit arcana verba*, and still less: *Gustavit arcana verba*, but *Audivit arcana verba quae non licet homini loqui* (He heard secret words which humans are not permitted to utter) [2 Cor 12:4]. It is thought that he saw God there as our Father Elijah also did in the whistling.

Since faith, as St. Paul also says [Rom 10:17], comes through hearing, so too that which faith tells us, the substance understood, comes through spiritual hearing. The prophet Job indicates this clearly in speaking with God who revealed Himself: *Auditu auris audivi te, nunc autem oculus meus videt te* (With the hearing of the ear I heard you and now my eye sees you) [Jb 42:5]. This passage points out clearly that to hear Him with the hearing of the soul is to see Him with the eye of the passive intellect. Consequently, he does not say I heard you with the hearing of my ears, but of my ear, nor I saw you with my eyes, but with my eye, which is the intellect. This hearing of the soul, therefore, is the vision of the intellect.

16. It must not be thought that, because what the soul understands is the naked substance, there is perfect and clear fruition as in heaven. Although the knowledge is stripped of accidents, it is not for this reason clear, but dark; for it is contemplation, which in this life, as St. Dionysius says, is a ray of darkness. We can say that it is a ray and image of fruition, since fruition takes place in the intellect.

THE SPIRITUAL CANTICLE

This substance that is understood, and which the soul calls whistling, is equivalent to "the eyes I have desired," of which the soul said, when they were being revealed to her, "Withdraw them, beloved," because her senses could not endure them. . . .

Stanza 16

Introduction

1. Since the virtues of the bride are perfect and she enjoys habitual peace in the visits of her beloved, she sometimes has a sublime enjoyment of their sweetness and fragrance when her beloved touches these virtues, just as people enjoy the sweetness and beauty of flowers and lilies when they have blossomed and are handled. In many of these visits the soul sees within herself all her virtues by means of the light the bridegroom causes. And then in a wonderful delight of love she gathers them together and offers them to him as a bouquet of beautiful flowers. And he, in accepting them—for indeed he accepts them—receives great service.

All of this occurs interiorly. The soul feels that the beloved is within her as in his own bed. She offers herself together with her virtues, which is the greatest service she can render him. Thus one of the most remarkable delights she receives in her interior communion with God comes from this gift of herself to her beloved.

2. The devil, who in his great malice is envious of all the good he sees in the soul, knowing of her prosperity, now employs all his ability and engages all his crafts to disturb even a slight part of this good. It is worth more to him to hinder a small fraction of this soul's rich and glorious delight than to make many others fall into numerous serious sins, for these others have little or nothing to lose and this soul has very much to lose because of all her precious gain. The loss of a little pure gold is much worse than the loss of many other base metals.

The devil at this point takes advantage of the sensory appetites, although most of the time he can do very little or nothing, since these appetites in persons having reached this state are already deadened. When he is unable to stir these appetites, he produces a great variety of images in the imagination. He is sometimes the cause of many movements of the sensory part of the soul and of many other disturbances, spiritual as well as sensory. It is not in a person's power to be free of these until the Lord sends His angel, as is said in the psalm, round about them that fear Him and delivers them [Ps 34:8], and until He brings peace and tranquillity, both in the sensory and spiritual part of the soul.

Referring to the devil's disturbances and distrustful of the wiles he uses to cause her harm at this time, the soul, seeking this favor from God, speaks to the angels whose duty it is to assist her now by putting the devil to flight. She recites the following stanza:

> Catch us the foxes,
> For our vineyard is now in flower,
> While we fashion a cone of roses
> Intricate as the pine's;
> And let no one appear on the hill.

Commentary

3. Desirous that neither the envious and malicious devils, nor the wild sensory appetites, nor the various wanderings of the imagination, nor any other knowledge or awareness hamper the continuance of this interior delight of love, which is the flower of her vineyard, the bride invokes the angels, telling them to catch all these disturbances and keep them from interfering with the interior exercises of love, in the delight of which the virtues and graces are communicated and enjoyed by the soul and the Son of God. . . .

Stanza 17

Introduction

1. For a greater understanding of the following stanza it should be pointed out that the absences of the beloved, which the soul suffers in this state of spiritual espousal, are very painful; some are of such a kind that there is no suffering comparable to them. The reason for such affliction is that since she has a singular and intense love for God in this state, His absence is a singular and intense torment for her. Added to this torment is the disturbance which at this time she receives from any kind of converse or communication with creatures. Since she lives with that driving force of a fathomless desire for union with God, any delay whatever is very burdensome and disturbing, just as anything in the

THE SPIRITUAL CANTICLE

path of a stone which is racing on toward its center would cause in that void a violent jolt. Since the soul has already received the delight of these sweet visits, they are more desirable than gold and all beauty. Fearing as a result the great lack—even if momentary—of so precious a presence, she speaks in this stanza both to dryness and to the spirit of her bridegroom:

> Be still deadening north wind;
> South wind come, you that waken love,
> Breathe through my garden,
> Let its fragrance flow,
> And the beloved will feed amid the flowers.

Commentary

2. Besides what was said in the previous stanza, spiritual dryness also hampers the interior satisfaction and sweetness of which she spoke. Dreading this, she does two things here:

First, she impedes dryness by closing the door to it through continual prayer and devotion.

Second, she invokes the Holy Spirit; it is He who will dispel this dryness and sustain and increase her love for the bridegroom. He also moves the soul to the interior exercise of the virtues, so that the Son of God, her bridegroom, may rejoice and delight more in His bride. She invokes the Holy Spirit because her entire aim is to please her bridegroom.

3.   Be still, deadening north wind;

The north wind is very cold; it dries up and withers the flowers and plants, or at least when striking them makes them shrink and close. Because the spiritual dryness and affective absence of the beloved produces this same effect in the soul by extinguishing the satisfaction, delight, and fragrance of the virtues she was enjoying, she calls it a deadening north wind. It deadens the virtues and affective exercise, and as a result the soul pleads: "Be still, deadening north wind."

It should be understood that this plea of the soul flows from prayer and the spiritual exercises and is directed toward a detainment of the dryness. Yet since God's communications to the soul are so interior that she cannot actively move her own faculties to the enjoyment of these

THE SPIRITUAL CANTICLE

communications, unless the spirit of the bridegroom causes this movement of love, she invokes him saying:

4.   South wind come, you that waken love,

The south wind is a delightful breeze: It causes rain, makes the herbs and plants germinate, opens the flowers, and scatters their fragrance. Its effects are the opposite of those of the north wind. The soul, by this breeze, refers to the Holy Spirit, who awakens love. When this divine breeze strikes her, it wholly enkindles and refreshes her, and quickens and awakens the will, and elevates the previously fallen appetites that were asleep to the love of God. It does so in such a way that she can easily add, you that waken love, both His love and hers.

What she asks of the Holy Spirit is expressed in the following verse:

5.   Breathe through my garden,

This garden is the soul. As the soul above calls herself a vineyard in flower, because the flowers of the virtues within her supply sweet-tasting wine, here she calls herself a garden because the flowers of perfections and virtues planted within her come to life and begin to grow.

It should be noted that the bride does not say "breathe into my garden," but "breathe through my garden," for there is a considerable difference between God's breathing into the soul and His breathing through the soul. To breathe into the soul is to infuse graces, gifts, and virtues. To breathe through the soul is to touch and put in motion the virtues and perfections already given, renewing and moving them in such a way that they of themselves afford the soul a wonderful fragrance and sweetness, as when you shake aromatic spices and they spread their abundant fragrance, which prior to this was neither so strong nor so highly perceptible. The soul is not always experiencing and enjoying the acquired or infused virtues actually, because, as we shall see later, they remain within her in this life like flowers enclosed in the bud or like aromatic spices whose scent is not perceived until shaken and uncovered.

6. God sometimes grants these favors to the soul, His bride. He breathes through her flowering garden, opens all these buds of virtues, and uncovers these aromatic spices of gifts, perfections, and riches; and, disclosing this interior treasure and wealth, He reveals all her beauty. And then it is something wonderful to behold and pleasant to

feel: the wealth of her gifts unveiled to the soul and the beauty of these flowers of virtues now in full bloom. And the fragrant scent each one with its own characteristics gives to her is inestimable. . . .

* * *

Stanza 20 and 21

Introduction

1. The attainment of so high a state of perfection as that which the soul here aims after, which is spiritual marriage, requires the purification of all the imperfections, rebellions, and imperfect habits of the lower part, which, by putting off the old self, is surrendered and made subject to the higher part; but there is also needed a singular fortitude and a very sublime love for so strong and intimate an embrace from God. The soul obtains not only a very lofty purity and beauty, but also an amazing strength because of the powerful and intimate bond effected between God and her by means of this union.

2. In order that she reach Him, it is necessary for her to attain an adequate degree of purity, fortitude, and love. The Holy Spirit, He who intervenes to effect this spiritual union, desiring that the soul attain the possession of these qualities in order to merit this union, speaks to the Father and the Son in the Canticle: *What shall we do for our sister on the day of her courtship, for she is little and has no breasts? If she is a wall, let us build upon it silver bulwarks and defenses; and if she is a door, let us reinforce it with cedar wood* [Sg 8:8–9]. The silver bulwarks and defenses refer to the strong and heroic virtues clothed with faith, which is signified by silver. These heroic virtues are those of spiritual marriage, and their foundation is in the strong soul, referred to by the wall. The peaceful bridegroom rests in the strength of these virtues without any weakness disturbing him. The cedar wood applies to the affections and properties of lofty love. This lofty love is signified by cedar, and it is the love proper to spiritual marriage. The bride must first be a door in order to receive the reinforcement of cedar wood; that is, she must hold the door of her will open to the bridegroom that he may enter through the complete and true yes of love. This is the yes of espousal, which is given before the spiritual marriage. The breasts of the bride also refer to this

perfect love that she should possess in order to appear before the bridegroom, Christ, for the consummation of this state.

3. The text, however, mentions that the bride answered immediately by stating her desire to be courted: *I am a wall and my breasts are as a tower* [Sg 8:10]. This means: My soul is strong and my love lofty, and so I should not be held back. Desiring this perfect union and transformation, the bride also manifested this strength in the preceding stanzas, especially in the one just explained, in which to oblige her spouse further she sets before him the virtues and preparative riches received from him. As a result the bridegroom, desiring to conclude this matter, speaks the two following stanzas in which he finishes purifying the soul, strengthening and disposing her in both sensory and spiritual parts for this state. He speaks these lines against all the oppositions and rebellions from the sensory part and the devil.

> Swift-winged birds,
> Lions, stags, and leaping roes,
> Mountains, lowlands, and river banks,
> Waters, winds, and ardors,
> Watching fears of night:
>
> By the pleasant lyres
> And the siren's song, I conjure you
> To cease your anger
> And not touch the wall,
> That the bride may sleep in deeper peace. . . .

Stanza 22

Introduction

1. Great was the desire of the bridegroom to free and ransom his bride completely from the hands of sensuality and the devil. Like the good shepherd rejoicing and holding on his shoulders the lost sheep for which he had searched along many winding paths [Lk 15:4–5], and like the woman who, having lit the candle and hunted through her whole house for the lost drachma, holding it up in her hands with gladness and calling to her friends and neighbors to come and celebrate, saying, rejoice with me, and so on [Lk 15:8–9], now, too, that the soul is lib-

THE SPIRITUAL CANTICLE

erated, this loving shepherd and bridegroom rejoices. And it is wonderful to see his pleasure in carrying the rescued, perfected soul on his shoulders, held there by his hands in this desired union.

Not only does he himself rejoice, but he also makes the angels and saintly souls share in his gladness, saying in the words of the Song of Songs: *Go forth daughters of Sion and behold king Solomon in the crown with which his mother crowned him on the day of his espousal and on the day of the joy of his heart* [Sg 3:11]. By these words he calls the soul his crown, his bride, and the joy of his heart, and he takes her now in his arms and goes forth with her as the bridegroom from his bridal chamber [Ps 19:6]. He refers to this in the following stanza.

> The bride has entered
> The sweet garden of her desire,
> And she rests in delight,
> Laying her neck
> On the gentle arms of her beloved.

Commentary

2. Now that the bride has diligently sought to catch the foxes, still the north wind, and calm the girls of Judea, all of which are obstacles to the full delight of the state of spiritual marriage; and now that she has also invoked and obtained the breeze of the Holy Spirit, as in the preceding stanzas, which entails the proper preparation and the instrument for the perfection of this state, we must treat of this state by explaining the stanza. Here the bridegroom speaks and, in calling the soul "bride," declares two things:

First he tells how, now victorious, she has reached this pleasant state of spiritual marriage, which was his as well as her ardent longing.

And second, he enumerates the properties of this state that the soul now enjoys, such as: resting in delight and laying her neck on the gentle arms of her beloved, as we will explain.

3.   The bride has entered.

To offer a more lucid explanation of the order of these stanzas and of what the soul usually passes through before reaching this state of spiritual marriage, which is the highest (that which, with the divine help, we will now speak of), it should be noted that before the soul reaches this state she first exercises herself both in the trials and the bitterness of mortification and in meditation on spiritual things. This is referred to from the first stanza until that which says: "Pouring out a thousand graces." Afterward she embarks on the contemplative way. Here she passes along the paths and straits of love about which she sings in the sequence of the verses until that stanza which begins, "Withdraw them, beloved," where the spiritual espousal is wrought. Afterward, she advances along the unitive way, in which she receives many remarkable communications, visits, gifts, and jewels from her bridegroom, and, as one betrothed, learns of her beloved and becomes perfect in loving him; this she relates starting at the stanza in which the espousal was made ("Withdraw them, beloved") until this one beginning with, "The bride has entered," where the spiritual marriage between the soul and the Son of God is effected.

This spiritual marriage is incomparably greater than the spiritual espousal, for it is a total transformation in the beloved in which each surrenders the entire possession of self to the other with a certain consummation of the union of love. The soul thereby becomes divine, becomes God through participation, insofar as is possible in this life. And thus I think that this state never occurs without the soul's being confirmed in grace, for the faith of both is confirmed when God's faith in the soul is here confirmed. It is accordingly the highest state attainable in this life.

Just as in the consummation of carnal marriage there are two in one flesh, as Sacred Scripture points out [Gn 2:24], so also when the spiritual marriage between God and the soul is consummated, there are two natures in one spirit and love, as St. Paul says in making this same comparison: *Whoever is joined to the Lord is one spirit with Him* [1 Cor 6:17]. This union resembles the union of the light of a star or candle with the light of the sun, for what then sheds light is not the star or the candle, but the sun, which has absorbed the other lights into its own.

The bridegroom speaks of the state in this verse saying: The bride has entered, that is, she has entered, leaving behind everything temporal and natural and all spiritual affections, modes, and manners, and has set aside and forgotten all temptations, disturbances, pains, solicitude, and cares, and is transformed in this high embrace.

The next line follows:

4.   The sweet garden of her desire.

This is like saying: She has been transformed into her God, here referred to as "the sweet garden," because of the sweet and pleasant dwelling she finds in Him. One does not reach this garden of full transformation, which is the joy, delight, and glory of spiritual marriage, without first passing through the spiritual espousal and the loyal and mutual love of betrothed persons. For after the soul has been for some time the betrothed of the Son of God in gentle and complete love, God calls her and places her in His flowering garden to consummate this most joyful state of marriage with Him. The union wrought between the two natures and the communication of the divine to the human in this state is such that even though neither changes its being, both appear to be God. Yet in this life the union cannot be perfect, although it is beyond words and thought.

5. The bridegroom points this out clearly in the Song of Songs where he invites the soul, now his betrothed, to this state: *Veni in hortum meum, soror mea sponsa, messui myrrham meam cum aromatibus meis* (Come and enter my garden, my sister, my bride, for now I have gathered my myrrh with my fragrant spices) [Sg 5:1]. He calls her sister and bride because she was a sister and bride in the love and surrender she had made of herself to him before he called her to this state of spiritual marriage, where, as he says, he has now gathered His fragrant myrrh and aromatic spices, which are the fruits of the flowers now ripe and ready for the soul. These are the delights and grandeurs that of himself and in himself he communicates to her in this state.

Consequently he is for her an enchanting, desirable garden. For her entire aim in all her works is the consummation and perfection of this state. She never rests until reaching it. She finds in this state a much greater abundance and fullness of God, a more secure and stable peace, and an incomparably more perfect delight than in the spiritual espousal; here it is as though she were placed in the arms of her bridegroom. As a result she usually experiences an intimate spiritual embrace, which is a veritable embrace, by means of which she lives the life of God. The words of St. Paul are verified in this soul: *I live, now not I, but Christ lives in me* [Gal 2:20].

Wherefore, since the soul lives in this state a life as happy and glorious as is God's, let each one consider here, if possible, how pleasant her life is. Just as God is incapable of feeling any distaste neither does she feel any, for the delight of God's glory is experienced and enjoyed in the substance of the soul now transformed in Him.

THE SPIRITUAL CANTICLE

As a result the next verse continues:

6.   And she rests in delight,
                        Laying her neck

The neck refers here to the soul's strength by means of which, as we said, is effected this union with her bridegroom, because she would be unable to endure so intimate an embrace if she were not now very strong. And because the soul labored it is right that with the strength by which she struggled and conquered she repose, laying her neck

7.   On the gentle arms of her beloved.

To recline her neck on the arms of God is to have her strength, or, better, her weakness, now united to the strength of God, for the arms signify God's strength. Accordingly this state of spiritual marriage is very aptly designated by the laying of her neck on the gentle arms of the beloved, for now God is the soul's strength and sweetness, in which she is sheltered and protected against all evils, and habituated to the delight of all goods.

Desirous of this state, the bride spoke to the bridegroom in the Song of Songs: *Who will give you to me for my brother, nursed at the breasts of my mother, that I may find you alone outside and kiss you, and no one despise me?* [Sg 8:1]. In calling him brother, she indicates the equality of love between the two in the espousal before this state is reached. And in saying, "nursed at the breasts of my mother," she means: You dried up and subdued in me the appetites and passions, which in our flesh are the breasts and milk of mother Eve, and an impediment to this state. And when this is accomplished "that I may find you alone outside," that is, outside of all things and of myself, in solitude and nakedness of spirit, which is attained when the appetites are dried up. And alone there, "kiss you" alone, that is, that my nature now alone and denuded of all temporal, natural, and spiritual impurity may be united with you alone, with your nature alone, through no intermediary. This union is found only in the spiritual marriage, in which the soul kisses God without contempt or disturbance from anyone. For in this state neither the flesh, nor the world, nor the devil molest her, nor do the appetites. Here we find also the fulfillment of what is said in the Song of Songs:

THE SPIRITUAL CANTICLE

Winter is now past, the rain is gone, and the flowers have appeared in our land [Sg 2:11].

Stanza 23

Introduction

1. In this high state of spiritual marriage the bridegroom reveals his wonderful secrets to the soul, as to his faithful consort, with remarkable ease and frequency, for true and perfect love knows not how to keep anything hidden from the beloved. He communicates to her, mainly, sweet mysteries of his Incarnation and of the ways of the redemption of humanity, which is one of the loftiest of his works, and thus more delightful to the soul. Even though he communicates many other mysteries to her, the bridegroom in the following stanza mentions only the Incarnation, as the most important. In speaking to the soul he says:

> Beneath the apple tree:
> There I took you for my own,
> There I offered you my hand,
> And restored you,
> Where your mother was corrupted.

Commentary

2. The bridegroom explains to the soul in this stanza his admirable plan in redeeming and espousing her to himself through the very means by which human nature was corrupted and ruined, telling her that as human nature through Adam was ruined and corrupted by means of the forbidden tree in the Garden of Paradise, so on the tree of the cross it was redeemed and restored when he gave it there, through his passion and death, the hand of his favor and mercy, and broke down the barriers between God and humans, which were built up through original sin.

Thus he says:

3.   Beneath the apple tree:

That is: beneath the favor of the tree of the cross (referred to by the apple tree), where the Son of God redeemed human nature and con-

THE SPIRITUAL CANTICLE

sequently espoused it to Himself, and then espoused each soul by giving it through the cross grace and pledges for this espousal.
And thus he says:

4. There I took you for my own,
There I offered you my hand,

That is: There I offered you my kind regard and help by raising you from your low state to be my companion and spouse.

5. And restored you,
Where your mother was corrupted.

For human nature, your mother, was corrupted in your first parents, under the tree, and you too under the tree of the cross were restored. If your mother, therefore, brought you death under the tree, I, under the tree of the cross, brought you life. In such a way God manifests the decrees of His wisdom; He knows how to draw good from evil so wisely and beautifully, and to ordain to a greater good what was a cause of evil.

The bridegroom himself literally speaks this stanza to the bride in the Song of Songs: *Sub arbore malo suscitavi te; ibi corrupta est mater tua, ibi violata est genetrix tua* (Under the apple tree I raised you up; there your mother was corrupted, there she who bore you was violated) [Sg 8:5].

6. The espousal made on the cross is not the one we now speak of. For that espousal is accomplished immediately when God gives the first grace, which is bestowed on each one at baptism. The espousal of which we speak bears reference to perfection and is not achieved save gradually and by stages. For though it is all one espousal, there is a difference in that one is attained at the soul's pace, and thus little by little, and the other at God's pace, and thus immediately. . . .

* * *

THE SPIRITUAL CANTICLE

Stanza 26

Introduction

1. What, then, is the state of this happy soul in her bed of flowers, where these things and so many others take place, in which she has for her couch the bridegroom, the Son of God, and love of this very bridegroom for a covering and hanging? She can certainly repeat the words of the bride: *His left hand is under my head* [Sg 2:6]. We can therefore assert truly that this soul is here clothed with God and bathed in divinity, not as though on the surface, but in the interior of her spirit, superabounding in divine delights. In the fullness of the spiritual waters of life, she experiences what David says of those who have reached God: *They shall be inebriated with the plenty of your house; and you will give them to drink of the torrent of your delight, because with you is the fountain of life* [Ps 36:9–10]. What fulfillment will the soul have in her being, since the drink given her is no less than a torrent of delight! This torrent is the Holy Spirit because, as St. John says, He is a resplendent river of living water that flows from the throne of God and of the Lamb [Rv 22:1]. These waters, since they are the intimate love of God, flow intimately into the soul and give her to drink of this torrent of love, which, as we said, is the Spirit of her bridegroom infused in this union. As a result she sings this stanza with abundant love:

> In the inner wine cellar
> I drank of my beloved, and when I went abroad
> Through all this valley
> I no longer knew anything,
> And lost the herd which I was following. . . .

> 13.   I no longer knew anything.

The reason is that the drink of highest wisdom makes her forget all worldly things. And it seems that her previous knowledge, and even all the knowledge of the world, in comparison with this knowledge is pure ignorance.

For a better understanding of this, it should be known that the most formal cause of the soul's knowing nothing of the world when in this state is that she is being informed with supernatural knowledge, in the presence of which all natural and political knowledge of the world is ignorance rather than knowledge. When the soul is brought into this lofty knowing, she understands by means of it that all other knowledge that has not the taste of this knowledge is not knowledge but ignorance, and that there is nothing to know in it. She declares the truth of the Apostle's words, that what is greater wisdom in the sight of humans is foolishness before God [1 Cor 3:19]. Hence she asserts that after drinking of that divine wisdom she no longer knew anything.

And this truth (that human wisdom and that of the whole world is pure ignorance and unworthy of being known) cannot be understood except by this favor of God's presence in the soul, by which He communicates His wisdom and comforts her with the drink of love that she may behold this truth clearly, as Solomon explains: *This is the vision that the man who is with God saw and spoke. And being comforted by God's dwelling within him, he said: I am the most foolish among humans, and human wisdom is not with me* [Prv 30:1–2].

The reason is that in the excess of the lofty wisdom of God lowly human wisdom is ignorance. The natural sciences themselves and the very works of God, when set beside what it is to know God, are like ignorance. For where God is unknown nothing is known. The high things of God are foolishness and madness to humans, as St. Paul says [1 Cor 2:14]. Hence the wise people of God and the wise people of the world are foolish in the eyes of each other, for the one group finds the wisdom and knowledge of God imperceptible, and the other finds the same of the knowledge of the world. Wherefore the knowledge of the world is ignorance to the knowledge of God, and the knowledge of God is ignorance to the knowledge of the world.

14. On the other hand, that elevation and immersion of the mind in God, in which the soul is as though carried away and absorbed in love, entirely transformed in God, does not allow attention to any worldly thing. She is not only annihilated before all things and estranged from them, but even from herself, as if she had vanished and been dissolved in love; all of which consists in passing out of self to the beloved. Thus the bride in the Song of Songs, after having treated of the transformation of her love into the beloved, refers to this unknowing, in which she was left, by the word *nescivi* (I did not know) [Sg 6:11].

In a way, the soul in this state resembles Adam in the state of innocence, who did not know evil. For she is so innocent that she does not understand evil, nor does she judge anything in a bad light. And she will hear very evil things and see them with her own eyes and be unable to understand that they are so, since she does not have within herself the habit of evil by which to judge them; for God by means of

THE SPIRITUAL CANTICLE

the perfect habit of true wisdom has destroyed her habitual imperfections and ignorances, which include the evil of sin.

15. And so too in regard to her words, "I no longer knew anything," she takes little part in the affairs of others, for she is not even mindful of her own. This is a characteristic of God's spirit in the soul: He gives her an immediate inclination toward ignoring and not desiring knowledge of the affairs of others, especially that which brings her no benefit. God's spirit is turned toward the soul to draw her away from external affairs rather than involve her in them. Thus she remains in an unknowing, in the manner she was accustomed to.

16. It should not be thought that because she remains in this unknowing that she loses there her acquired knowledge of the sciences; rather these habits are perfected by the more perfect habit of supernatural knowledge infused in her. Yet these habits do not reign in such a way that she must use them in order to know; though at times she may still use them since this supernatural knowledge does not impede their use. For in this union with divine wisdom these habits are joined to the superior wisdom of God. When a faint light is mingled with a bright one, the bright light prevails and is that which illumines. Yet the faint light is not lost, but rather perfected, even though it is not the light that illumines principally.

Such, I believe, will be the case in heaven. The habits of knowledge that were acquired by the just will not be supplanted, but they will not be of great benefit either, since the just will have more knowledge through the divine wisdom than through these habits.

17. Yet particular knowledge, forms of things, imaginative acts, and any other apprehensions involving form and figure are all lost and ignored in that absorption of love. There are two reasons for this:

First, since the soul is absorbed and imbibed in that drink of love, she cannot advert actually to any other thing.

Second, and principally, that transformation in God makes her so consonant with the simplicity and purity of God, in which there is no form or imaginative figure, that it leaves her clean, pure, and empty of all forms and figures, purged, and radiant in simple contemplation. The effect of this contemplation is like that of the sun on a window. In shining on the window, the sun makes it look bright, and all the stains and smudges previously apparent are lost sight of; yet when the sunlight passes, the stains and smudges reappear.

Since the effect of that act of love endures a while, the unknowing also continues, so that the soul cannot advert to anything in particular until the effect of that act of love passes. Since that act of love inflamed and transformed her into love, it annihilated her and did away with all that was not love, as is understood in what we mentioned above concerning David: *Because my heart was inflamed, my reins were also changed, and I was brought to nothing and knew not* [Ps 73:21–22]. The change of the reins because of this inflammation of the heart is a change of the soul, according to her operations and appetites, into God, into a new kind of life in which she is undone and annihilated before all the old things she formerly made use of. The prophet thus says that he was brought to nothing and did not know, for these are the two effects we mentioned of this drink from the wine cellar of God. . . .

Stanza 27

Introduction

1. In this interior union God communicates Himself to the soul with such genuine love that no mother's affection, in which she tenderly caresses her child, no brother's love, nor friendship is comparable to it. The tenderness and truth of love by which the immense Father favors and exalts this humble and loving soul reaches such a degree—O wonderful thing, worthy of all our awe and admiration—that the Father Himself becomes subject to her for her exaltation, as though He were her servant and she His lord. And He is as solicitous in favoring her as He would be if He were her slave and she His good. So profound is the humility and sweetness of God!

In this communication of love, He exercises in some way that very service that He says in the gospel He will render to His elect in heaven, that is: Girding Himself and passing from one to another, He will minister to them [Lk 12:37]. He is occupied here in favoring and caressing the soul like a mother who ministers to her child and nurses it at her own breasts. The soul thereby comes to know the truth of Isaiah's words: *You shall be carried at the breast of God and upon His knees you will be caressed* [Is 66:12].

2. What then will be the soul's experience among such sovereign graces! How she will be dissolved in love! How thankful she will be to see the breasts of God given to her with such supreme and generous love! Aware that she has been set among so many delights, she makes a complete surrender of herself and gives Him the breast of

her will and love. She experiences this surrender of her soul in the way the bride did in the Canticle when speaking to her bridegroom: *I turn to my beloved, and his turning is toward me. Come my beloved, let us go into the field, let us abide together on the grange; let us rise very early and go to the vineyards to see if the vine is in flower and if the flowers bear fruit, if the pomegranates flourish; there will I give you my breasts* (that is, I shall employ the delights and strength of my will in your love) [Sg 7:11–13]. . . .

Stanza 28

Introduction

1. Because we said that God makes use of nothing other than love, it may prove beneficial to explain the reason for this, prior to commenting on the stanza. The reason is that all our works and our trials, even though they are the greatest possible, are nothing in the sight of God. For through them we cannot give Him anything or fulfill his only desire, which is the exaltation of the soul. Of these other things He desires nothing for Himself, since He has no need of them. If anything pleases Him, it is the exaltation of the soul. Since there is no way by which He can exalt her more than by making her equal to Himself, He is pleased only with her love. For the property of love is to make the lover equal to the object loved. Since the soul in this state possesses perfect love, she is called the bride of the Son of God, which signifies equality with Him. In this equality of friendship the possessions of both are held in common, as the bridegroom himself said to his disciples: *I have now called you my friends because all that I have heard from my Father I have manifested to you* [Jn 15:15].

She then recites the stanza:

Now I occupy my soul
And all my energy in his service;
I no longer tend the herd,
Nor have I any other work
Now that my every act is love.

Commentary

2. Since in the last stanza the soul—or better the bride—said she surrendered herself entirely to the bridegroom without keeping anything

THE SPIRITUAL CANTICLE

back, she now tells of her mode and method in accomplishing this, saying that now she occupies her soul and body, her faculties and all her ability, in nothing other than the service of her bridegroom. And she says that on this account she no longer goes about in search of her own gain or pleasures, nor occupies herself with things and matters foreign to God; and that even with God Himself she has no other style or manner of dealing than the exercise of love, since she has now traded and changed for love all her first manner of dealing with Him, as is now said:

3.   Now I occupy my soul

By saying that she occupies her soul, she refers to her surrender to the beloved in that union of love where now the soul and all the faculties (intellect, memory, and will) are dedicated and devoted to his service. She employs the intellect in understanding and carrying out the things that are more for his service, and the will in loving all that is pleasing to him and attaching it to him in all things, and her memory and care in what most pleases and serves him.

And she adds:

4.   And all my energy in his service;

By "all her energy" she refers to all that pertains to the sensory part of the soul. The sensory part includes the body with all its senses and faculties, interior and exterior, and all the natural ability (the four passions, the natural appetites, and other energies).

All of this, she says, she occupies, as she does the rational and spiritual part referred to in the preceding verse, in the service of her beloved. By directing the activity of the interior and exterior senses toward God, her use of the body is now conformed to His will. She also binds the four passions of the soul to Him, for she does not rejoice except in God, nor hope in anything other than God; she fears only God and has no sorrow unless in relation to Him. And likewise all her appetites and cares go out only to God.

5. All this energy is occupied in God, and so directed to Him that even without advertence all its parts, which we have mentioned, are inclined from their first movements to work in and for God. The intellect, will, and memory go out immediately toward God, and the affections, senses, desires, appetites, hope, joy, and all the energy from the first instant incline toward God, although, as I say, the soul may not advert to the fact that she is working for Him.

THE SPIRITUAL CANTICLE

As a result she frequently works for God, and is occupied in Him and in His affairs without thinking or being aware that she is doing so. For her custom and habit of acting in this way causes her to lack advertence and care and even the fervent acts she used to make in beginning some work.

Because this energy is now all employed in God, the soul necessarily achieves the condition described in the following verse:

6.   I no longer tend the herd

This is like saying: I no longer follow after my pleasures and appetites. For having placed them in God and given them to Him, she no longer feeds them nor keeps them for herself.

She does not merely say she no longer tends this herd, but even more:

7.   Nor have I any other work

Before reaching this gift and surrender of herself and her energy to the beloved, the soul usually has many unprofitable occupations, by which she endeavors to serve her own appetite and that of others. For we can say she had as much work as she had many habitual imperfections. These habitual imperfections can be, for example, the trait or "work" of speaking about useless things, thinking about them, and also carrying them out, or of not making use of these actions in accord with the demands of perfection. She usually has desires to serve the appetites of others, which she does through ostentatiousness, compliments, flattery, human respect, the effort to impress and please people by her actions, and many other useless things. In this fashion she strives to satisfy people, employing for them all her care, desires, work, and finally energy.

She says she no longer has all this work, because all her words, thoughts, and works are of God and directed toward Him without any of the former imperfections. Thus the verse means: I no longer tend to giving satisfaction to my appetite or that of others, neither am I occupied or detained with other useless pastimes or things of the world.

8.   Now that my every act is love.

This is like saying that now all this work is directed to the practice of love of God, that is: All the ability of my soul and body (memory, intellect, and will, interior and exterior senses, appetites of the sensory and spiritual part) moves in love and because of love. Everything I do,

I do with love, and everything I suffer, I suffer with the delight of love. David meant this when he said: *I shall keep my strength for you* [Ps 59:10].

9. It should be known that when the soul reaches this state, all the activity of the spiritual and sensory part (in which it does, or in what it suffers, and in whatever manner) always causes more love and delight in God, as we have said. Even the very exercise of prayer and communion with God, in which she was accustomed to considerations and methods, is now wholly the exercise of love. Hence whether her work is temporal or spiritual, this soul can always say, "Now that my every act is love."

10. Happy is the life and state, and happy the person who attains it, where everything is now the substance of love and the pleasure and delight of espousal. The bride in this state can indeed say to the divine bridegroom those words she spoke to him out of pure love in the Song of Songs: *All the new and old apples I have kept for you* [Sg 7:14], which is equivalent to saying: My beloved, all that is rough and toilsome I desire for your sake, and all that is sweet and pleasant I desire for your sake. Yet the accommodated sense of this verse is that the soul in this state of spiritual espousal ordinarily walks in the union of love of God, which is a habitual and loving attentiveness of the will to God.[14]

Stanza 29

Introduction
1. This soul indeed, lost to all things and won over to love, no longer occupies her spirit in anything else. She even withdraws in matters pertinent to the active life and exterior occupations for the sake of fulfilling the one thing the bridegroom said was necessary [Lk 10:42], and that is: attentiveness to God and continual love of Him. This the Lord values and esteems so highly that He reproved Martha when she tried to call Mary away from her place at His feet in order to busy her with

---

14. In the first redaction, this stanza was number 19, where John was speaking about the spiritual betrothal but not with great precision. From this stanza to stanza 34 there is a fluctuating between the spiritual betrothal and the spiritual marriage. Actually, the stanzas could be interpreted to speak of either. St. Therese of Lisieux found in this stanza the substance of her experience. It gave a beautiful little summary of the spiritual message given to her by her esteemed Holy Father John of the Cross.

other active things in His service. And Martha thought that she herself was doing all the work and that Mary, because she was enjoying the Lord's presence, was doing nothing [Lk 10:39–41]. Yet, since there is no greater or more necessary work than love, the contrary is true. He also defends the bride in the Song of Songs, conjuring all creatures of the world, referred to by the daughters of Jerusalem, not to hinder the bride's spiritual sleep of love or cause her to awaken or open her eyes to anything else until she desires [Sg 3:5].

2. It should be noted that until the soul reaches this state of union of love, she should practice love in both the active and contemplative life. Yet once she arrives, she should not become involved in other works and exterior exercises that might be of the slightest hindrance to the attentiveness of love toward God, even though the work be of great service to God. For a little of this pure love is more precious to God and the soul and more beneficial to the Church, even though it seems one is doing nothing, than all these other works put together.

Because of her determined desire to please her spouse and benefit the Church, Mary Magdalene, even though she was accomplishing great good by her preaching and would have continued doing so, hid in the desert for thirty years in order to surrender herself truly to this love. It seemed to her, after all, that by such retirement she would obtain much more because of the notable benefit and gain a little of this love brings to the Church.

3. Great wrong would be done to those who possess some degree of this solitary love, as well as to the Church, if we should urge them to become occupied in exterior or active things, even if the works are very important and demand only a short time. Since God has solemnly entreated that no one awaken a soul from this love [Sg 3:5], who will dare do so and remain without reproof? After all, this love is the end for which we were created.

Let those, then, who are singularly active, who think they can win the world with their preaching and exterior works, observe here that they would profit the Church and please God much more, not to mention the good example they would give, were they to spend at least half of this time with God in prayer, even though they may not have reached a prayer as sublime as this. They would then certainly accomplish more, and with less labor by one work than they otherwise would by a thousand. For through their prayer they would merit this result, and themselves be spiritually strengthened. Without prayer they would

THE SPIRITUAL CANTICLE

do a great deal of hammering but accomplish little, and sometimes nothing, and even at times cause harm.

God forbid that the salt should begin to lose its savor [Mt 5:13], for however much they may appear to achieve externally, they will in substance be accomplishing nothing; it is beyond doubt that good works can be performed only by the power of God.

4. Oh, how much could be written here on this subject! But this is not the place. I have mentioned it only in explanation of the next stanza. In this stanza the soul replies to all those who impugn her holy idleness, and who desire every work to be the kind that shines outwardly and satisfies the eye, and do not know the secret source from which the water flows and all fruit is produced.[15]

And thus she recites the stanza

> If, then, I am no longer
> Seen or found on the common,
> You will say that I am lost;
> That stricken by love,
> I lost myself, and was found.

Commentary

5. In this stanza the soul answers a tacit reproof of those in the world who usually criticize persons who are entirely given to God and think these persons excessive in their conduct, estrangement, and withdrawal, and assert that they are useless in important matters and lost to what the world esteems. The soul skillfully answers this reprimand, boldly facing it and all the other possible reproofs of the world; for in having reached the intimate love of God, she considers everything else of little consequence.

But this is not all. She even proclaims how she has acted, and rejoices and glories in having lost the world and herself for her beloved. This is what she means in the stanza when she addresses the worldly: that, if they no longer see her engaged in her former worldly conversations and pastimes, they should believe and declare that she has lost

---

15. The longest of the *Canticle*, this introduction is written with deep conviction and passion. The love of God is the supreme value in one's personal life and in the service of the Church. But these words cannot be taken to imply that pure love could ever exclude the making of conscientious choices; cf. C. 28, 3–9.

these things and withdrawn; and that she has counted this loss such a good that she herself, searching for her beloved and intensely enamored of him, desired it. That they might see the gain of her loss and not think it an absurdity or a delusion, she declares that her loss was her gain, and that as a result she became lost purposely.

> 6. If, then, I am no longer
> Seen or found on the common

The place where people often gather for diversion and recreation, and where shepherds also feed their flocks, is usually called the common. Thus, by the common the soul refers to the world, where worldlings engage in their pastimes and conversations and feed the flock of their appetites. In this verse she tells those who are of the world that if they neither see nor find her as they did before her complete surrender to God, they should consider her, by this fact, lost, and they should therefore say (because she rejoices in their saying this and desires them to do so):

> 7. You will say that I am lost;

Those who love are not abashed before the world because of the works they perform for God, nor even if everybody condemns them do they hide them in shame. Those who are ashamed to confess the Son of God before others, by failing to perform His works, will discover that the Son of God, as is recorded in Luke, will be ashamed to confess them before the Father [Lk 9:26]. The soul possessing the spirit of love glories rather in beholding that she has achieved this work in praise of her beloved and lost all things of the world. Hence she says: "You will say that I am lost."

8. Few spiritual persons reach such daring and determination in their works. Though some do act this way, and are considered far advanced, they never lose themselves entirely in some matters, whether worldly or natural, and never execute works for Christ with perfection and nakedness of spirit and without thought of what others will say or how their work will appear. Since these persons are not lost to themselves in their work, they cannot declare: "You will say that I am lost." They are still ashamed to confess Christ before others by their works. Because of their human respect they do not live entirely in Christ.

THE SPIRITUAL CANTICLE

9. *That, stricken by love*

This means that, through the practice of virtue, stricken with love,

10. *I lost myself and was found.*

Aware of the bridegroom's words in the gospel, that no one can serve two masters, but must necessarily fail one [Mt 6:24], the soul claims here that in order not to fail God, she failed all that is not God, that is, herself and all other creatures, losing all these for love of Him. Those who truly walk in love let themselves lose all things immediately in order to be found more attached to what they love. On this account the soul affirms here that she lost herself. She achieved this in two ways: She became lost to herself by paying no attention to herself in anything, by concentrating on her beloved and surrendering herself to him freely and disinterestedly, with no desire to gain anything for herself; secondly, she became lost to all creatures, paying no heed to all her own affairs, but only to those of her beloved. And this is to lose herself purposely, which is to desire to be found.

11. Those who walk in the love of God seek neither their own gain nor their reward, but only to lose all things and themselves for God; and this loss they judge to be their gain. And thus it is as St. Paul asserts: *Mori lucrum* [Phil 1:21], that is, my death for Christ is the spiritual gain of all things and of myself. And consequently the soul declares, "I was found." Those who do not know how to lose themselves, do not find themselves, but rather lose themselves, as our Lord teaches in the gospels: *Those who desire to gain their soul shall lose it, and those who lose it for my sake shall gain it* [Mt 16:25].

Should we desire to interpret this verse more spiritually and in closer accord with what we are discussing here, it ought to be known that when a soul treading the spiritual road has reached such a point that she has lost all roads and natural methods in her communion with God, and no longer seeks Him by reflections, or forms, or sentiments, or by any other way of creatures and the senses, but has advanced beyond them all and beyond all modes and manners, and enjoys communion with God in faith and love, then it is said that God is her gain, because she has certainly lost all that is not God. . . .

* * *

THE SPIRITUAL CANTICLE

Stanza 36

Introduction

1. Strange it is, this property of lovers, that they like to enjoy each other's companionship alone, apart from every creature and all company. If some stranger is present, they do not enjoy each other freely, even though they are together and may speak to each other just as much when the other is present as when absent, and even though this stranger does not talk to them. The reason they desire to commune with each other alone is that love is a union between two alone. . . .

> Let us rejoice, beloved,
> And let us go forth to behold ourselves in your beauty,
> To the mountain and to the hill,
> To where the pure water flows,
> And further deep into the thicket. . . .

4.   *Let us rejoice, beloved*

That is: Let us rejoice in the communication of the sweetness of love, not only in that sweetness we already possess in our habitual union, but in that which overflows into the effective and actual practice of love, either interiorly with the will in the affective act, or exteriorly in works directed to the service of the beloved. As we mentioned, when love takes root it has this characteristic: It makes one always desire to taste its joys and sweetnesses, which are the inward and outward exercise of love.[16] All this the lover does in order to resemble the beloved more.

And thus she continues:

5. *And let us go forth to behold ourselves in your beauty*

This means: Let us so act that by means of this loving activity we may attain to the vision of ourselves in your beauty in eternal life. That is: That I may be so transformed in your beauty that we may be alike in beauty, and both behold ourselves in your beauty, possessing now your very beauty; this, in such a way that looking at each other we may see in each other our own beauty since both of us are your beauty alone, I being absorbed in your beauty; hence, I shall see you in your beauty,

---

16. The joy and sweetness of love is found not only in contemplation but also in action, or in John's traditional terminology, in both the contemplative and the active life.

THE SPIRITUAL CANTICLE

and you shall see me in your beauty, and I shall see myself in you in your beauty, and you will see yourself in me in your beauty; that I may resemble you in your beauty, and you resemble me in your beauty, and my beauty be your beauty and your beauty be my beauty; wherefore I shall be you in your beauty, and you will be me in your beauty, because your very beauty will be my beauty; and therefore we shall behold each other in your beauty.[17]

This is the adoption of the children of God, who will indeed declare to God what the very Son said to the Eternal Father through St. John: *All my things are yours, and yours mine* [Jn 17:10]. He says this by essence since He is the natural Son of God, and we say it by participation, since we are adopted children. He declared this not only for Himself, the head, but for His whole mystical body, the Church, which on the day of her triumph, when she sees God face to face, will participate in the very beauty of the bridegroom. Hence the soul makes the petition that she and her bridegroom go forth to behold each other in his beauty. . . .

Stanza 37

1. One of the main reasons for the desire to be dissolved and to be with Christ [Phil 1:23] is to see Him face to face and thoroughly understand the profound and eternal mysteries of His Incarnation, which is by no means the lesser part of beatitude. As Christ Himself says to the Father in St. John's gospel: *This is eternal life that they might know you, the one true God, and your Son Jesus Christ whom you have sent* [Jn 17:3]. The first thing a person desires to do after having come a long distance is to see and converse with the one deeply loved. Similarly, the first thing the soul desires on coming to the vision of God is to know and enjoy the deep secrets and mysteries of the Incarnation and the ancient ways of

---

17. This passage is actually a prayer in which John forgets the reader and is carried away by the beauty of the beloved. He speaks not of beauty in general but of "your beauty," and he uses the word beauty twenty-three times. Francisca de la Madre de Dios, a discalced Carmelite nun in Beas, recounted that one day John asked her how she spent her time in prayer. She told him that she spent it beholding the beauty of God and rejoicing that He possessed it. John became so happy over the reply that for some days he spoke very elevated things about the beauty of God. Impelled by this love he composed at the time (1582–1584) five stanzas, which began with "Let us rejoice, beloved."

THE SPIRITUAL CANTICLE

God dependent on it. Hence after expressing her desire to see herself in the beauty of God, the soul declares in the following stanza:

> And then we will go on
> To the high caverns in the rock
> Which are so well concealed;
> There we shall enter
> And taste the fresh juice of the pomegranates.

Commentary

2. One of the reasons urging the soul most to enter this thicket of God's wisdom and know its beauty from further within is her wish to unite her intellect with God in the knowledge of the mysteries of the Incarnation, in which is contained the highest and most savory wisdom of all His works. The bride states in this stanza that once she has entered further into the divine wisdom (further into the spiritual marriage she now possesses, which will be the face-to-face vision of God in glory as well as union with the divine wisdom, who is the Son of God), she will know the sublime mysteries of God and of humanity. These mysteries are exalted in wisdom, and the soul enters the knowledge of them, engulfing and immersing herself in them. And both the bride and bridegroom will taste the savor and the delight caused by the knowledge of these mysteries together with the powers and attributes of God uncovered in them such as: justice, mercy, wisdom, power, charity, and so on.

> 3. And then we will go on
> To the high caverns in the rock

The rock mentioned here, as St. Paul says, is Christ [1 Cor 10:4]. The high caverns of this rock are the sublime, exalted, and deep mysteries of God's wisdom in Christ, in the hypostatic union of the human nature with the divine Word, and in the corresponding union of human beings with God, and the mystery of the harmony between God's justice and mercy with respect to the manifestations of His judgments in the salvation of the human race. These mysteries are so profound that she very appropriately calls them high caverns; high, because of the height of the sublime mysteries; caverns, because of the depth of God's wisdom in them. As caverns are deep and have many recesses, so each of the mysteries in Christ is singularly deep in wisdom and contains many recesses of His secret judgments of predestination and foreknowledge concerning the children of this earth.

She then adds:

4.   Which are so well concealed

They are so well concealed that however numerous are the mysteries and marvels that holy doctors have discovered and saintly souls understood in this earthly life, all the more is yet to be said and understood. There is much to fathom in Christ, for He is like an abundant mine with many recesses of treasures, so that however deep people go they never reach the end or bottom, but rather in every recess find new veins with new riches everywhere. On this account St. Paul said of Christ: *In Christ dwell hidden all treasures and wisdom* [Col 2:3]. The soul cannot enter these caverns or reach these treasures if, as we said, she does not first pass over to the divine wisdom through the straits of exterior and interior suffering. For one cannot reach in this life what is attainable of these mysteries of Christ without having suffered much, and without having received numerous intellectual and sensible favors from God, and without having undergone much spiritual activity; for all these favors are inferior to the wisdom of the mysteries of Christ in that they serve as preparations for coming to this wisdom. When Moses asked God to reveal His glory, he was told by God that he would be unable to receive such a revelation in this life, but that he would be shown all good, that is all the good revealable in this life. So God put Moses in the cavern of the rock, which is Christ, as we said, and showed His back to him, which was to impart knowledge of the mysteries of the humanity of Christ.

5. The soul, then, earnestly longs to enter these caverns of Christ in order to be absorbed, transformed, and wholly inebriated in the love of the wisdom of these mysteries, and hide herself in the bosom of the beloved. In the Song of Songs he invites her to these clefts, saying: *Arise, make haste, my love, my beautiful one, and come into the clefts of the rock and into the cavern of the wall* [Sg 2:13–14]. . . .

THE SPIRITUAL CANTICLE

Stanza 38

Introduction

1. In the two preceding stanzas the bride's song focused on the good that the bridegroom will offer her in that eternal bliss. That is, the spouse will really transform her into the beauty of both his created and uncreated wisdom, and also into the beauty of the union of the Word with his humanity, in which she will know him face to face as well as from the back.

In the next stanza she discusses two things: first, the manner in which she will taste that divine juice of the sapphires, or rather the pomegranates; second, the glory she will give to her bridegroom through her predestination.

It should be noted that even though she refers to these goods as successive parts, they are all contained in one essential glory.

She says:

> There you will show me
> What my soul has been seeking,
> And then you will give me,
> You, my life, will give me there
> What you gave me on that other day:

Commentary

2. The reason the soul desired to enter these caverns was to reach the consummation of the love of God, which she had always been seeking; that is, to love God as purely and perfectly as He loves her in order to repay Him by such love. She declares to the bridegroom in this stanza that there he will show her what was her desire in all her acts, how to love the spouse as perfectly as he loves her. The second gift she will receive there is the essential glory to which he predestined her from the day of his eternity.

Thus she declares:

3.   There you will show me
     What my soul has been seeking

The soul's aim is a love equal to God's. She always desired this equality, naturally and supernaturally, for lovers cannot be satisfied if they fail to feel that they love as much as they are loved. Since the soul sees that through her transformation in God in this life she cannot, even though her love is immense, equal the perfection of God's love for her, she desires the clear transformation of glory in which she will reach this equality. Even though there is a true union of will in this high state she now enjoys, she cannot attain the excellence and power of love that she will possess in the strong union of glory. Just as the soul, according to St. Paul, will know then as she is known by God [1 Cor 13:12], so she will also love God as she is loved by Him. As her intellect will be the intellect of God, her will then will be God's will, and thus her love will be God's love. The soul's will is not destroyed there, but it is so firmly united with the strength of God's will, with which He loves her, that her love for Him is as strong and perfect as His love for her, for the two wills are so united that there is only one will and love, which is God's. This strength lies in the Holy Spirit, in whom the soul is there transformed, for by this transformation of glory He supplies what is lacking in her since He is given to the soul for the sake of the strength of this love. Even in the perfect transformation of this state of spiritual marriage, which the soul reaches in this life, she superabounds with grace and, as above, loves in some way through the Holy Spirit who is given [Rom 5:5] in this transformation of love.

4. It should be noted that the soul does not say that there He will give her His love—although He really does—because she would in this way manifest only that God loves her. She states rather that there He will show her how to love Him as perfectly as she desires. Insofar as He gives her there His love, He shows her how to love as she is loved by Him. God makes her love Him with the very strength with which He loves her. Transforming her into His love, as we said, He gives her His own strength by which she can love Him. As if He were to put an instrument in her hands and show her how it works by operating it jointly with her, He shows her how to love and gives her the ability to do so. . . .

THE SPIRITUAL CANTICLE

Stanza 39

* * *

> The breathing of the air,
> The song of the sweet nightingale,
> The grove and its living beauty
> In the serene night,
> With a flame that is consuming and painless. . . .

3.   The breathing of the air,

This breathing of the air is an ability that the soul states God will give her there in the communication of the Holy Spirit. By His divine breath-like spiration, the Holy Spirit elevates the soul sublimely and informs her and makes her capable of breathing in God the same spiration of love that the Father breathes in the Son and the Son in the Father, which is the Holy Spirit Himself, who in the Father and the Son breathes out to her in this transformation, in order to unite her to Himself. There would not be a true and total transformation if the soul were not transformed in the three Persons of the Most Holy Trinity in an open and manifest degree.

And this kind of spiration of the Holy Spirit in the soul, by which God transforms her into Himself, is so sublime, delicate, and deep a delight that a mortal tongue finds it indescribable, nor can the human intellect, as such, in any way grasp it. Even that which comes to pass in the communication given in this temporal transformation is unspeakable, for the soul united and transformed in God breathes out in God to God the very divine spiration that God—she being transformed in Him—breathes out in Himself to her.

4. In the transformation that the soul possesses in this life, the same spiration passes from God to the soul and from the soul to God with notable frequency and blissful love, although not in the open and manifest degree proper to the next life. Such I believe was St. Paul's meaning when he said: *Since you are children of God, God sent the Spirit of His Son into your hearts, calling to the Father* [Gal 4:6]. This is true of the Blessed in the next life and of the perfect in this life according to the ways described.

One should not think it impossible that the soul be capable of so sublime an activity as this breathing in God, through participation, as

God breathes in her. For, granted that God favors her by union with the Most Blessed Trinity, in which she becomes deiform and God through participation, how could it be incredible that she also understand, know, and love—or, better, that this be done in her—in the Trinity, together with it, as does the Trinity itself! Yet God accomplishes this in the soul through communication and participation. This is transformation in the three Persons in power and wisdom and love, and thus the soul is like God through this transformation. He created her in His image and likeness that she might attain such resemblance. . . .

12. In the serene night,

This night is the contemplation in which the soul desires to behold these things. Because of its obscurity, she calls contemplation night. On this account contemplation is also termed mystical theology, meaning the secret or hidden knowledge of God. In contemplation God teaches the soul very quietly and secretly, without its knowing how, without the sound of words, and without the help of any bodily or spiritual faculty, in silence and quietude, in darkness to all sensory and natural things. Some spiritual persons call this contemplation knowing by unknowing. For this knowledge is not produced by the intellect that the philosophers call the agent intellect, which works on the forms, phantasies, and apprehensions of the corporal faculties; rather it is produced in the possible or passive intellect. This possible intellect, without the reception of these forms, and so on, receives passively only substantial knowledge, which is divested of images and given without any work or active function of the intellect.

13. This contemplation, in which the soul, by means of her transformation, has sublime knowledge in this life of the divine grove and its living beauty, is consequently called night. Yet, however sublime this knowledge may be, it is still a dark night when compared with the beatific knowledge she asks for here. In seeking clear contemplation, she asks that this enjoyment of the grove and its fascination, as well as the other goods mentioned, take place now in the serene night, that is, in beatific and clear contemplation, the night of the dark contemplation of this earth changing into the contemplation of the clear and serene vision of God in heaven. Therefore, by saying, "in the serene night," she means in the clear and serene contemplation of the vision of God. David declares of this night of contemplation: *The night will be my illumination in my delights* [Ps 138:11], which is like saying: When I shall

delight in the essential vision of God, then the night of contemplation will have changed into day and light for my intellect.

14. With a flame that is consuming and painless.

By the flame she here indicates the love of the Holy Spirit. To consummate means to bring to completion or perfection. The soul, then, in affirming that the beloved will give her all the things she mentioned in this stanza, and that she will possess them with consummate and perfect love, and that these goods will all be absorbed—and she with them—in perfect love that is painless, affirms all this in order to reveal the complete perfection of this love. For love to be perfect it must have these two properties: It must consummate and transform the soul in God; and the inflaming and transformation engendered by this flame must give no pain to the soul, which cannot be true except in the beatific state where this flame is delightful love. For by the transformation of the soul in this flame, there is a beatific conformity and satisfaction of both lover and beloved, and thus the flame gives no pain from the variety of greater or less intensity, as it did before the soul reached the capacity of this perfect love. Having reached perfection, the soul possesses a love so comforting and conformed to God that, even though God is a consuming fire, as Moses says [Dt 4:24], He is now a consummator and restorer. This transformation is not like the one the soul possesses in this life, for although the flame in this life is very perfect and consummating in love, it is still also somewhat consuming and destructive, acting as fire does on coal; although the coal is conformed with and transformed into the fire, and does not fume as it did before the transformation, still the flame which consummated the coal in fire consumed and reduced it to ashes.

Stanza 40

No one looked at her,
Nor did Aminadab appear;
The siege was still;
And the cavalry,
At the sight of the waters, descended.

THE SPIRITUAL CANTICLE

Introduction and Commentary
1. The bride knows that now her will's desire is detached from all things and attached to her God in most intimate love; that the sensory part of her soul, with all its strength, faculties, and appetites, is in harmony with the spirit, and its rebelliousness brought into subjection; that the devil is now conquered and far withdrawn as a result of her varied and prolonged spiritual activity and combat; that her soul is united and transformed with an abundance of heavenly riches and gifts; and that consequently she is now well prepared, disposed, and strong, leaning on her beloved, coming up from the desert of death, flowing with delights, to the glorious thrones of her bridegroom [Sg 8:5]. Desiring the spouse to conclude this matter now, she sets all these facts before him in this last stanza in order to urge him the more to do so. In this stanza she mentions five blessings:

First, her soul is detached and withdrawn from all things.
Second, the devil is conquered and put to flight.
Third, the passions are subjected and the natural appetites mortified.
Fourth and fifth, the sensory and lower part is reformed, purified, and brought into conformity with the spiritual part. The sensory part not only offers no obstacle to the reception of these spiritual blessings, but is even accommodated to them since it participates according to its capacity in the goods the soul now possesses. . . .

7. The bride sets all this perfection and preparedness before her beloved, the Son of God, with the desire that He transfer her from the spiritual marriage, to which He desired to bring her in this Church Militant, to the glorious marriage of the Triumphant. May the most sweet Jesus, bridegroom of faithful souls, be pleased to bring all who invoke His name to this glorious marriage. To Him be honor and glory, together with the Father and the Holy Spirit, *in saecula saeculorum*. Amen.

The Living Flame of Love

Editor's Introduction

In his writings, John of the Cross shows much more interest in the dynamic process that leads to the life of union and in that life itself than he does in the concept of perfection or sanctity. The key symbols that serve as the basis for each of his works focus in different ways on this interest. The "Mount of Perfection" places before us the path that leads to the top of the mountain. *The Dark Night* tells of an escape in darkness, a radical passing over to new life. *The Spiritual Canticle* sings of love between bride and bridegroom, about experiences of presence and absence, and gift, and final surrender. Now *The Living Flame of Love* marvels at the wood converted into a fire that continues to grow hotter, bursting frequently into lifelike flames.

The symbol of fire and flame appeared also in *The Dark Night* to illustrate the purification that the flame must first achieve, making the log of wood sputter and steam and turn black. Only after this preliminary work may the wood be transformed by the fire. The *Canticle*, too, turned to the images of night and flame. In it we find "the serene night with a flame that is consuming and painless."[1] The symbolism here suggests both a calm stability and an activity, the activity of a consuming fire.

This calm stability in the midst of activity, John manages to express with wonderful poetic genius in this new poem *The Living Flame of Love*. By using six lines in each stanza rather than the five that were characteristic of his lyric poems, he creates an atmosphere of serenity and stability. And then with the use of exclamations and interjections, he conveys something of the strong activity of the divine fire. But the four stanzas do not show, as do the other poems explained by John, any

---

1. C. 39, 12–14.

progression in the activity. Rather, they bring to light in different ways experiences that all belong to the same high level.

This sublime work of poetry was composed, according to John's own words, for Doña Ana de Penalosa, a lay person, whom the author was directing in Granada.[2] It was she who gave lodging to the discalced Carmelite nuns when they first came to Granada (1582). The little group had been led, according to St. Teresa's wishes, by John himself and Ana de Jesús, the one for whom he had written the *Canticle*. In his prologue to this commentary on the *Flame*, John manifests his reluctance to write about such interior and spiritual matters, but he also reveals something of the close bond that must have grown between himself and Doña Ana, so familiarly could he speak with her about the things of the spirit. John furthermore confesses that he had to wait for a moment of deep spiritual recollection before attempting the commentary, "for one speaks badly of the intimate depths of the spirit if one does not do so with a deeply recollected soul."[3]

In this work, then, the explanations of the verses carry over a good deal of the fervor and lyricism contained in the poem. They keep close to the poem, often seeming to be an actual expansion of the poetic language and mood.

Written in the heat of this fervor, while John as vicar provincial was immersed in many pressing business activities, this commentary was completed within a fortnight. Later, during his days at La Peñuela, in the final months of his life, the author went over his work and made some revisions, clarifying things here and there and adding further explanations and biblical passages. This revised text has come to be known as *Flame B*. But the modifications in this second redaction in no way compare in extent with those made in the second redaction of the *Canticle*; nothing substantially new or different was added to the first draft written in Granada.

The prologue at once situates the poem, telling us that the stanzas were written within the state of "transformation in God," that period of which *The Spiritual Canticle* was treating in its last stanzas. If we have no new state here, John nonetheless does insist that the fire can grow much hotter and that we are dealing with a more intense love within

---

2. F. prol. 1.
3. Ibid.

the stage of spiritual marriage. The wood transformed by the fire becomes "much more incandescent and inflamed, even to the point of flaring up and shooting out flames from itself."[4] The poem, then, sings of these moments of actual union within this final state of transformation in which the soul united with the fire bursts into living flames.

Here and there throughout his works, John explains that there are different aspects to union with God and that the total union experienced in the substance and faculties of the soul may be either a habitual union or an actual one. The actual union never becomes permanent on this earth, but is always a passing phenomenon. The total union that is habitual is a union of likeness brought about through love, in which the lives of the two, God's and the soul's, are so alike that they appear to be one. The soul's cognitive-affective activity is said to be divine because of its likeness, through participation, to God's activity. The person in this state is not moved to act by passions, appetites, or purely natural motives, but by the divine movement of the Holy Spirit. "The intellect, will, and memory go out immediately toward God and the affections, senses, desires, appetites, hope, joy, and all the energy from the first instant incline toward God, although, as I say, the soul may not advert to the fact that she is working for Him."[5] This union of love is experienced habitually by the soul in its substance. "Thus in the soul in which neither any appetite nor other images or forms, nor any affections for created things, dwell, the beloved dwells secretly with an embrace so much the closer, more intimate, and interior, the purer and more alone the soul is to everything other than God."[6]

This habitual union of love is the everyday life of union, less intense in form. But here on earth, as shown in the *Canticle* and even more in the *Flame*, there may come moments in which the experience of union becomes through God's special communication more alive and intense and of greater or lesser quality, length, and frequency. In this poem, John refers to these actual unions symbolically: living flames, delightful wounds, splendors from the lamps of fire, and awakenings of the beloved.

These experiences are for John so sublime that he seems to foresee how some readers will be skeptical, thinking that the matters of which

---

4. F. prol. 3.
5. C. 28, 5.
6. F. 4, 14.

he writes are too extraordinary for human credence.[7] As a result, he urges his readers to turn their attention to God. Might they not be placing limits on the divine generosity? Readers should even realize that the seemingly unbelievable things the author does say are still "as far from the reality as a painting from the living object represented."[8]

An important characteristic of the entire work brought into relief right at the outset is the trinitarian nature of this life of full union with God. God does not appear in these pages as some undetermined absolute but as the Father, the Son, and the Holy Spirit dwelling and acting in those who love Him. In the first stanza, the Holy Spirit dominates, being identified with the principal image, the living flame of love. In the second stanza, each of the Persons of the Trinity share the action in the soul through appropriation. In the third stanza, all three Persons work as one, communicating their attributes in the deep caverns of the soul's spiritual faculties. In the fourth stanza, the Word, the bridegroom, at first takes center stage, but then as the verses go on, the scene changes and one's attention is turned back to the Holy Spirit. The work concludes in a tone similar to the one in which it opened.

If in previous works John spoke much of the purgative character of the flame of love, now in this stage the fire of love no longer works at purification. The focal point is glorification. These heightened periods of sublime union are like glimpses of glory offered to the spirit. It is as though the Holy Spirit were summoning a person to the next life by the "immense glory He marvelously and with gentle affection places before its eyes."[9] This is made possible by a highly illumined faith;[10] the veil is now so thin that it no longer cloaks the light with darkness but allows it to begin to seep through. This soul finds as well a new remarkable delight in all of creation, for it now knows creatures in God.[11] Absorbed in God, enlivened by His loving presence and communication, it receives a foretaste of eternal life. At the time of these glorious encounters, the soul comes within a step of departing from earth. A person lives on the borderlines of life and death and glory.

These selections from *The Living Flame of Love* may be briefly divided as follows:

---

7. F. prol. 2; 1, 15–16.
8. F. prol. 1.
9. F. 1, 28.
10. F. 3, 80.
11. F. 4, 4–5.

THE LIVING FLAME OF LOVE

Stanza 1
a. The nature and the work of the flame
b. The desire for glory

Stanza 2
a. The work of the Father, the Son, and the Holy Spirit in the substance of the soul
b. The hundredfold reward

Stanza 3
a. The splendors produced by the lamps of fire
b. The soul's gift to God

Stanza 4
a. Communion with the Word in the depths of the soul and the knowledge of all creation in Him
b. A participation in the breathing of the Holy Spirit

The copies of *Flame B* most respected by editors are the codex of Burgos in the Silverian archives in Burgos and the codices of Seville and Baeza in the National Library of Madrid.

The Living Flame of Love

A commentary on the stanzas that treat of the very intimate and exalted union and transformation of the soul in God, written at the request of Doña Ana de Peñalosa by the author of the stanzas.

Prologue

1. I have felt, very noble and devout lady, somewhat reluctant to explain these four stanzas, as you asked. Since they deal with matters so interior and spiritual, for which words are usually lacking—in that the spiritual surpasses sense—I find it difficult to say something of their content. Also one speaks badly of the intimate depths of the spirit if one does not do so with a deeply recollected soul. Because of my want of such recollection, I have deferred this commentary until now, a period in which the Lord seems to have uncovered some knowledge and bestowed some fervor. This must be the result of your holy desires; perhaps since I have composed the stanzas for you, His Majesty wants me to explain them for you.

I have been encouraged in knowing certainly that through my own ability I shall say nothing worthwhile, especially in matters so sublime and vital, and thus only the faults and mistakes of this commentary will be mine. Submitting it to the judgment and better opinion of our Holy Mother the Roman Catholic Church, by whose rule no one errs, depending on Sacred Scripture, and knowing the reader understands that everything I say is as far from the reality as is a painting from the living object represented, I will venture to declare what I know.

2. There is no reason to marvel at God's granting such sublime and strange gifts to souls He determines to favor. If we consider that He is God and that He bestows them as God, with infinite love and goodness, it does not seem unreasonable. For He declared that the Father, the Son, and the Holy Spirit would take up their abode in anyone who

THE LIVING FLAME OF LOVE

loved Him [Jn 14:23]. He takes up His abode in individuals by making them live the life of God and dwell in the Father, the Son, and the Holy Spirit, as the soul points out in these stanzas.

3. Although in the stanzas we have already commented on,[1] we speak of the highest degree of perfection one can reach in this life (transformation in God), these stanzas treat of a love within this very state of transformation that is more exalted and perfect. Even though it is true that what these and other stanzas describe is all one state of transformation, and that as such one cannot pass beyond it; yet, with time and practice, love can receive added quality, as I say, and become more intensified. We have an example of this in the activity of fire: Although the fire has penetrated the wood, transformed it, and united it with itself, yet as this fire grows hotter and continues to burn, the wood becomes much more incandescent and inflamed, even to the point of flaring up and shooting out flames from itself.

4. It should be understood that the soul now speaking has reached this enkindled degree, and is so inwardly transformed and exalted in the fire of love that it is not merely united to this fire but produces within it a living flame. The soul feels this and speaks of it thus in these stanzas with intimate and delicate sweetness of love, burning in love's flame, and stressing in these stanzas some of its effects.

I will use in this commentary the method I have used before. First I will quote all the stanzas together, and then, after recording each stanza separately, I will present a brief explanation of it; finally, I will quote each verse and comment on it.

Stanzas that the soul recites in the intimate union with God

1. O living flame of love
That tenderly wounds my soul
In its deepest center! Since
Now you are not oppressive,
Now Consummate! if it be your will:
Tear through the veil of this sweet encounter!

2. O sweet cautery,
O delightful wound!

---

1. He is probably referring to *The Spiritual Canticle;* he implies that Ana de Peñalosa was familiar with it.

THE LIVING FLAME OF LOVE

O gentle hand! O delicate touch
That tastes of eternal life
And pays every debt!
In killing you changed death to life.

3. O lamps of fire!
In whose splendors
The deep caverns of feeling,
Once obscure and blind,
Now give forth, so rarely, so exquisitely,
Both warmth and light to their beloved.

4. How gently and lovingly
You wake in my heart,
Where in secret you dwell alone;
And in your sweet breathing,
Filled with good and glory,
How tenderly you swell my heart with love.

Stanza 1

O living flame of love
That tenderly wounds my soul
In its deepest center! Since
Now you are not oppressive,
Now Consummate! if it be your will:
Tear through the veil of this sweet encounter!

Commentary

1. The soul now feels that it is all inflamed in the divine union and that its palate is all bathed in glory and love, that in the most intimate part of its substance it is flooded with no less than rivers of glory, abounding in delights, and that from its bosom flow rivers of living water [Jn 7:38], which the Son of God declared will rise up in such souls. Accordingly it seems, because the soul is so vigorously transformed in God, so sublimely possessed by Him, and arrayed with such rich gifts and virtues, that it is singularly close to beatitude—so close that only a thin veil separates it.

THE LIVING FLAME OF LOVE

And the soul sees that every time that delicate flame of love, burning within, assails it, it does so as though glorifying it with gentle and powerful glory. Such is the glory this flame of love imparts that each time it absorbs and attacks, it seems that it is about to give eternal life and tear the veil of mortal life, that very little is lacking, and that because of this lack the soul does not receive eternal glory completely. Hence with ardent desire the soul tells the flame, the Holy Spirit, to tear now the veil of mortal life by that sweet encounter in which He truly communicates entirely what He is seemingly about to give each time He encounters it, that is, complete and perfect glory.

And thus it says:

2.   O living flame of love

To lay stress on the sentiment and esteem with which it speaks in these four stanzas, the soul uses in all of them the exclamations "O" and "how," which stress affection. Each time they are uttered, they reveal more about the interior than the tongue expresses. "O" serves to speak of intense desire and to use persuasion in petitioning. The soul uses this expression for both reasons in this stanza because it intimates and stresses its immense desire, persuading love to loose it.

3. This flame of love is the Spirit of its bridegroom, which is the Holy Spirit. The soul feels Him within itself not only as a fire which has consumed and transformed it, but as a fire that burns and flares within it, as I mentioned. And that flame, every time it flares up, bathes the soul in glory and refreshes it with the quality of divine life. Such is the activity of the Holy Spirit in the soul transformed in love: The interior acts He produces shoot up flames, for they are acts of inflamed love in which the will of the soul united with that flame, made one with it loves most sublimely.

Thus these acts of love are most precious; one of them is more meritorious and valuable than all the deeds one may have performed in the whole of life before this transformation, however great they may have been.

The same difference that lies between a habit and an act lies between the transformation in love and the flame of love; it is like the difference between the wood that is on fire and the flame that leaps up from it, for the flame is the effect of the fire that is present there.

4. Hence we can compare the soul in its ordinary condition in this state of transformation of love to the log of wood that is ever immersed in fire, and the acts of this soul to the flame that blazes up from the fire

of love. The more intense the fire of union, the more vehemently does this fire burst into flames. The acts of the will are united to this flame and ascend, carried away and absorbed in the flame of the Holy Spirit, just as the angel mounted to God in the flame of Manue's sacrifice [Jgs 13:20].

Thus in this state the soul cannot make acts because the Holy Spirit makes them all and moves it toward them. As a result all the acts of the soul are divine, since the movement toward these acts and their execution stem from God. Hence the soul thinks that every time this flame shoots up, making it love with delight and divine quality, that it is being given eternal life, since it is being raised by the flame to the activity of God in God.

5. This is the language and these the words God speaks in souls that are purged, cleansed, and all enkindled. As David exclaimed: *Your word is exceedingly enkindled* [Ps 119:140], and the prophet: *Are not my words, perchance, like a fire?* [Jer 23:29]. As God Himself says through St. John, these words are spirit and life [Jn 6:63]. This spirit and life is perceived by souls who have ears to hear it, those souls, as I say, that are cleansed and enamored. Those who do not have a sound palate, but seek other tastes, cannot taste the spirit and life of God's words; His words, rather, are distasteful to them.

Hence the loftier were the words of the Son of God, the more tasteless they were to the impure, as happened when He preached the savory and loving doctrine of the Holy Eucharist; for many turned away [Jn 6:60-61, 66].

6. Those who do not taste this language God speaks within them must not think on this account that others do not taste it. St. Peter tasted it in his soul when he said to Christ: *Lord, where shall we go; you have the words of eternal life?* [Jn 6:68]. And the Samaritan woman forgot the water and the water pot because of the sweetness of God's words [Jn 4:28].

Since this soul is so close to God that it is transformed into a flame of love, in which the Father, the Son, and the Holy Spirit are communicated to it, what is so unbelievable about saying that it enjoys a foretaste of eternal life? Yet, it does not enjoy this perfectly since the conditions of life here below do not allow for this. But the delight that the flaring up of the Holy Spirit generates in the soul is so sublime that it makes the soul know that which savors of eternal life. Thus it refers to this flame as living, not because the flame is not always living, but because of this effect; it makes the soul live in God spiritually and experience the life of God in the manner David mentions: *My heart and my flesh rejoiced in the living God* [Ps 84:3]. David did not refer to God as living because of a necessity to do so, for God is always living, but in order to manifest that the spirit and the senses, transformed in God, enjoy Him in a living way, which is to taste the living God—that is God's life, eternal life. Nor did David call Him the living God other than because he enjoyed Him in a living way, although not perfectly, but as though by a glimpse of eternal life. Thus in this flame the soul experiences God so vividly and tastes Him with such delight and sweetness that it exclaims: O living flame of love!

7.   That tenderly wounds my soul

That is: O living flame of love that with your ardor tenderly touches me. Since this flame is a flame of divine life, it wounds the soul with the tenderness of God's life, and it wounds and stirs it so deeply as to make it dissolve in love. What the bride affirmed in the Song of Songs is fulfilled in the soul. She was so moved that her soul melted, and thus she says: *As soon as he spoke my soul melted* (Sg 5:4). For God's speech is the effect He produces in the soul.

8. But how can one claim that the flame wounds the soul since there is nothing left in it to wound now that it is all cauterized with the fire of love? It is something splendid that since love is never idle, but in continual motion, it is always emitting flames everywhere like a blazing fire, and, since its duty is to wound in order to cause love and delight, and it is present in this soul as a living flame, it dispatches its wounds like most tender flares of delicate love. Joyfully and festively it practices the arts and games of love, as though in the palace of its nuptials, as Ahasuerus did with Esther [Est 2:17–18]. God shows His graces there, manifests His riches and the glory of His grandeur that in this soul might be fulfilled what he asserted in Proverbs: *I was delighted every day, playing before Him all the time, playing in the world. And my delights were to be with the children of men* [Prv 8:30–31], that is, by bestowing delights on them. Hence these wounds (His games) are flames of tender touches; arising from the fire of love, which is not idle, they suddenly touch the soul. These, it says, occur inwardly and wound the soul.

9.   In its deepest center!

This feast takes place in the substance of the soul, where neither the center of the senses nor the devil can reach. Therefore, it is the more secure, substantial, and delightful the more interior it is, because the more interior it is, the purer it is. And the greater the purity, the more abundantly, frequently, and generously God communicates Himself. Thus the delight and joy of the soul is so much the more intense because God is the doer of all without the soul's doing anything. Since the soul cannot do any work of its own save by the means and aid of the corporal senses, from which in this event it is very free and far removed, its sole occupation now is to receive from God, who alone can move the soul and do His work in its depths. Thus all the movements of this soul are divine. Although they belong to it, they belong to it because God works them in it and with it, for it wills and consents to them. . . .

13. It is noteworthy, then, that love is the soul's inclination, strength, and power in making its way to God, for love unites it with God. The more degrees of love it has, the more deeply it enters into God and centers itself in Him. We can say that there are as many centers in God possible to the soul, each one deeper than the other, as there are degrees of love of God possible to it. A stronger love is a more unitive love, and we can understand in this manner the many dwelling places the Son of God declared were in His Father's house [Jn 14:2].

Hence, that the soul be in its center—which is God, as we have said—it is sufficient for it to possess one degree of love, for by one degree alone it is united with Him through grace. Should it have two degrees, it will have become united and concentrated in God in another deeper center. Should it reach three, it will have centered itself in a third. But once it has attained the final degree, God's love will have arrived at wounding the soul in its ultimate and deepest center, which is to transform and clarify it in its whole being, power, and strength, and according to its capacity, until it appears to be God.

When light shines on a clean and pure crystal, we find that the more intense the degree of light, the more light the crystal has concentrated within it and the brighter it becomes; it can become so brilliant due to the abundance of light it receives that it seems to be all light. And then the crystal is indistinguishable from the light, since it is illumined according to its full capacity, which is to appear to be light. . . .

15. . . . And it should not be held as incredible in a soul now examined, purged, and tried in the fire of tribulations, trials, and many kinds of temptations, and found faithful in love, that the promise of the Son of God be fulfilled, the promise that the Most Blessed Trinity will come and dwell within anyone who loves Him [Jn 14:23]. The Blessed

Trinity inhabits the soul by divinely illumining its intellect with the wisdom of the Son, delighting its will in the Holy Spirit, and by absorbing it powerfully and mightily in the delightful embrace of the Father's sweetness.

16. If He acts thus in some souls, as it is true He does, it should be believed that this soul we are speaking of will not be left behind in regard to receiving these favors from God. For what we are explaining about the activity of the Holy Spirit within it is something far greater than what occurs in the communication and transformation of love. This latter resembles the glowing embers, whereas the former is similar to embers not merely glowing but embers that have become so hot they shoot forth a living flame.[2]

And thus these two kinds of union (union of love alone, and union with an inflaming of love) are somehow comparable to the fire of God that, Isaiah says, is on Sion and to His furnace that is in Jerusalem [Is 31:9]. The one signifies the Church Militant, in which the fire of charity is not enkindled to an extreme; the other signifies the vision of peace, which is the Church Triumphant, where this fire is like a furnace blazing in the perfection of love.[3]

Although, as we said, the soul has not attained such great perfection as this vision of peace, yet, in comparison with the other common union, this union resembles a blazing furnace in which there is a vision so much more peaceful and glorious and tender, just as the flame is clearer and more resplendent than the burning coal.

17. Wherefore the soul, feeling that this living flame of love is vividly communicating to it every good, since this divine love carries all things with it, exclaims: "O living flame of love that tenderly wounds my soul." This is like saying: O enkindled love, with your loving movements you are pleasantly glorifying me according to the greater capacity and strength of my soul, bestowing divine knowledge according to all the ability and capacity of my intellect, and communicating love according to the greater power of my will, and rejoicing the substance of my soul with the torrent of your delight by your divine contact and

---

2. These kinds of union are the equivalent of the habitual union and the actual union. The former is permanent on this earth, the latter transitory. The former is the state of union, or transformation, or spiritual marriage. Cf. prol. 3; 1, 3–4; C. 22, 2–3; A. 2, 5.

3. This text is influenced by the liturgy for the Dedication of a Church. The hymn for first Vespers read: *Caelestis urbs Jerusalem, beata pacis visio* (Heavenly city Jerusalem, blessed vision of peace).

substantial union, in harmony with the greater purity of my substance and the capacity and breadth of my memory!

And this is what happens, in an indescribable way, at the time this flame of love rises up within the soul. Since the soul is completely purged in its substance and faculties (memory, intellect, and will), the divine substance, which because of its purity, as the Wise Man says, touches everywhere profoundly, subtly, and sublimely [Wis 7:24], absorbs the soul in itself with its divine flame. And in that immersion of the soul in wisdom, the Holy Spirit sets in motion the glorious flickerings of His flame. . . .

27. . . . However intimate the union with God may be, individuals will never have satisfaction and rest until God's glory appears [Ps 17:15], especially since they now experience its savor and sweetness. This experience is so intense that if God had not favored their flesh, by fortifying the sensory part with His right hand, as He did Moses in the rock, enabling him to behold His glory without dying [Ex 33:22], nature would be torn apart and death would ensue, since the lower part is unequipped to suffer so much and such a sublime fire of glory.

28. Affliction, then, does not accompany this desire and petition, for the soul is no longer capable of such affliction, but with a gentle and delightful desire it seeks this in the conformity of both spirit and sense to God's will. As a result it says in this verse, "Now Consummate! if it be your will," for its will and appetite are so united with God that it considers the fulfillment of God's will to be its glory.

Yet the sudden flashes of glory and love that appear vaguely in these touches at the door of entry into the soul, and which are unable to fit into it because of the narrowness of the earthly house, are so sublime that it would rather be a sign of little love not to try to enter into that perfection and completion of love.

Moreover, a soul is conscious that in that vigor of the bridegroom's delightful communication, the Holy Spirit rouses and invites it by the immense glory He marvelously and with gentle affection places before its eyes, telling it what He told the bride in the Song of Songs. The bride thus refers to this: *Behold what my spouse is saying to me: Arise and make haste, my love, my dove, my beautiful one, and come* [Sg 2:10]. . . .

29.   Tear through the veil of this sweet encounter!

The veil is what impedes so singular an event. It is easy to reach God when all the impediments are removed and the veils that separate the soul from union with Him are torn. We can say there are three veils that constitute a hindrance to this union with God, and which must be torn if the union is to be effected and possessed perfectly by the soul, that is: the temporal veil, comprising all creatures; the natural, embodying the purely natural inclinations and operations; and the sensitive, which consists only of the union of the soul with the body, that is, the sensitive and animal life of which St. Paul speaks: *We know that if this our earthly house is dissolved, we have a building of God in heaven* [2 Cor 5:1].

The first two veils must necessarily be torn in order to obtain this union with God in which all the things of the world are renounced, all the natural appetites and affections mortified, and the natural operations of the soul divinized.

All of this was accomplished, and these veils were torn by means of the oppressive encounters of this flame. Through the spiritual purgation we referred to above, the soul tears these two veils completely and is united with God, as it here is; only the third veil of this sensitive life remains to be torn. As a result it mentions a veil and not veils, since there is only this one to tear. Because the veil is now so tenuous, thin, and spiritualized through this union with God, the flame is not harsh in its encounter as it was with the other two, but savorous and sweet. The soul hence calls it a sweet encounter; so much the sweeter and more savorous, the more it seems about to tear through the veil of mortal life.

30. It should be known that the death of persons who have reached this state is far different in its cause and mode than the death of others, even though it is similar in natural circumstances. If the death of other people is caused by sickness or old age, the death of these persons is not so induced, in spite of their being sick or old; their soul is not wrested from them unless by some impetus and encounter of love, far more sublime than previous ones, of greater power, and more valiant, since it tears through this veil and carries off the jewel, which is the soul.[4]

The death of such persons is very gentle and very sweet, sweeter and more gentle than was their whole spiritual life on earth. For they die with the most sublime impulses and delightful encounters of love, resembling the swan whose song is much sweeter at the moment of death. Accordingly, David affirmed that the death of the saints is precious in the sight of the Lord [Ps 116:15]. The soul's riches gather to-

---

4. John is not speaking rhetorically; he definitely affirms the possibility of a death (physical death, separation of body and soul) produced by the impulse of divine love.

gether here, and its rivers of love move on to enter the sea, for these rivers, because they are blocked, become so vast that they themselves resemble seas. The first treasures of the just and their last are heaped together to accompany them when they depart and go off to their kingdom, while praises are heard from the ends of the earth, which, as Isaiah says, are the glory of the just one [Is 24:16].

31. The soul, then, conscious of the abundance of its enrichment, feels at the time of these glorious encounters to be almost at the point of departing for the complete and perfect possession of its kingdom, for it knows that it is pure, rich, full of virtues, and prepared for such a kingdom. God permits it in this state to discern its beauty and He entrusts to it the gifts and virtues He has bestowed, for everything is converted into love and praises. And the soul has no touch of presumption or vanity, since it no longer bears the leaven of imperfection, which corrupts the mass [1 Cor 5:6; Gal 5:9]. Since it is aware that nothing is wanting other than to tear the weak veil of this natural life, in which it feels the entanglement, hindrance, and captivity of its freedom, and since it desires to be dissolved and to be with Christ [Phil 1:23], it laments that a life so weak and base impedes another so mighty and sublime and asks that the veil be torn, saying: Tear through the veil of this sweet encounter!

32. There are three reasons for the term "veil": first, because of the union between the spirit and the flesh; second, because this union separates the soul from God; third, because a veil is not so thick and opaque that a brilliant light cannot shine through it; and in this state the bond seems to be so tenuous a veil, since it is now very spiritual, thin, and luminous, that it does not prevent the divinity from vaguely appearing through it. Since the soul perceives the power of the other life, it is conscious of the weakness of this one and that the veil is of delicate fabric, as thin as a spider's web; in David's words: *Our years shall be considered as the spider* [Ps 90:9], and according to Isaiah, all nations are as though they were not [Is 40:17]. These things carry the same weight in the soul's view: All things are nothing to it, and it is nothing in its own eyes; God alone is its all. . . .

THE LIVING FLAME OF LOVE

Stanza 2

O sweet cautery,
O delightful wound!
O gentle hand! O delicate touch
That tastes of eternal life
And pays every debt!
In killing you changed death to life.

1. In this stanza the soul proclaims how the three Persons of the Most Blessed Trinity, the Father, the Son, and the Holy Spirit, are they who effect in it this divine work of union. Thus the hand, the cautery, and the touch are substantially the same. The soul applies these terms to the Persons of the Trinity because of the effect each of the Persons produces. The cautery is the Holy Spirit; the hand is the Father; and the touch is the Son. The soul here magnifies the Father, the Son, and the Holy Spirit, stressing the three admirable favors and blessings they produce in it, having changed its death to life, transforming it in the Trinity. . . .

8. O happy wound, wrought by One who knows only how to heal! O fortunate and choicest wound; you were made only for delight, and the quality of your affliction is delight and gratification for the wounded soul! You are great, O delightful wound, because He who caused you is great! And your delight is great because the fire of love is infinite and makes you delightful according to your capacity and greatness. O, then, delightful wound, so much more sublimely delightful the more the cautery touched the intimate center of the substance of the soul, burning all that was burnable in order to give delight to all that could be delighted!

It is understandable that this cautery and this wound are of the highest degree possible in this state. For there are many other ways God cauterizes the soul that are unlike this one and fail to reach such a degree. For this cautery is a touch only of the divinity in the soul, without any intellectual or imaginative form or figure.

9. There is another way of cauterizing the soul by an intellectual form, usually very sublime, which is as follows. It will happen that while the soul is inflamed with the love of God, although not with a love of as deep a quality as that we mentioned (yet it is fitting that it be so for what I want to say), it will feel that a seraph is assailing it by

means of an arrow or dart that is all afire with love. And the seraph pierces and cauterizes this soul which, like a red-hot coal, or, better, a flame, is already enkindled. And then in this cauterization, when the soul is transpierced with that dart, the flame gushes forth, vehemently and with a sudden ascent, like the fire in a furnace or an oven when someone uses a poker or bellows to stir and excite it. And being wounded by this fiery dart, the soul feels the wound with unsurpassable delight. Besides being fully stirred in great sweetness by the blowing or impetuous motion of the seraph, in which it feels in its intense ardor to be dissolving in love, it is aware of the delicate wound and the herb (which serves as a keen temper to the dart) as though it were a sharp point in the substance of the spirit, in the heart of the pierced soul.[5]

10. Who can fittingly speak of this intimate point of the wound, which seems to be in the middle of the heart of the spirit, there where the soul experiences the excellence of the delight? The soul feels that that point is like a tiny mustard seed, very much alive and enkindled, sending into its surroundings a living and enkindled fire of love. The fire issuing from the substance and power of that living point, which contains the substance and power of the herb, is felt to be subtly diffused through all the spiritual and substantial veins of the soul in the measure of the soul's power and strength. The soul feels its ardor strengthen and increase and its love become so refined in this ardor that seemingly there are seas of loving fire within it, reaching to the heights and depths of the earthly and heavenly spheres, imbuing all with love. It seems to it that the entire universe is a sea of love in which it is engulfed, for, conscious of the living point or center of love within itself, it is unable to catch sight of the boundaries of this love.

11. There is nothing else to say about the soul's enjoyment here except that it realizes how appropriately the kingdom of heaven was compared in the gospel to a grain of mustard seed which, by reason of its intense heat, grows into a large tree, despite its being so small [Mt 13:31–31]. For the soul is converted into an immense fire of love, which emanates from that enkindled point at the heart of the spirit.

---

5. He describes here the transpiercing of the soul, a grace that St. Teresa also explains in her *Life* 29, 13–14. Teresa speaks of an imaginative vision, whereas John speaks of a sublime intellectual vision, but with forms not purely spiritual. For John the transpiercing is the work of a seraph. Teresa thinks the agent is from the cherubim. Banez noted in the autograph, "It seems to be rather from those called the seraphim."

12. Few persons have reached these heights. Some have, however; especially those whose virtue and spirit were to be diffused among their children. For God accords to founders, with respect to the first fruits of the spirit, wealth and value commensurate with the greater or lesser following they will have in their doctrine and spirituality.[6]

13. Let us return to the work of that seraph, for he truly inflicts a sore and wounds inwardly in the spirit. Thus, if God sometimes permits an effect to extend to the bodily senses in the fashion in which it existed interiorly, the wound and sore appears outwardly, as happened when the seraph wounded St. Francis.[7] When the soul is wounded with love by the five wounds, the effect extends to the body and these wounds are impressed on the body, and it is wounded just as the soul is wounded with love. God usually does not bestow a favor on the body without bestowing it first and principally on the soul. Thus the greater the delight and strength of love the wound produces in the soul, so much the greater is that produced by the wound outside on the body, and when there is an increase in one there is an increase in the other. This so happens because these souls are purified and established in God, and that which is a cause of pain and torment to their corruptible flesh is sweet and delectable to their strong and healthy spirit. It is, then, a wonderful experience to feel the pain augment with the delight.

Job, with his wounds, clearly beheld this marvel when he said to God: *Returning to me, you torment me wondrously* [Jb 10:16]. This is an unspeakable marvel and worthy of the abundance and sweetness God has hidden for them that fear Him [Ps 31:20]: to cause them to enjoy so much the more savor and sweetness the more pain and torment they experience.

Nevertheless, when the wound is made only in the soul without being communicated outwardly, the delight can be more intense and sublime. The spirit has the flesh curbed in this state, but when the goods of the spirit are communicated also to the flesh, the flesh pulls the reins, bridles the mouth of this swift horse of the spirit, and restrains its great impetuosity; for if the spirit makes use of its power, the reins will break. Yet until the reins are broken, the flesh does not fail

---

[6]. John is probably referring to St. Teresa, although not solely to her. These souls destined to have a spiritual following in the Church experience in a living way the Gospel parable of the mustard seed.

[7]. St. Francis of Assisi received the marks of the wounds of Christ on his hands, feet, and right side in the autumn of 1224 on Mount Alvernia.

to oppress the spirit's freedom, as the Wise Man asserts: *The corruptible body is a load on the soul, and the earthly dwelling oppresses the spiritual mind which of itself comprehends many things* [Wis 9:15].

14. I say this in order to make it clear that he who would go to God relying on natural ability and reasoning will not be very spiritual. There are some who think that by pure force and the activity of the senses, which of itself is lowly and no more than natural, they can reach the strength and height of the supernatural spirit. One does not attain to this peak without restraining and leaving aside the activity of the senses.

Yet it is something quite different when an effect of the spirit overflows in the senses. When this is true, the effect in the senses proceeds from an abundance of spirit, as in the event of the wounds that proceed from the inner strength and appear outwardly. This happened with St. Paul, whose immense compassion for the sufferings of Christ redounded into the body, as he explains to the Galatians: *I bear the wounds of the Lord Jesus in my body* [Gal 6:17]. . . .

16. . . . And your only begotten Son, O merciful hand of the Father, is the delicate touch by which you touched me with the force of your cautery and wounded me.

17. O you, then, delicate touch, the Word, the Son of God, through the delicacy of your divine being, you subtly penetrate the substance of my soul and, lightly touching it all, absorb it entirely in yourself in divine modes of delights and sweetnesses unheard of in the land of Canaan and never before seen in Teman [Bar 3:22]! O, then, very delicate, exceedingly delicate, touch of the Word, so much the more delicate for me insofar as, after overthrowing the mountains and smashing the rocks to pieces on Mount Horeb with the shadow of might and power that went before you, you gave the prophet the sweetest and strongest experience of yourself in the gentle breeze [1 Kgs 19:11–12]! O gentle breeze, since you are a delicate and mild breeze, tell us: How do you, the Word, the Son of God, touch mildly and gently, since you are so awesome and mighty? Oh, happy is the soul that you, being terrible and strong, gently and lightly touch! Proclaim this to the world! But you are unwilling to proclaim this to the world because it does not know of a mild breeze and will not experience you, for it can neither receive nor see you [Jn 14:17]. But they, O my God and my life, will see and experience your mild touch, who withdraw from the world and become mild, bringing the mild into harmony with the mild, thus enabling themselves to experience and enjoy you. You touch them the

more gently the more you dwell permanently hidden within them, for the substance of their soul is now refined, cleansed, and purified, withdrawn from every creature and every touch and trace of creature. As a result, *you hide them in the secret of your face*, which is the Word, *from the disturbance of men* [Ps 31:21].

18. O, then again, repeatedly delicate touch, so much the stronger and mightier the more you are delicate! Since you detach and withdraw the soul from all the other touches of created things by the might of your delicacy, and both reserve it for and unite it to yourself alone, you leave so mild an effect in the soul that every other touch of all things both high and low seems coarse and spurious. It displeases the soul to look at these things, and to deal with them is a heavy pain and torment to it. . . .

21.   That tastes of eternal life

Although that which the soul tastes in this touch of God is not perfect, it does in fact have a certain savor of eternal life, as was mentioned. And this is not incredible if we believe, as we should, that this is a touch of substances, that is, of the substance of God in the substance of the soul. Many saints have attained to this substantial touch during their lives on earth. . . .

23.   And pays every debt!

The soul affirms this because in the taste of eternal life, which it here enjoys, it feels the reward for the trials it passed through in order to reach this state. It feels not only that it has been compensated and satisfied justly but that it has been rewarded exceedingly. It thoroughly understands the truth of the bridegroom's promise in the gospel, that he would repay a hundredfold [Mt 19:29]. It has endured no tribulation, or penance, or trial to which there does not correspond a hundredfold of consolation and delight in this life, and it can truly say: And pays every debt. . . .

Stanza 3

O lamps of fire!
In whose splendors
The deep caverns of feeling,

THE LIVING FLAME OF LOVE

Once obscure and blind,
Now give forth, so rarely, so exquisitely,
Both warmth and light to their beloved.

Commentary

1. . . . The soul exalts and thanks its bridegroom in this stanza for the admirable favors it receives from its union with him. It states that by means of this union it receives abundant and lofty knowledge of God, which is all loving, and which communicates light and love to its faculties and feeling. That which was once obscure and blind can now receive illumination and the warmth of love, as it does, so as to be able to give forth light and love to the one who illumined and filled it with love. True lovers are only content when they employ all that they are in themselves, are worth, have, and receive, in the beloved; and the greater all this is, the more satisfaction they receive in giving it. The soul rejoices on this account because from the splendors and love it receives, it can shine brightly in the presence of its bridegroom and give him love. The verse follows:

2.   O lamps of fire!

First of all it should be known that lamps possess two properties: They transmit both light and heat. To understand the nature of these lamps and how they shine and burn within the soul, it ought to be known that God in His unique and simple being is all the powers and grandeurs of His attributes. He is almighty, wise, and good; and He is merciful, just, powerful, and loving, and so on. And He is the other infinite attributes and powers of which we have no knowledge. Since He is all of this in His simple being, the soul views distinctly in Him, when He is united with it and deigns to disclose this knowledge, all these powers and grandeurs, that is: omnipotence, wisdom, goodness, and mercy, and so on. Since each of these attributes is the very being of God in His one and only *suppositum*, which is the Father, the Son, and the Holy Spirit, and since each one is God Himself, who is infinite light or divine fire, we deduce that the soul, like God, gives forth light and warmth through each of these innumerable attributes. Each of these attributes is a lamp that enlightens it and transmits the warmth of love.

3. Insofar as the soul receives the knowledge of these attributes in only one act of this union, God Himself is for it many lamps together, which illumine and impart warmth to it individually, for it has clear knowledge of each, and through this knowledge is inflamed in love. By

means of all the lamps the soul loves each individually, inflamed by each one and by all together, because all these attributes are one being, as we said. All these lamps are one lamp which, according to its powers and attributes, shines and burns like many lamps. Hence the soul in one act of knowledge of these lamps loves through each one and, in so doing, loves through them all together, bearing in that act the quality of love for each one and from each one, and from all together and for all together.

The splendor of this lamp of God's being, insofar as He is omnipotent, imparts light to the soul and the warmth of love of Him according to His omnipotence. God is then to the soul a lamp of omnipotence which shines and bestows all knowledge in respect to this attribute. And the splendor of this lamp of God's being insofar as He is wisdom grants the soul light and the warmth of the love of God according to His wisdom. God is then a lamp of wisdom to it. And the splendor of this lamp insofar as it is goodness imparts to the soul light and the warmth of love according to His goodness. God is then a lamp of goodness to it. He is also to the soul a lamp of justice, fortitude, and mercy, and of all the other attributes that are represented to it together in God. The light communicated to it from all these attributes together is enveloped in the warmth of love of God by which it loves Him because He is all these things. In this communication and manifestation of Himself to the soul, which in my opinion is the greatest possible in this life, He is to it innumerable lamps giving forth knowledge and love of Himself.

4. Moses beheld these lamps on Mount Sinai where, when God passed by, he prostrated himself on the ground and began to call out and enumerate some of them: *Emperor, Lord, God merciful, clement, patient, of much compassion, true, who keeps mercy unto thousands, who takes away iniquities and sins, no one is of himself innocent before you* [Ex 34:6–7]. In this passage it is clear that the greatest attributes and powers Moses knew there in God were those of God's omnipotence, dominion, deity, mercy, justice, truth, and righteousness, which was the highest knowledge of God. Because love was communicated to him in accord with the knowledge, the delight of love and fruition he enjoyed were most sublime.

5. It is noteworthy that the delight the soul receives in the rapture of love, communicated by the fire of the light of these lamps, is wonderful and immense, for it is as abundant as it would be if it came from many lamps. Each lamp burns in love, and the warmth from each fur-

thers the warmth of the other, and the flame of one, the flame of the other, just as the light of one sheds light on the other, because through each attribute the other is known. Thus all of them are one light and one fire, and each of them is one light and one fire.

Immensely absorbed in delicate flames, subtly wounded with love through each of them, and more wounded by all of them together, more alive in the love of the life of God, the soul perceives clearly that that love is proper to eternal life. Eternal life is the aggregation of all goods,[8] and the soul somehow experiences this here and fully understands the truth of the bridegroom's assertion in the Song of Songs, that the lamps of love are lamps of fire and of flames [Sg 8:6]. . . .

76. This feeling, then, of the soul that was once obscure, without this divine light, and blind through the soul's appetites and affections, has now together with the deep caverns of the soul's faculties become not only bright and clear, but like a resplendent light.

77. Now give forth, so rarely, so exquisitely,
    Both warmth and light to their beloved.

When these caverns of the faculties are so wonderfully and marvelously pervaded with the admirable splendors of those lamps that are burning within them, they give forth to God in God with loving glory, besides their surrender to Him, these very splendors they have received. Inclined in God toward God, having become enkindled lamps within the splendors of the divine lamps, they render the beloved the same light and heat they receive.[9] In the very manner they receive it, they return it to the one who gave it, and with the same beauty in which it was given; just as the window when the sun shines on it, for it then too reflects the splendors. Yet the soul reflects the divine light in a more excellent way because of the active intervention of its will.

78. "So rarely, so exquisitely," means: in a way rare or foreign to every common thought, every exaggeration, and every mode and manner.

---

8. Being simple, God is not a collection of parts. In Him all attributes or qualities are His being, are not simply attached to it as with humans. No terms we use of God mean the same as when we use them of creatures. In this section John brings out beautifully the supereminence of God with respect to all created perfections. The definition of eternal life comes from Boethius, *De Consolatione Philosophiae* 3, 2, 2–4 (Migne PL 63, 724).

9. The commentary on these last verses was very much influenced by *De Beatitudine*, the work of pseudo-Thomas. Cf. C. 14–15, 14, note 13.

THE LIVING FLAME OF LOVE

Corresponding to the exquisiteness or to the excellence with which the intellect receives the divine wisdom, being made one with God's intellect, is the excellence with which the soul gives this wisdom, for it cannot give it save according to the mode in which it was given.

And corresponding to the excellence by which the will is united to goodness is the excellence by which it gives in God the same goodness to God, for it only receives it in order to give it.

And, no more nor less, according to the excellence by which it knows in the grandeur of God, being united to it, the soul shines and diffuses the warmth of love.

And according to the excellence of the divine attributes (fortitude, beauty, justice, and so on), which the beloved communicates, is the excellence with which the soul's feeling gives joyfully to Him the very light and heat it receives from Him. Having been made one with God, the soul is somehow God through participation. Although it is not God as perfectly as it will be in the next life, it is like the shadow of God. Being the shadow of God through this substantial transformation, it performs in this measure in God and through God what He through Himself does in it. For the will of the two is one will, and thus God's operation and the soul's is one. Since God gives Himself with a free and gracious will, so too the soul (possessing a will the more generous and free the more it is united with God) gives to God, God Himself in God; and this is a true and complete gift of the soul to God.

It is conscious there that God is indeed its own and that it possesses Him by inheritance, with the right of ownership, as His adopted child, through the grace of His gift of Himself. Having Him for its own, it can give Him and communicate Him to whomever it wishes. Thus it gives Him to its beloved, who is the very God who gave Himself to it. By this donation it repays God for all it owes Him, since it willingly gives as much as it receives from Him.[10]

79. Because the soul in this gift to God offers Him the Holy Spirit, with voluntary surrender, as something of its own (so that God loves Himself in the Holy Spirit as He deserves), it enjoys inestimable delight and fruition, seeing that it gives God something of its own which is suited to Him according to His infinite being. Although it is true that

---

10. This mutual giving between God and the soul is especially characteristic of the spiritual marriage.

the soul cannot give God again to Himself, since in Himself He is ever Himself, nevertheless it does this truly and perfectly, giving all that was given it by Him in order to repay love, which is to give as much as is given. And God, who could not be considered repaid with anything less, is considered repaid with that gift of the soul, and He accepts it gratefully as something it gives Him of its own. In this very gift He loves it anew, and in the re-surrender of God to the soul, the soul also loves as though again.

A reciprocal love is thus actually formed between God and the soul, like the marriage union and surrender, in which the goods of both (the divine essence which each possesses freely by reason of the voluntary surrender between them) are possessed by both together. They say to each other what the Son of God spoke to the Father through St. John: *Omnia mea tua sunt et tua mea sunt et clarificatus sum in eis* (All my goods are yours and yours are mine, and I am glorified in them) [Jn 17:10]. In the next life this will continue unintermittently in perfect fruition, but in this state of union it occurs, although not as perfectly as in the next, when God produces in the soul this act of the transformation.

Clearly the soul can give this gift, even though the gift has greater entity than the soul's own being and capacity, for an owner of many nations and kingdoms, which have more entity than the owner does, can give them at will to anyone.

80. This is the soul's deep satisfaction and happiness: to see that it gives to God more than in itself it is worth; and this it does with that very divine light and divine heat and solitude. It does this in heaven by means of the light of glory and in this life by means of a highly illumined faith. Accordingly, the deep caverns of feeling give forth with rare excellence to their beloved heat and light together.

Stanza 4

> How gently and lovingly
> You wake in my heart,
> Where in secret you dwell alone;
> And in your sweet breathing,

THE LIVING FLAME OF LOVE

Filled with good and glory,
How tenderly you swell my heart with love!

Commentary . . .

3. And thus it is as though the soul were to say: How gentle and loving (that is, extremely loving and gentle) is your awakening, O Word, Spouse, in the center and depth of my soul, which is its pure and intimate substance, in which secretly and silently, as its only lord, you dwell alone, not only as in your house, nor only as in your bed, but also as in my own heart, intimately and closely united to it. And how delicately you captivate me and arouse my affections toward you in the sweet breathing you produce in this awakening, a breathing delightful to me and full of good and glory.

The soul uses this comparison because its experience here is similar to that of one who upon awakening breathes deeply.

The verse follows:

4.   How gently and lovingly
       You wake in my heart

There are many kinds of awakening that God effects in the soul, so many that we would never finish explaining them all. Yet this awakening of the Son of God, which the soul wishes to refer to here, is one of the most elevated and most beneficial. For this awakening is a movement of the Word in the substance of the soul containing such grandeur, dominion, and glory, and intimate sweetness that it seems to the soul that all the balsams and fragrant spices and flowers of the world are commingled, stirred, and shaken so as to yield their sweet odor, and that all the kingdoms and dominions of the world and all the powers and virtues of heaven are moved; and not only this, but it also seems that all the virtues and substances and perfections and graces of every created thing glow and make the same movement all at once.

Since, as St. John says, *all things in Him are life* [Jn 1:3–4], and, as the Apostle declares, *in Him they live and are and move* [Acts 17:28], it follows that when, within the soul, this great Emperor moves (whose principality, as Isaiah says, He bears on His shoulders [Is 9:6]—which consists of the three spheres, celestial, terrestrial, and infernal, and the things contained in them—upholding them all, as St. Paul says [Heb 1:3], with the word of His power), all things seem to move in unison.

This happens in the same manner as when at the movement of the earth all material things in it move as though they were nothing. So it is when this Prince moves, who Himself carries His court, instead of His court carrying Him.[11]

5. Even this comparison is most inadequate, for in this awakening they not only seem to move, but they all likewise disclose the beauties of their being, power, loveliness, and graces, and the root of their duration and life. For the soul is conscious of how all creatures, earthly and heavenly, have their life, duration, and strength in Him, and it clearly realizes what He says in the Book of Proverbs: *By me kings reign and princes rule and the mighty exercise justice and understand it* [Prv 8:15–16]. Although it is indeed aware that these things are distinct from God, insofar as they have created being, nonetheless that which it understands of God, by His being all these things with infinite eminence, is such that it knows these things better in God's being than in themselves.

And here lies the remarkable delight of this awakening: The soul knows creatures through God and not God through creatures. This amounts to knowing the effects through their cause and not the cause through its effects. The latter is knowledge *a posteriori*, and the former is essential knowledge. . . .

14.   Where in secret you dwell alone

The soul says He dwells in its heart in secret because this sweet embrace is wrought in the depths of its substance.

It should be known that God dwells secretly in all souls and is hidden in their substance, for otherwise they would not last. Yet there is a difference, a great difference, in His dwelling in them. In some souls He dwells alone, and in others He does not dwell alone. Abiding in some, He is pleased; and in others, He is displeased. He lives in some as though in His own house, commanding and ruling everything; and in others as though a stranger in a strange house, where they do not permit Him to give orders or do anything.

It is in that soul in which less of its own appetites and pleasures dwell that He dwells more alone, more pleased, and more as though in

---

11. It would seem that John accepted the Copernican theory, which was disputed in his time but taught at the University of Salamanca, the first to accept the theory. When the first edition of John's works was published, this text was altered because Copernicus's work was by then on the Index.

His own house, ruling and governing it. And He dwells more in secret, the more He dwells alone. Thus in this soul, in which neither any appetite nor other images or forms nor any affections for created things dwell, the beloved dwells secretly with an embrace so much the closer, more intimate, and interior, the purer and more alone the soul is to everything other than God. His dwelling is in secret, then, because the devil cannot reach the area of this embrace, nor can one's intellect understand how it occurs.

Yet it is not secret to the soul itself that has attained this perfection, for within itself it has the experience of this intimate embrace. It does not, however, always experience these awakenings, for when the beloved produces them, it seems to the soul that he is awakening in its heart, where before he remained as though asleep. Although it was experiencing and enjoying him, this took place as though with a loved one who is asleep, for knowledge and love are not communicated mutually while one is still asleep.

15. Oh, how happy is this soul that ever experiences God resting and reposing within it! Oh, how fitting it is for it to withdraw from things, flee from business matters, and live in immense tranquillity, so that it may not even with the slightest mote or noise disturb or trouble its heart where the beloved dwells.

He is usually there, in this embrace with his bride, as though asleep in the substance of the soul. And it is very well aware of him and ordinarily enjoys him. Were he always awake within it, communicating knowledge and love, it would already be in glory. For if, when he does waken, scarcely opening his eyes, he has such an effect on the soul, what would it be like were he ordinarily in it fully awake?

16. Although he is not displeased with other souls that have not reached this union, for after all they are in the state of grace, yet insofar as they are not well disposed, his dwelling is secret to them, even though he does dwell in them. They do not experience him ordinarily, except when he grants them some delightful awakening. But such an awakening is not of this kind and high quality, nor is it comparable to these, nor as secret to the intellect and the devil, which are still able to understand something through the movements of the senses. For the senses are not fully annihilated until the soul reaches this union, and they still have some activity and movements concerning the spiritual, since they are not yet totally spiritual.

But in this awakening of the bridegroom in the perfect soul, everything that occurs and is caused is perfect, for he is the cause of it all.

And in that awakening, which is as though one were to awaken and breathe, the soul feels a strange delight in the breathing of the Holy Spirit in God, in which it is sovereignly glorified and taken with love. Hence it says in the subsequent verses:

17.   And in your sweet breathing,
       Filled with good and glory,
       How tenderly you swell my heart with love!

I do not desire to speak of this spiration, filled for the soul with good and glory and delicate love of God, for I am aware of being incapable of so doing; and were I to try, it might seem less than it is.[12] It is a spiration that God produces in the soul, in which, by that awakening of lofty knowledge of the Godhead, He breathes the Holy Spirit in it in the same proportion as was its knowledge and understanding of Him, absorbing it most profoundly in the Holy Spirit, rousing its love with divine excellence and delicacy according to what it beheld in Him. Since the breathing is filled with good and glory, the Holy Spirit, through this breathing, filled the soul with good and glory, in which He enkindled it in love of Himself, indescribably and incomprehensibly, in the depths of God, to whom be honor and glory forever and ever. Amen.

---

12. Actually John does not finish his work but abandons it, giving as his excuse, now at the end of his writings, the ineffable character of the mystical experience of God.

Selected Bibliography

Bibliographies

Archivum Bibliographicum Carmelitanum. Rome: Edizioni del Teresianum, 1956–.

Bibliographia Internationalis Spiritualitatis. Rome: Edizioni del Teresianum, 1966–.

Benno a S. Joseph. "Bibliographiae S. Joannis a Cruce, O.C.D., specimen (1891–1940)," in *Ephemerides Carmeliticae* 1 (1947): 163–210, 367–81; 3 (1949): 407–24, interrupted and partly completed in the following: "Bibliographia Carmelitana recentior" (ab anno 1946 et deinceps), ibid. 1 (1947): 393–416; 2 (1948): 561–610; 3 (1949): 133–219.

Ruano, Lucinio. "Guión bibiliográfico." In *Vida y Obras de San Juan de la Cruz*, 10th ed., pp. 1105–33. Madrid: B.A.C., 1978: 1105–33.

Pacho, Eulogio. "Orientación Bibliográfica." In *Iniciación a S. Juan de la Cruz*, pp. 243–94. Burgos: Editorial Monte Carmelo, 1982.

Works

Obras de San Juan de la Cruz, Doctor de la Iglesia. Edited with notes by Silverio de Santa Teresa. 5 vols. Burgos: Editorial El Monte Carmelo, 1929–1931.

San Juan de la Cruz: Obras Completas. Edited with introductions, notes, and revisions of the text by Eulogio Pacho. Burgos: Editorial Monte Carmelo, 1982.

San Juan de la Cruz: Obras Completas. Edited with textual revision, introductions, and notes to the text by José Vicente Rodríguez. With doctrinal introductions and notes by Federico Ruiz Salvador. 2nd ed. Madrid: Editorial de Espiritualidad, 1980.

San Juan de la Cruz: Cántico Espiritual Primera Redacción Y Texto Retocado. Edited with introduction and notes by Eulogio Pacho. Madrid: Fundación Universitaria Española, 1981.

BIBLIOGRAPHY

Vida y Obras de San Juan de la Cruz. Edited, with notes and appendices, by Lucinio Ruano. With a biography by Crisógono de Jesús Sacramentado, revised and enlarged by Matías del Niño Jesús. 10th ed. Madrid: Biblioteca de Autores Cristianos, 1978.

English Translations

The Complete Works of Saint John of the Cross. Translated and edited by E. Allison Peers, from the critical edition of Silverio de Santa Teresa. New ed., ref. 3 vols. Westminster, Md.: Newman Press, 1953. Reprinted by Sheed & Ward, 1 vol., 1978.

The Collected Works of St. John of the Cross. Translated by Kieran Kavanaugh and Otilio Rodriguez. With introductions by Kieran Kavanaugh. 2d ed. Washington, D.C.: I.C.S. Publications, 1979.

The Poems of St. John of the Cross. Translated by Roy Campbell. Preface by Martin D'Arcy. London: Harvill Press, 1951.

The Poems of Saint John of the Cross. Translated with introduction by Willis Barnstone. New York: New Directions, 1972.

The Poems of St. John of the Cross. Translated by John Frederick Nims. 3rd ed. Chicago: Chicago University Press, 1979.

Resources

San José, Luis de. *Concordancias de las Obras y escritos del Doctor de la Iglesia san Juan de la Cruz*. 2d ed. Burgos: Editorial Monte Carmelo, 1980.

Peers, E. Allison. *Handbook to The Life and Times of St. Teresa and St. John of the Cross*. London: Burns Oates, 1954.

Florisoone, Michel. *Jean de la Croix: Iconographie Générale*. Bruges, Belgium: Desclee de Brouwer, 1975.

Biographies

Bruno de Jésus-Marie. *Saint John of the Cross*. Edited by Benedict Zimmerman. New York: Sheed & Ward, 1932.

Crisógono de Jesús Sacramentado. *The Life of St. John of the Cross*. Translated by Kathleen Pond. London: Longmans, Green & Co., 1958.

BIBLIOGRAPHY

Hardy, Richard. *Search for Nothing: The Life of John of the Cross.* New York: Crossroad, 1982.

Studies

Ahern, Barnabas. "The Use of Scripture in the Spiritual Theology of St. John of the Cross." *Catholic Biblical Quarterly* 14 (January 1952): 6–17.
Asín Palacios, Miguel. *Saint John of the Cross and Islam.* Translated by Elmer H. Douglas and Howard W. Yoder. New York: Vantage, 1981.
Baruzi, Jean. *Saint Jean de la Croix et le problème de l'expérience mystique.* Paris: Felix Alcan, 1924.
Bendick, Johannes. "God and World in John of the Cross." *Philosophy Today* 16 (Winter 1972): 281–94.
A Benedictine of Stanbrook Abbey. *Medieval Mystical Tradition and Saint John of the Cross.* Westminster, Md.: Newman Press, 1954.
Bord, André. *Mémoire et espérance chez Jean de la Croix.* Paris: Beauchesne, 1971.
Brenan, Gerald. *St. John of the Cross: His Life and Poetry.* With a translation of his poetry by Lynda Nicholson. Cambridge: Cambridge University Press, 1973.
Brice, Fr. *Journey in the Night: A Practical Introduction to St. John of the Cross.* New York: Frederick Pustet Co., 1945.
———. *Spirit in Darkness: A Companion to Book Two of the "Ascent of Mt. Carmel."* New York: Frederick Pustet Co., 1946.
Buckley, Michael J. "Atheism and Contemplation." *Theological Studies* 40 (1979): 680–99.
Centner, David. "Christian Freedom and The Nights of St. John of the Cross." *Carmelite Studies* 2 (1982): 3–80.
Crisógono de Jesús Sacramentado. *San Juan de la Cruz: su obra científica y su obra literaria.* 2 vols. Madrid: Mensajero de Santa Teresa y de San Juan de la Cruz, 1929.
Cugno, Alain. *St. John of the Cross: Reflections on Mystical Experience.* Translated by Barbara Wall. New York: Seabury, 1982.
Culligan, Kevin G. "Toward a Contemporary Model of Spiritual Direction: A Comparative Study of St. John of the Cross and Carl Rogers." *Ephemerides Carmeliticae* 31 (1980): 29–90. Reprinted in *Carmelite Studies* 2 (1982): 95–166.
Dictionnaire de Spiritualité, Ascétique et Mystique, Doctrine et Histoire. Paris:

BIBLIOGRAPHY

Beauchesne, 1937–. S.v. "Jean de la Croix (Saint)." By Lucien-Marie de Saint-Joseph.

Edward, Denis. "Experience of God and Explicit Faith: A Comparison of John of the Cross and Karl Rahner." *Thomist* 46 (1982): 33–74.

Ferraro, Joseph. "Sanjuanist Doctrine on the Human Mode of Operation of the Theological Virtue of Faith". *Ephemerides Carmeliticae* 22 (1971): 250–94.

Foresti, Fabrizio. "Le radici bibliche della 'Salita del Monte Carmelo' di S. Giovanni della Croce." *Carmelus* 28 (1981): 226–55.

Frost, Bede. *Saint John of the Cross: An Introduction to His Philosophy, Theology, and Spirituality*. New York: Harper & Bros., 1937.

Gabriel of St. Mary Magdalen. *St. John of the Cross: Doctor of Divine Love and Contemplation*. Cork: The Mercier Press, 1947.

———. *The Spiritual Director According to the Principles of St. John of the Cross*. Translated by a Benedictine of Stanbrook Abbey. Westminster, Md.: Newman Press, 1950.

———. *Visions and Revelations in the Spiritual Life*. Translated by a Benedictine of Stanbrook Abbey. Westminster, Md.: Newman Press, 1950.

Galilea, Segundo. *The Future of Our Past: The Spanish Mystics Speak to Contemporary Spirituality*. Notre Dame, Ind.: Ave Maria Press, 1985.

Garrigou-Lagrange, Reginald. *Christian Perfection and Contemplation According to St. Thomas Aquinas and St. John of the Cross*. Translated by M. Timothea Doyle. St. Louis, Mo.: B. Herder Book Co., 1937.

Gaudreau, Marie M. *Mysticism and Image in St. John of the Cross*. Frankfurt am Main: Peter Lang, 1976.

Herrera, Robert A. "Mysticism: St. John of the Cross." In *God and Contemporary Thought: A Philosophical Perspective*, pp. 573–85. Edited by Sebastian A. Matczak. New York: Learned Publications, 1977.

———. *St. John of the Cross: Introductory Studies*. Madrid: Editorial de Espiritualidad, 1968.

Juan de Jesús María. "Le amará tanto como es amada." *Ephemerides Carmeliticae* 6 (1955): 3–103.

———. "El díptico Subida-Noche." In *Sanjuanistica*, pp. 27–83. Edited by the Theological Faculty. Rome: Teresianum, 1943.

Lucien-Marie de Saint-Joseph. "Spiritual Direction According to St. John of the Cross." *Carmelite Studies* 1 (1980): 3–34.

McCann, Leonard A. *The Doctrine of the Void: The Doctrine of the Void as Propounded by St. John of the Cross in his Major Prose Works and as*

BIBLIOGRAPHY

Viewed in the Light of Thomistic Principles. Toronto: Basilian Press, 1955.

Maio, Eugene A. *St. John of the Cross: The Imagery of Eros.* Madrid: Playor, 1973.

Mallory, Marilyn May. *Christian Mysticism: Transcending Techniques: A Theological Reflection on the Empirical Testing of the Teaching of St. John of the Cross.* Amsterdam: Van Gorcum Assen, 1977.

Mamic, Jakov. *S. Giovanni Della Croce E Lo Zen-Buddismo: Un confronto nella problematica dello "svuotamento" interiore.* Rome: Edizioni del Teresianum, 1982.

Maritain, Jacques. *Distinguish to Unite, or The Degrees of Knowledge.* Translated from the 4th French edition under the direction of Gerald B. Phelan. New York: Charles Scribner's Sons, 1959.

Merton, Thomas. *The Ascent to Truth.* New York: Harcourt, Brace & Co., 1951.

———. "Light in Darkness: The Ascetic Doctrine of St. John of the Cross." In *Disputed Questions*, pp. 208–17. New York: Farrar, Straus and Cudahy, 1960.

Morel, Georges. *Le Sens de l'existence selon S. Jean de la Croix.* 3 vols. Paris: Editions Montaigne, Aubier, 1960–1961.

Nemeck, Francis Kelly. *Teilhard de Chardin et Jean de la Croix.* Montreal: Bellarmin, 1975.

Nieto, Jose C. *Mystic, Rebel, Saint: A Study of St. John of the Cross.* Geneva: Librarie Droz, 1979.

Orcibal, Jean. "Le Rôle de l'intellect possible chez Jean de la Croix: ses sources scolastiques et nordiques." In *La Mystique Rhénane*, pp. 235–279. Edited by Phillipe Dollinger, et al. Paris: Presses Universitaires de France, 1963.

———. *Saint Jean de la Croix et les mystiques rhénoflamands.* Bruges, Belgium: Desclee de Brouwer, 1966.

Pacho, Eulogio (de la Virgen del Carmen). "El 'Cántico Espiritual' retocado." *Ephemerides Carmeliticae* 27 (1976): 382–452.

———. *El Cántico Espiritual: trayectoria histórica del texto.* Rome: Teresianum, 1967.

———. "La antropología Sanjuanistica." *El Monte Carmelo* 69 (1961): 47–70.

———. *San Juan de la Cruz y sus escritos.* Madrid: Ediciones Cristianidad, 1969.

Panakal, Justin. *The Theology of Private Revelations According to St. John of the Cross.* Kerala, India: Piusnagar, 1969.

BIBLIOGRAPHY

Peers, E. Allison. *Spirit of Flame: A Study of St. John of the Cross*. Wilton, Conn.: Morehouse-Barlow Co., 1979. Reprint edition.

Poslusney, Venard. *Attaining Spiritual Maturity for Contemplation According to St. John of the Cross*. Locust Valley, N.Y.: Living Flame Press, 1973.

Ruiz Salvador, Federico. *Introducción a San Juan de la Cruz: El hombre, los escritos, el sistema*. Madrid: Biblioteca de Autores Cristianos, 1968.

Sanson, Henri. *L'Esprit humain selon Saint Jean de la Croix*. Paris: Presses Universitaires de France, 1953.

Stein, Edith. *The Science of the Cross*. Edited by Lucy Gelber and Romaeus Leuven. Translated by Hilda Graef. Chicago: Henry Regnery, 1960.

Sullivan, John. "Night and Light. The Poet John of the Cross and the 'Exultet' of the Easter Liturgy." *Ephemerides Carmeliticae* 30 (1979): 52–68.

Sullivan, Lawrence. "The 'Moralia' of Pope St. Gregory the Great and its influence on St. John of the Cross." *Ephemerides Carmeliticae* 27 (1976): 453–88.

Thibon, Gustave. *Nietzsche und der heilige Johannes vom Kreuz: Eine characterologische Studie*. Paderborn: Verlag Ferdinand Schoningh, 1957.

Thompson, Colin P. *The Poet and the Mystic: A Study of the Cantico Espiritual of San Juan de la Cruz*. Oxford: Oxford University Press, 1977.

Vilnet, Jean. *Bible et mystique chez Saint Jean de la Croix*. Bruges, Belgium: Desclee de Brouwer, 1949.

Wojtyla, Karol. *Faith According to Saint John of the Cross*. Translated by Jordan Aumann. San Francisco: Ignatius Press, 1981.

———. "The Question of Faith in St. John of the Cross." *Carmelite Studies* 2 (1982): 223–73.

Zabalza, Laureano de la Inmaculada. *El Desposorio Espiritual segun San Juan de la Cruz*. Burgos: El Monte Carmelo, 1963.

Index

Accidents, 35
Alonzo, Damaso, 27
Alumbrados movement, 12, 22
Alvarez, Catalina, 8
Anger, 173
Appetites: freedom from all, 73–74; harm caused by, 72, 74–76; mortification of, 49, 65–72; and night, 63–64
Aquinas, Saint Thomas, 35
Ark of the Covenant, 71–72
Ascent of Mount Carmel, The (*See also* specific topics in): Book One of, 61–80; Book Three of, 143–53; Book Two of, 81–142; and *Dark Night, The*, 43, 46, 157–58; difficulty in reading, 46–47; divisions of, 47–48, 53–54; and *Living Flame of Love, The*, 46; and passions, 36; prologue of, 57–60; stanzas of, 56–57; structure of, 48–53; symbolism in, 47; theme of, 55–56; writing of, 38–39, 43, 46
Avarice, spiritual, 168–69

Benedict XIII, 24
Bible, 28–32
Book of the First Monks, The, 9

Carmelites: and Dominicans, 16–20; formation of, 12–15; and Teresa of Avila, Saint, 12–13
Christ (*See* Jesus)
Contemplation: description of signs for passing on to, 109–11; natural apprehensions of, 118–20; necessity of signs for passing on to, 111–18; and proficients, 118–20; purgative, 162–63; supernatural apprehensions of, 120–21
Crisostomo, Padre, 24

Darkness, 178–80 (*See also* Night of senses; Night of spirit)
Dark Night, The (*See also* specific topics in): and *Ascent of Mount Carmel, The*, 43, 46, 157–58; background of, 157–60; Book One of, 167–97; Book Two of, 198–209; divisions of, 158, 160–61; and personal histories of Old Testament, 29; symbolism in, 157–58; writing of, 38–39, 43, 46
Deification, 33
Dejados movement, 12
Discalced, 14–15 (*See also* Carmelites)
Divinization, 33
Dominicans, 16–20
Doria, Nicolas, 21, 23

Envy, spiritual, 177–78

Faith (*See also* Intellect; Knowledge; Meditation; Soul): dimensions of, 50–53; and faculties of soul, 92–98; guidance by, for soul, 85–88; and habit of soul, 82–84; and intellect, 98–103; and petitioning God through supernatural means, 127–35; and procedure of God in communicating goods, 122–27; of soul, 236–38; symbolism of, 81–82; and union with God, 88–92
Feelings, spiritual, 136
Ferdinand, 12
Fernandez, Pedro, 16–17, 19

INDEX

Gluttony, spiritual, 174–76
God (*See also* Union): and communication of love, 265–66; freedom of, 67; goodness of, 67; grace of, 65–67; intention of, in bestowing goods, 122–27; knowledge of, 138–40; petitioning of, through supernatural means, 127–35; presence of, 230–35; sovereignty of, 67; transcendence of, 48–49; and use of love, 266–69; wisdom of, 67–68
Grace, 65–67, 81–82
Gracian, Jeronimo, 18
Gregory XIII, 18, 20

Heredia, Antonio de, 15
Holy Spirit, 254, 280

Incarnation, 260, 275
Inquisition, 12
Intellect (*See also* Soul): and class of apprehensions of, 49; division of apprehensions of, 103–4; and faith, 98–103; harm caused by apprehensions of, 104–5; nakedness of, 93–98; natural apprehensions of, 105–9; spiritual apprehensions of, 135–37; supernatural apprehensions of, 104–5; and union with God, 98–103
Isabella, 12

Jesus (*See also* Union): facing of, 275–77; love of, with soul, 219–27
Jimena, 23
John of the Cross, Saint (*See also* specific works of): and anthropology, 34–37; and Bible, 28–32; biographies of, 7; birth of, 8; and Carmelites, 9, 12–20; death of, 24; and discalced, 14–15; doctrine of, 9, 30–34; and Dominicans, 16–20; early years of, 8; governing by, 22–23; importance of, 7; influences of, 27–28; last years of, 23–24; monastic life of, 10; as mystic, 24–28, 32–34; personality of, 21–23; as poet, 24–27; sketches of, 43; and Spanish reform, 10–12; as superior, 20–21; and symbolism, 25–26, 38; and Teresa of Avila, Saint, 10–14, 24–25; as theologian, 27–32; as writer, 20–21; writings of, 38–39; youth of, 8

Joy, 152–53
Juan de la Cruz (*See* John of the Cross)
Juan de Santo Maria (*See* John of the Cross)

Knowledge (*See also* Memory): and disclosure of secrets and hidden mysteries, 140–41; kinds of, 137–40; of memory, 143–48; and recollection of spirit, 141–42

Life, eternal, 93–98
Light, 204–5
Living Flame of Love, The (*See also* specific topics in): and *Ascent of Mount Carmel, The*, 46; background of, 287–90; divisions of, 290–91; prologue of, 292–94; Stanza 1, 292–94; Stanza 2, 303–7; Stanza 3, 307–12; Stanza 4, 313–16; symbolism of, 287; writing of, 38–39
Locutions, 136, 141–42
Love: between soul and Christ, 219–27; communication of, by God, 265–66; and night of senses, 186–88; and night of spirit, 208–9; and soul, 79–80
Lust, 169–73

Madre Ana de Jesus, 23
Maxime cuperemus, 15
Meditation: description of signs for giving up, 109–11; natural apprehensions of, 118–20; necessity of signs for giving up, 111–18; and proficients, 118–20; supernatural apprehensions of, 120–21
Memory (*See also* Soul): benefits from forgetting knowledge of, 147–48; class of apprehensions of, 49; harm resulting from remembering knowledge of, 143–47; rule of conduct in using, 149–50; as spiritual faculty, 35

New Testament, 29
Night of senses (*See also* Appetites; Faith; Memory; Night of spirit; Will): and anger of beginners, 173; and avarice of beginners, 168–69; benefits of, other, 193–97; benefits of, to soul, 189–93; conduct required of souls in, 184–86; entering, 76–79; and envy of beginners, 177–78; and gluttony of beginners, 174–76; and

INDEX

imperfection of beginners, 163–64; and kinds of darkness, 178–80; and love, 79–80, 186–88; and lust of beginners, 169–73; passing through, 56–57, 65–68; and pride of beginners, 164–67; reasons for calling journey, 63–64; and senses, 162–63; signs for treading, 18–84; and sloth of beginners, 177–78; term of, 61–63

Night of spirit (*See also* Night of senses): and affliction of soul, 200–204; comparison of, 205–8; and light, 204–5; and love, 208–9; term of, 198–200

Nights (*See* Night of senses; Night of spirit)

Old Testament, 29
Ormaneto, Nicolas, 18–19
Osuna, Francisco de, 11

Passions, 36
Pelayo, Menendez, 27
Philip II, 13
Pius V, 15
Pius XI, 24
Prayers, 230–31
Pride, 164–67
Proficients: and contemplation, 118–20; and meditation, 118–20; passing to, from beginners' state, 163; state of, 198–99
Purgations, 62, 178–80 (*See also* Night of senses; Night of spirit)

Revelations, 136, 140–41
Rossi, John Baptists (*See* Rubeo)
Rubeo, 13–15, 17
Ruiz, Federico, 32

Salazar, Angel de, 20
Santo, Magdalena del Espiritu, 43
Scriptures, 28–32
Sega, Felipe, 19–20
Sense, 36–37 (*See also* Night of senses)
Sins (*See* specific types of)
Sloth, spiritual, 177–78
Soul (*See also* Intellect; Knowledge; Memory; Union; Will): and absence of God, 251–54; affliction of, 200–4; and attentiveness to God, 269–73; awakening of, by God, 313–16; benefits to, of night of senses, 189–93; and communication of God, 245–50; and communication of love, 265–66; and communication of mysteries, 260–61; conduct required of, for treading night of senses, 184–86; entering of, into night of senses, 163; and facing Jesus, 275–77; faculties of, 92–98; faith of, 236–38; and flame of love, 294–302; fulfillment of, 262–65; and glory of predestination, 278–79; and God's use of love, 266–69; and guidance by faith, 85–88; habit of, 82–84; and Holy Spirit, 280–82; and Jesus, love between, 219–27; and ladder of faith, 81–82; and light, 204–5; and love, 79–80, 208–9; offering of, 250–51; prayers of, 230–31; preparedness of, 283; and presence of God, 230–35; purification of, 254–55; rejoicing of, 255–60; signs of, for treading night of senses, 180–84; and strangers, 274–75; suffering of, 239–44; traits of, in sickness of love of God, 227–30; transformation of, in God, 292–94; and Trinity, 303–7; union of parts of, 198–99; and union with God, 88–92, 307–12

Spanish reform, 10–13
Spirit, 36–37 (*See also* Night of spirit)
Spiritual Canticle, The (*See also* specific topics in): background of, 213–18; CA redaction of, 215; CB redaction of, 215; divisions of, 218; overview of stanzas of, 215–18; prologue of, 219–21; and reality, 26; Stanza 10, 227–30; Stanza 11, 230–35; Stanza 12, 236–38; Stanza 13, 239–44; Stanza 14, 245–50; Stanza 15, 245–50; Stanza 16, 250–51; Stanza 17, 251–54; Stanza 20, 254–55; Stanza 21, 254–55; Stanza 22, 255–60; Stanza 23, 260–61; Stanza 26, 262–65; Stanza 27, 265–66; Stanza 28, 266–69; Stanza 29, 269–73; Stanza 36, 273–75; Stanza 37, 275–77; Stanza 38, 277–79; Stanza 39, 280–82; Stanza 40, 282–83; stanzas between Soul and Bridegroom, 221–27; summary of, 213–14; and union with Christ, 53; writing of, 19, 38–39

Spiritual feelings, 136

INDEX

Substance, 35
Superioribus mensibus, 15
Symbolism (*See also* Night of senses; Night of spirit): in *Ascent of Mount Carmel, The*, 47; in *Dark Night, The*, 157–58; of faith, 81–82; of fire, 287; of flame, 287; and John of the Cross, 25–26, 38

Teresa of Avila, Saint: and Domincans, 16–20; and John of the Cross, Saint, 10–14; letters of, 24-25; and Spanish reform, 10–13
Toledo, Don Alonso Alvarez de, 9
Tostado, Jeronimo, 17–19
Trinity, 303–7
Truths (*See* Knowledge)

Union, divine (*See also* Appetites; Faith; Intellect; Memory; Will): in *Ascent of Mount Carmel, The*, 55–60, 63; and intellect, 98–103; and love, 79–80; nature of, 88–92; in *Spiritual Canticle, The*, 53

Vargas, Francisco, 16–17
Vices (*See* specific types of)
Villacreces, Pedro de, 11
Visions, 135–36

Will: detachment of, 283; division of emotions of, 150–52; and joy, 152–53
Wisdom, divine, 67–68

Yepes, Gonzalo de, 8
Yepes, Juan de (*See* John of the Cross)

Other Volumes in this Series

Julian of Norwich • SHOWINGS
Jacob Boehme • THE WAY TO CHRIST
Nahman of Bratslav • THE TALES
Gregory of Nyssa • THE LIFE OF MOSES
Bonaventure • THE SOUL'S JOURNEY INTO GOD, THE TREE OF LIFE, and THE LIFE OF ST. FRANCIS
William Law • A SERIOUS CALL TO DEVOUT AND HOLY LIFE, and THE SPIRIT OF LOVE
Abraham Isaac Kook • THE LIGHTS OF PENITENCE, LIGHTS OF HOLINESS, THE MORAL
    PRINCIPLES, ESSAYS, and POEMS
Ibn 'Ata' Illah • THE BOOK OF WISDOM and Kwaja Abdullah Ansari • INTIMATE CONVERSATIONS
Johann Arndt • TRUE CHRISTIANITY
Richard of St. Victor • THE TWELVE PATRIARCHS, THE MYSTICAL ARK, and BOOK THREE OF THE TRINITY
Origen • AN EXHORTATION TO MARTYRDOM, PRAYER AND SELECTED WORKS
Catherine of Genoa • PURGATION AND PURGATORY, THE SPIRITUAL DIALOGUE
Native North American Spirituality of the Eastern Woodlands • SACRED
    MYTHS, DREAMS, VISIONS, SPEECHES, HEALING FORMULAS, RITUALS AND CEREMONIALS
Teresa of Avila • THE INTERIOR CASTLE
Apocalyptic Spirituality • TREATISES AND LETTERS OF LACTANTIUS, ADSO OF
    MONTIER-EN-DER, JOACHIM OF FIORE, THE FRANCISCAN SPIRITUALS, SAVONAROLA
Athanasius • THE LIFE OF ANTONY, A LETTER TO MARCELLINUS
Catherine of Siena • THE DIALOGUE
Sharafuddin Maneri • THE HUNDRED LETTERS
Martin Luther • THEOLOGIA GERMANICA
Native Mesoamerican Spirituality • ANCIENT MYTHS, DISCOURSES, STORIES,
    DOCTRINES, HYMNS, POEMS FROM THE AZTEC, YUCATEC, QUICHE-MAYA AND OTHER SACRED TRADITIONS
Symeon the New Theologian • THE DISCOURSES
Ibn Al'-Aribī • THE BEZELS OF WISDOM
Hadewijch • THE COMPLETE WORKS
Philo of Alexandria • THE CONTEMPLATIVE LIFE, THE GIANTS, AND SELECTIONS
George Herbert • THE COUNTRY PARSON, THE TEMPLE
Unknown • THE CLOUD OF UNKNOWING
John and Charles Wesley • SELECTED WRITINGS AND HYMNS
Meister Eckhart • THE ESSENTIAL SERMONS, COMMENTARIES, TREATISES AND DEFENSE
Francisco de Osuna • THE THIRD SPIRITUAL ALPHABET
Jacopone da Todi • THE LAUDS
Fakhruddin 'Iraqi • DIVINE FLASHES
Menahem Nahum of Chernobyl • THE LIGHT OF THE EYES
Early Dominicans • SELECTED WRITINGS

John Climacus • THE LADDER OF DIVINE ASCENT
Francis and Clare • THE COMPLETE WORKS
Gregory Palamas • THE TRIADS
Pietists • SELECTED WRITINGS
The Shakers • TWO CENTURIES OF SPIRITUAL REFLECTION
Zohar • THE BOOK OF ENLIGHTENMENT
Luis de León • THE NAMES OF CHRIST
Quaker Spirituality • SELECTED WRITINGS
Emanuel Swedenborg • THE UNIVERSAL HUMAN AND SOUL-BODY INTERACTION
Augustine of Hippo • SELECTED WRITINGS
Safed Spirituality • RULES OF MYSTICAL PIETY, THE BEGINNING OF WISDOM
Maximus Confessor • SELECTED WRITINGS
John Cassian • CONFERENCES
Johannes Tauler • SERMONS
John Ruusbroec • THE SPIRITUAL ESPOUSALS AND OTHER WORKS
Ibn 'Abbād of Ronda • LETTERS ON THE SŪFĪ PATH
Angelus Silesius • THE CHERUBINIC WANDERER
The Early Kabbalah •
Meister Eckhart • TEACHER AND PREACHER